Tracing Your Family Tree

The Comprehensive Guide
to Discovering your Family History

JEAN COLE

and

JOHN TITFORD

COUNTRYSIDE BOOKS
NEWBURY, BERKSHIRE

First published 1988
Second enlarged edition 1997
Third Edition, 2000
© Jean Cole and John Titford 1997, 2000

Revised and reprinted 2001

COUNTRYSIDE BOOKS
3 Catherine Road
Newbury, Berkshire

To view our complete range of books,
please visit us at
www.countrysidebooks.co.uk

ISBN 1 85306 656 7

Produced through MRM Associates Ltd., Reading
Printed by Woolnough Bookbinding Ltd., Irthlingborough

Contents

Foreword

In 1987 I was approached by Thorsons Publishing of Wellingborough and asked if I knew of someone who would write a book on how to begin your family history. My view at that time was that there were already more than enough basic books on the market, but what was lacking was a good all-round handbook which, besides being helpful to the beginner, would provide useful information and sources as the researcher progressed further along the family history trail.

This view was accepted, and in partnership with Jean Cole, who from 1985 had so admirably conducted the 'Questions and Answers' column in our magazine, I was co-author of the first edition of *Tracing Your Family Tree*. It was published in 1988, and over the next few years sold around 50,000 copies, but as time progressed and much of the information became increasingly out of date, it was apparent that reprints were no longer satisfactory, and a complete revision was required.

Jean, to her credit, worked for many months on her part of the project but unfortunately, due mainly to professional commitments, my own contribution didn't come along as well as it should have done, nor did it look like doing so in the immediate future. I was more than pleased therefore that John Titford agreed to team up with Jean to complete the second edition.

Jean and John between them have a tremendous knowledge of family history. They have both worked in a freelance capacity for *Family Tree Magazine* for a number of years, so knowing their capabilities I am pleased, but not in the least surprised, to see that the second edition is far better than the first. I offer my heartiest congratulations to the pair of them on a job well done.

Michael Armstrong FSG
Family Tree Magazine
Ramsey, Huntingdon

Introduction

The reasons why people set out on the family history trail are many and varied. For some, it may be that family stories handed down through the generations will have provided the motivation, or the discovery of an old photograph, family letters, a diary or a family bible. Others are simply driven by curiosity or a need to know at least something about their roots.

The subject fascinates people from all walks of life. We can be as different from one another as chalk from cheese, and yet have this one common, all-absorbing need to discover where, when and how our ancestors lived. The long-term aim is to find out everything possible about them. After all, our forebears will have had at least some influence upon the kind of people we are today. Are you tall and red-haired like your paternal grandfather, or short and dark like your maternal grandmother? Is there a predisposition to have twins in your family, or a talent for music, painting, carpentry, needlework or some other skill? Tracing your family history could throw some light on why you are the way you are, with all your physical and mental characteristics, your temperament, your interests and your skills.

It is essential to realise that most families have had their 'ups and downs' over the generations, may have been at various times landed gentry, yeomen, members of a profession, tradesmen or labourers. Some forebears will have been hard-working members of the community, outgoing and cheerful; maybe some were reserved or taciturn, melancholic or feckless; perhaps a few were capable of breaking the law. You could discover ancestors in gaol or the poor-house, whilst others may have been churchwardens, lawyers or magistrates. Time and circumstance may have changed the lifestyle of the family - the rich becoming poor, and the poor becoming rich.

The art of tracing the history of any family lies in the researcher's ability to locate and to read the appropriate records, and then to make an interpretation of them which is both intelligent and imaginative. The amount of official and unofficial documentation concerning individuals has grown steadily throughout the centuries. From birth to death the average person nowadays leaves behind a trail of clues as to his or her life - the *where*, the *when* and the *how* of it all. This trail can start off even before birth with pre-natal records, but the first important record in a person's life is, of course, his or her birth certificate. From this we learn where a person was born, the names of the parents, the maiden name of the mother, and the occupation of the father. This gives the researcher several clues with which to step back to a previous generation.

Family photographs. *George Phillips and Sarah Nickols on their wedding day in 1865 at Cruwys Morchard, Devon.*

As life progresses, other written records may be made: of baptism, school attendance, marriage, the birth of children, sporting achievements, occupation or profession, membership of a union or a professional body, civic office held, retirement, pension - and ultimately death and the probate of a will or the issuing of Letters of Administration. Much may have survived as unofficial documentation in a private family archive: apprenticeship indentures, business accounts, invoices, diaries, photographs, newspaper cuttings, records of divorce proceedings, criminal files, armed service or merchant navy records - and, if you're lucky, a family bible.

As you pursue your family history, you'll find that old leads eventually peter out, only to be replaced by a whole new set of exciting possibilities. Many of our ancestors led such eventful lives that it seems wrong to leave their stories hidden in the archives; others had a more ordinary existence without seemingly making their mark on society. Here are some details concerning a very ordinary family which show that there may still be a tale to tell.

The Bidgood and Elston Families

Abraham Bidgood, the youngest son of Abraham Bidgood, farmer and wheelwright, and his wife Agnes (née Gillard), of Halberton in Devon, was born in 1838. Six years later, his wife-to-be, Selina Elston, daughter of Samuel Elston, yeoman farmer, and Elizabeth (née Harris) was born at Newcott, later known as Higher Way Farm, on the outskirts of Tiverton. By 1864 the Bidgood family had moved to work the neighbouring farm of Lower Way, and it was here that Abraham and Selina met. They married at Tiverton Register Office by notice of marriage in 1864; the names of the witnesses to the ceremony would suggest that neither family was present at the time. The couple moved around to various places in Devon and Somerset, wherever Abraham could find dairy work, and within a few years four children were born to them, two boys and two girls. Tragedy soon struck the little family when Selina died from typhoid pneumonia in 1874, shortly after the birth of her daughter Elizabeth, known as Bessie. Abraham's sight was now failing and he moved back to Lower Way Farm to live with his widowed father (his mother having died from consumption in 1848), taking three of his children with him. His third child, Annie, went to live with John Bidgood, Abraham's elder brother, who was a farmer and schoolmaster at Bradninch. Abraham's sight failed completely, but he still rode around the countryside selling tea and was a well-known character in the locality.

Details of letters from New Zealand, family memories and other papers from quite unexpected quarters, were to reveal further information concerning the Elston and Bidgood families.

Selina's father, Samuel Elston, died in 1862, leaving a will and effects of £600 to be shared amongst his wife and numerous children. Shortly after this, one of his sons, Henry Elston, then aged 23, sailed for New Zealand - according to his great grandson, Murray Elston. In 1912, on his official application in his own handwriting for the New Zealand War Medal, he supplied details about his service with the No.2 Company of the élite Forest Rangers (known as the 'Von Tempskys') from 1865 to 1869, relating that the company had been under fire several times during the time of the Maori Wars, and how, at the time of the Bay Massacre near Gisbourne, his house and store had been burnt to the ground and he had lost everything he owned. He added on his medal application that he considered that the New Zealand government should give a grant of land to all those who suffered through the results of the massacre. James McCurk JP, of Harepope, Waikato, confirmed that Henry Elston of Palmerston

South had been under fire with him in May 1865 and again later in the same year. In 1913 Henry eventually received his medal for services rendered.

According to his great grandson, Henry had been known as a 'wild one' during his younger days in Palmerston, always keeping about 18 gallons of beer in his hut, until he decided to reform and settle down. He married Susannah Wakefield in 1872 at St. Paul's Chapel of Ease at Palmerston and shortly afterwards joined the Salvation Army. In the late 1880s he eventually resumed contact with his mother and family back home in Devon, much to his mother's great joy. Elizabeth Elston must have been a strong-minded woman, as she wrote to Henry that although she and her family were pleased to hear he was a Christian man, they definitely did not approve of his being a member of the Salvation Army, as they were 'church going people', and he was never to write anything more about the 'Army' in his letters. The original letters from 'the old country' are still in the possession of the New Zealand Elstons, giving news about the family and the prevailing conditions and low prices affecting the farming community in England at this time. Henry's mother, Elizabeth, died in 1892 without seeing her son again, and it is clear from a letter written by one of her sons to New Zealand that her last words had been about him. Henry died in 1920, still a staunch member of the Salvation Army, and a glowing obituary to 'Dad Elston' appeared in the New Zealand War Cry *of 12 June 1920.*

During the 1860s Abraham Bidgood's sisters, Sarah and Maria, also emigrated - this time to America. Sarah Chave and her husband had emigrated to New York a few years before her sister Maria followed, together with her husband William Jarman and their two children, Maria and Albert. After being baptised into the Mormon faith at Exmouth, the family set sail from Liverpool in 1866 and settled in Albany, New York, for two years. After the cessation of the Black Hawk Wars in 1868, the Jarman family made the journey by railroad to Fort Laramie, and from there by wagon to Salt Lake City in Utah. Their journey lasted three months and they were among the last of the pioneers before the railroad from east to west was joined at Promontory Point near Ogden, Utah. Maria's fortunes were mixed: shortly after the family's arrival in Salt Lake City, heavily pregnant as she was, she divorced her husband on grounds of extreme cruelty and was given back her maiden name by the court. Although Maria was to marry twice more, she had no more children. In 1888 she made a last journey back to see her family and friends in England and to gather family information for her genealogy as required by the Church. All these details she noted in her journal which, together with more recorded information from her daughter and some friends, is now held in the Church Historic Archives and in the Daughters of the Pioneers Museum in Salt Lake City. As Maria finally left these shores to return to America, she wrote in her journal that she was so sad to say goodbye to her blind brother Abraham and her sister, but how she rejoiced to return home to her family, her friends and her Church.

Towards the end of the nineteenth century Abraham and Selina

Bidgood's second son William, now aged 18, decided that he would seek his fortunes in Australia. He never married, but always maintained contact with his brother and sisters, coming home just once in 1914 to see them, bringing expensive presents for all the family - a fact related by his eldest nephew and his nieces. Opinions within the family as to William's exact occupation were divided: was he a farmer, a lawyer or a bookmaker? William Bidgood died in the 1940s, leaving a substantial sum of money to his brother, John Charley in London and to his sisters, Annie in Swindon and Bessie in Uffculme, with an equal share to his housekeeper in Australia.

Abraham and Selina's daughter, Annie Alice Elston Bidgood, married Walter Phillips of Way Village, Cruwys Morchard, at Halberton parish church on a July day in 1896 and moved to Swindon with her husband, where they set up business and raised a family of six boys and two girls. Jean (Cole), their eldest son Elton's daughter, is the historian of the family.

This résumé is only a very small part of the story to be told about these two families at a certain period of time. They were just ordinary families working hard and getting on with life as best they knew how. The information gathered from letters, newspapers, books and journals written well over a hundred years ago, shows just how much family history can be gained from such sources through contact with other family descendants and somehow brings the families to life again. The usual mainstream sources outlined in this book applied to the rest of the research, which has taken the Elston family back to the early seventeenth century and the Bidgood family to the early eighteenth century in Devon. Surely there must be many other such family stories still waiting to be discovered?

Maybe after all there is no such thing as an 'ordinary' family? In 1985 John Titford was awarded first prize in a competition organised by the Institute of Heraldic and Genealogical Studies (in celebration of its premises in Canterbury being 700 years old) to find the best written family history. *The Titford Family 1547–1947* was subsequently published by Phillimore in 1989. The original intention was to give the book a sub-title: The story of an ordinary family. Yet in the event, even this family of modest means, originating with artisans in Wiltshire and Somerset, was not entirely ordinary. The story encompasses a planter and slave-owner in Jamaica, a master mariner who died of fever off the coast of Honduras, a man arrested for blaspheming the Holy Ghost in London in 1651, a wife excluded from the local baptist chapel in Frome, Somerset, for 'dishonesty, intemperance and falsehood'. One branch of the family runs through generations of humble shepherds and agricultural labourers on the Wiltshire downs, culminating in a Rear Admiral who is now retired and lives not so far from his original ancestral village. Above all, the family travelled and migrated - to Australia, New Zealand, Newfoundland and America. Few families are so ordinary, after all - and even fewer stayed put in one place for very long, despite what the history books may tell us.

Don't rush things. It is so easy to browse through books such as this one, and on the spur of the moment decide to attempt to trace your family tree. It is also all too easy to set about it in a haphazard fashion and cause yourself many problems and a great deal of unnecessary expense.

If, for instance, your name is Turpin, and family stories tell you that you are connected with the famous highwayman, never let this idea obsess you throughout your research; just treat it as an interesting possibility. You must start with yourself, work back through your parents to your grandparents, and from there on take each generation as it comes. Above all, you must be methodical. Devise a simple system of collecting and storing your information at the beginning, as more complicated files for cross-referencing can be developed as time goes on. The Federation of Family History Societies publishes a number of easy-to-use recording sheets. By all means use a computer to store, retrieve and organise information once you feel confident enough to do so.

One of the most important things to do is to read as many books for beginners as possible. Scattered throughout this handbook you will find highly-recommended publications, either of a general nature or specialising in certain aspects of the subject. Some of these can be borrowed through your inter-library loan service, or purchased from the publisher or from bookshops. The Society of Genealogists and the Institute of Heraldic and Genealogical Studies have bookshops and publish book catalogues, and *Family Tree Magazine* lists many books for sale by post.

After reading this book, and before jumping in at the 'deep end', just spend some time deep in thought. We will show you the sensible way to approach the subject to enable you to save time and money, and will suggest a large number of possible basic sources; there are many more, of course, but you will discover these mainly as spin-offs from current research. The early part of the book is arranged in the order in which your initial research should naturally progress.

Addresses and even titles of archive offices, libraries and the like have a habit of changing over the years. We have done all we can to ensure that the information contained in this book is as up-to-date as possible, but you would be well advised to telephone in advance before making a personal visit to any record repository. Major changes affecting the location and availability of records within the London area took place during 1996 and 1997; the Family Records Centre was established in Myddelton Street and the Public Record Office in Chancery Lane was closed, most of its archives being transferred to the existing repository at Kew. The situation is still developing as we write. In particular, the exact division of original and microfilm records between the Public Record Office at Kew and the Family Records Centre in Myddelton Street is still subject to some degree of uncertainty, so do check before committing yourself to a visit to either place.

The 'Further reading' sections featured throughout this book have a bias towards printed, rather than microform, works. Some of the books listed are easy to locate, others less so. Some were published abroad.

Speaking of bias...You will notice, perhaps, that both authors (by sheer coincidence) have a particular connection with Wiltshire, and have used this county extensively when it comes to references and illustrations. We have tried to play to our strength, if you like. We hope you won't feel that this in any way distorts what we have to say, and we wouldn't pretend that any one county is 'typical' when it comes to family history research. Beyond that, this is primarily a book for English researchers, though we've made every attempt to include a wider British and even international context wherever possible.

One final thought before you start. As you set off in hot pursuit of your ancestors, do bear in mind the outside possibility (depending upon your susceptibility to such things) that maybe, just maybe, your ancestors are really looking for you. You will soon discover that family history research has as much to do with intuition as with intellect, and that you are entering a world in which coincidence and serendipity (that is, the discovery of something important by chance, while you are looking for something else) are commonplace. Don't be alarmed by this - let it work for you. Henry Z.('Hank') Jones, genealogist and one-time Hollywood film actor, has made a fascinating study of this subject in his book *Psychic roots: serendipity and intuition in genealogy* (1993) and its follow-up, *More psychic roots* (1997).

We wish you good luck and hope you spend many enjoyable hours as you go back in time. You will be pleasantly surprised at the number of people interested in the subject, and in the way this pastime encourages friendship and companionship amongst its participants.

Jean Cole
John Titford

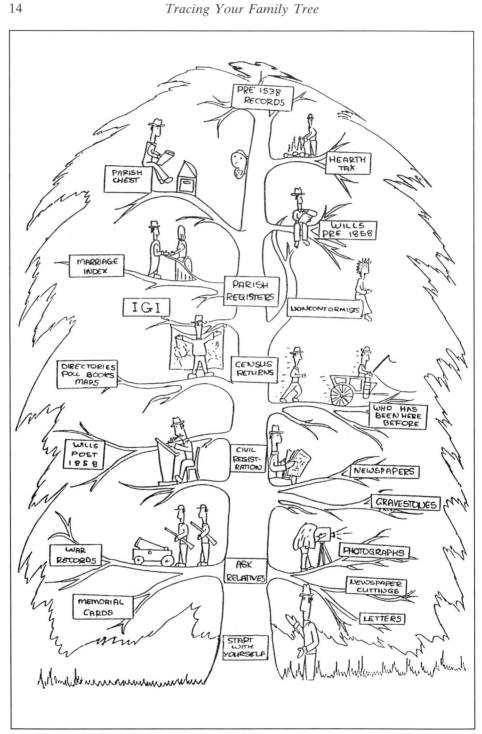

Climbing the tree: *an illustration of sources constructed in 1987 by 14 year old J.P. Bloore.* (Family Tree Magazine)

CHAPTER 1

Where and How To Start

There are many ways to record the results of your research, but initially it is wise to use the system below, known as a drop-line chart or pedigree. It is simple, straightforward, and easy to read.

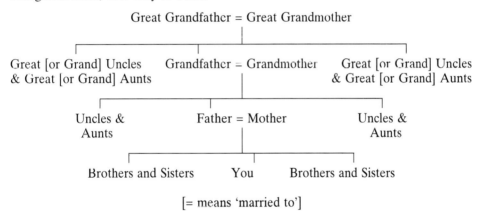

Great Grandfather = Great Grandmother

Great [or Grand] Uncles & Great [or Grand] Aunts   Grandfather = Grandmother   Great [or Grand] Uncles & Great [or Grand] Aunts

Uncles & Aunts   Father = Mother   Uncles & Aunts

Brothers and Sisters   You   Brothers and Sisters

[= means 'married to']

First, it is wise to make a basic family tree from the facts and information you already know. Arrange such a tree in a horizontal, vertical or circular fashion as you wish. The vertical option as shown in the illustration overleaf is the one most usually adopted, with the earliest known ancestor at the top and successive generations arranged at horizontal levels below. From this tree it is possible to see at a glance what family information you have acquired. Many questions will remain to be asked of other members of the family, who may be able to fill in some of the gaps and supply documents and papers to give more names, dates, places and facts.

Begin with the birth of the eldest child on the left-hand side of the tree and so on along the line to the youngest at the right-hand side. Fill in dates of births, deaths and marriages as far as you know them on your basic tree.

Which family are you going to trace?

Which family line are you going to trace? Your father's, the paternal line? Your mother's, the maternal or distaff line? All families can offer at least some

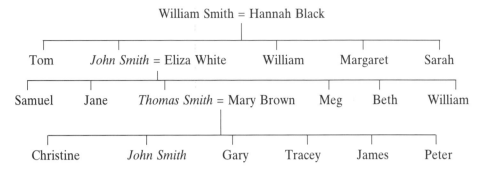

The Smith Family — an example

fascinating research possibilities, taking different directions and social patterns in their lifetimes. One family may have been extremely affluent, another reasonably well-off, while another may have been poor, surviving on parish hand-outs or maybe eking out an existence in the workhouse. Another family may have had more than its fair share of wrong-doers and eccentrics.

Some researchers decide to trace their paternal ancestry only, but it can be just as interesting to have a close look at the families of the females who married your direct male-line ancestors. If you happen to be 'stuck' on one line for a while, you may be more likely to have success with another family whilst waiting to solve that particular problem. You may choose to trace a family about which you know the most, or whose members live nearest to you. Whichever choice or choices you make, always make a separate chart for each line you are researching.

Family history research is a step-by-step process, from the known to the unknown, starting with yourself. From the information given on your birth certificate you go back a generation to your parents and their marriage certificate. From the details given on this certificate you will then need to find your parents' birth certificates. From their births back to your grandparents' marriage, and back to their births, and so on, following this pattern. Unless cousins have married cousins, you will find you have four grandparents, eight great-grandparents, sixteen great-great-grandparents, doubling up every generation. Of course, many close or distant cousins *have* married each other throughout the centuries, each often unaware that any relationship existed between them. In this way the number of your ancestors is reduced - a phenomenon referred to by Cecil Humphery-Smith as 'implection'.

Obviously, as you research back in time the blood line will become somewhat diluted, as it were, but tracing a number of ancestral paths can make research an intriguing and gripping pursuit. Truth can be stranger than fiction, they say, and truth can be a great deal more interesting than fiction when it comes to one's very own family!

Ask the family

Your first point of contact must be your parents, grandparents, aunts, uncles, cousins, second cousins, and close family friends. Conversations or correspondence with such people could well lead you to other relatives and cousins of whose existence you had previously been unaware. With luck, you will find that

George and Sarah Phillips was married
the 21st of October 1865. George Phillips son
of george and mary ann Phillips was born the
25th of October 1844 Sarah Nickols daughter
of john an Elizabeth Nickols was born the
28 of april 1847 —

Walter john Phillips son of george an Sarah
Phillips was born the 9th of November 1866

William. Thomas. Phillips was born the 27th March 1869

George. Henery. Phillips was born the 10th October 1870

Elizabeth ann Phillips was Born May 1st — 1872

Albart George Phillips was Born September 27th 1874

Clara jane Phillips was born March 25th 1877 —

Ernest Phillips was Born March 13th 1879

Lily Maud Phillips was Born Dec 20th 1880

Minnie Phillips was Born February 9th 1883

Fredrick Phillips Born March 10th 1885

Mina Phillips Born October 15th 1886

Harold Emilyn Phillips Born Dec 4th 1891

Elsie Eveline Mary Phillips Born Oct 5th 1896

A page from the Phillips family bible.

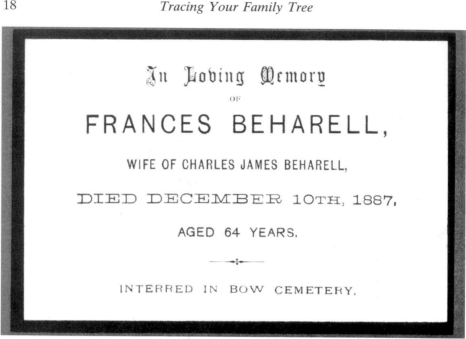

In Loving Memory

OF

FRANCES BEHARELL,

WIFE OF CHARLES JAMES BEHARELL,

DIED DECEMBER 10TH, 1887,

AGED 64 YEARS.

INTERRED IN BOW CEMETERY.

A 'Loving Memory' card, *especially popular in Victorian and Edwardian times.*

one or two of these will be interested in the family history and will be prepared to help with information. You will discover that every member of the family has a different piece which will fit into the overall jig-saw puzzle picture which is steadily coming to life.

Ask all your contacts about their own memories and about what they have been told by others. Do they have any documents, letters, diaries, memorial cards, certificates, wills, and so on? Visit people in person if you can, and record everything you are told - do not rely on memory, which will only fail when you try to remember crucial names, dates and facts. The unobtrusive use of a tape-recorder can be a great help at this time. Perhaps someone else from the family could go with you to write down the information in a notebook?

Prepare a list of questions to ask your informant:

- Is there a family bible, giving dates of events such as births, christenings, marriages, deaths and burials?
- Are there any certificates of birth, marriage or death?
- Has anyone kept baptismal certificates, confirmation cards, books with dedications on the fly leaf, wills, burial or grave records, memorial cards?
- Has anyone in the family kept a diary? Are there any letters, birthday books?
- What about a family photograph album and other photographs? Ideally, individuals need to be named, with dates and places added.
- Has anyone been an apprentice? If so, are there any apprenticeship indentures?
- What are the occupations and trades followed by members of the family? Are there any trade union records?
- Where did members of the family go to school? Are there any school reports, certificates, school prizes or other records of achievement? Any Sunday School prizes?

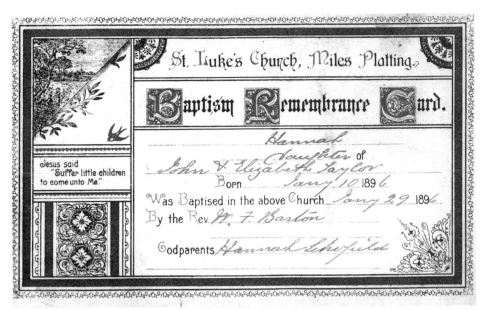

A **Baptism Remembrance card** *for Hannah Taylor, 1896.* (Heather Flockton)

- Has anyone served in the forces - army, navy, air force, marines? Are there any certificates of service or of discharge, details of a pension, any medals? Is there a family tradition of service in the armed forces? Was anyone in the territorials or the Home Guard? Was an ancestor in the merchant navy in times of peace or war, in the police force or in the customs and excise service?
- Are there any other family papers - passports, driving licences, ration books, identity cards?
- Has a particular first or second name been handed down throughout the family? Has a surname been used as a first name?
- Did the family come from a certain town or county, or did they come from elsewhere to settle in this country? Did anyone emigrate?
- Does the family subscribe to the beliefs of the Church of England, or have individuals been members of a local chapel or embraced some other religion?
- Does anyone have any information, however anecdotal, of the earliest-known members of the family?
- Has anyone researched the family history before?

Has it been done before?

Reinventing the wheel may be fun, but ultimately it's a waste of valuable time. Do try and contact anyone else in the family who has done any relevant ancestral research, though at some stage you should check the information to satisfy yourself that it is accurate. Amend it or extend it where necessary. Not every researcher may have been as thorough as we hope you will be! Do check the surnames which interest you in the various genealogical guides shown at the end of this chapter (especially those by Marshall, Whitmore and Barrow) which should be available at a larger reference library in your area or may be borrowed through the inter-library loan service. Useful sources for finding out if

Lancashire & Cheshire Band of Hope & Temperance Union: Certificate of Merit *awarded to Edwin Flockton, 1905 for his essay on alcohol and the human body.* (Heather Flockton)

someone else is researching the same family in the same area as you include: *Genealogical Research Directory* (GRD), published annually and also now on CD-ROM; lists of members' interests published by individual Family History Societies; the *BIG R* (The British Isles Genealogical Register, produced by the Federation of Family History Societies) and the Readers' Interests and Connections Sought pages which appear each month in *Family Tree Magazine*.

Recording information

At the very beginning of your research it is vital to decide on a system for recording all the information gathered. It may be that a card index system with a card for each ancestor and his or her family is the best for you, or a ring-file for each family in which you can insert the results of research, together with civil registration certificates and other records, with acid-free pocket files for photocopies and original documents. You may decide right from the start to enter all your research onto a computer; if so, make a decision at the outset and save yourself time in the long run.

Keep a family tree for each family line you research: the Smith Tree, the Jones Tree, and so on.

Meticulously record your research findings with complete references and catalogue numbers. Always transcribe exactly what has been written and not what you think it should be. If you have found nothing, still record the fact as a 'negative search' so that you do not go over the same ground again.

Friendly Society policy, 1919–1929. *Margaret Titford paid a penny a week to assure the life of her young son Sidney 'for funeral expenses'.*

As more information is gathered it can be added to your basic family tree. If you are compiling this tree by hand, it will not be long before a larger sheet of paper is required. Use the blank side of a sheet of wallpaper if you wish! A comprehensive family tree should always include names, dates of events, places and other necessary information. Compile a separate 'skeleton' tree, too, if you like, which shows in barest outline the various branches of the family as you discover them.

A special research file with plenty of paper should be kept for visits to record offices and libraries, together with an ordnance survey map of the area you are going to search (preferably one-inch or half-inch to the mile) and a county parish map which shows every parish and probate jurisdiction (these are obtainable from the Institute of Heraldic and Genealogical Studies in Canterbury). You will also need a magnifying glass, a good supply of pencils (no pens), and a working family tree to enable you to see where your next path of research lies. Do your homework before setting out for a record office, and during your work keep a notebook handy to jot down any ideas or sources as they occur to you. If this is not done then valuable time will be wasted.

In an ideal family, we may say, births, marriages and deaths should have been properly recorded during the years of centralised civil registration, and records of baptism and burial should be there waiting for us when we need to refer to them. Alas, few families comply with this ideal. Various rules and regulations have always been broken by those unwilling to conform, who have always thought that rules were made for everyone else but them! So, always think around a problem, keep an open mind and never take anything for granted.

In the long run you may wish to donate copies of your research files to a local or national library or other repository; family history flourishes on the sharing of information, and it's always nice to be able to put something back into the system as well as take something out.

Surnames

It can never be too early in a book such as this to give you a timely warning about surnames. It is the very existence of hereditary surnames that makes it possible to trace pedigrees of even the most ordinary families in the British Isles and elsewhere. But beware: most surnames have varied significantly over the centuries, being affected by local dialect, intonation, the inability of parish clerks to spell consistently, and illiteracy or speech impediments on the part of our ancestors. In fact, it was not until the nineteenth century and the advent of compulsory education that some kind of real stability came to surnames, establishing them in the way that we spell them today.

The possibility of variation in surname spelling should always be taken into account from the outset. It has been said that the biggest single difference between professionals and amateurs in this field is that the professional takes a more flexible approach to the form and spelling of a surname. The reason for this is simple: the professional has no emotional attachment to a particular form of a name, whereas if you are researching your own surname, you can feel very protective about its modern-day 'correct' spelling, exclaiming that 'I'm not prepared to welcome a man with the surname Belitha into my family, when I know that the name is Billiter!' Take care: if you become too emotionally attached to your surname in its present form only, you may never get very far in your pedigree. All that being said, surnames can vary in spelling from one branch of a family to the next. The Fysons with a 'y' might be distinguishable in more recent times from the Fisons with an 'i', even though the original ancestors would have used either letter indiscriminately. The letters 'v' and 'f' can be interchangeable, as in the names Fosse and Vosse or Volkes and Folkes. The letter 'h' may be put in front of a name beginning with a vowel, so that Alford or Elford become Halford and Helford. Letters may be added to or taken from a surname, and the dialect of an ancestral county must always be considered when searching for a name. In two actual examples from Cheshire, Alice Pilsbury appears in a marriage entry as Alice Spilsbury, and James Pierpoint as James Spearpoint, the 's' sound from the end of each Christian name having become attached to the beginning of the surname.

The West Country family of Phillips was known variously as Philipe, Philpe, Phelps and even Filp in the 1500s, and the standard 'Phillips' as it is spelt today only became stable in the late 1800s. One branch of the Vavasor family of Yorkshire became Vavister and then Bavister once it moved south, while another family line settled for the alternative Vawser in the fenlands of Cambridgeshire. The surnames Bavister and Vawser might appear to have no connection with each other; in fact they originate from the same stem.

Above all, vowels in surnames are notoriously unstable, since you do not use your tongue, your lips or your teeth to affect the sound as it comes up from your voice-box. The merest difference in the shape of your mouth can move you from one vowel to another. Expect to find the surname Titford as Tutford, Tatford, Tetford or Totford. This principle, of course, applies as much to place names as it does to surnames. The settlement called Totford in Hampshire eventually became Tutford, just as North Tidworth in Wiltshire was originally Todeworth and then Tuddeworth. Even during the last ten years or so, well into the age of general literacy, the following variations on the one surname have appeared on correspondence received: Tidford, Tedford, Tetford, Titferd, Titforth, Titfort, Titfield, Titfeild, Titsore, Titsort, Titsord, Titsford, Titfsord, Tissord, Tifford, Tiford, Tittford, Titfordd, Tichford, Titchford, Titfoed, Titfoot, Titlord, Tilford, Telford, Tipford, Tippford, Tiltford, Ttitford, Tictord, Titofrd, Totford, Tidmarsh, Titmarsh, Twyford, Pickford, Pitford, Pitsford, Fitford, Mitford, Citford, Sitford, Stitford. As it happens, many of the historical spelling varieties of the name appear here in the twentieth century. In some cases, a typist's finger has obviously hit the wrong key in error; but what can we make of more surreal varieties such as Thord, Tittoral, Alford and Lidgard? Please, be flexible and imaginative - anything is possible!

An unusual surname can often be traced through telephone directories to discover the location of today's families, and *The homes of family names* by H.B. Guppy (1890) can give you a good lead on more common surnames and their location in the late nineteenth century. You might like to contact an organisation called the Guild of One-Name Studies (GOONS for short) to discover if anyone else is collecting references to surnames which interest you. Write to: The Registrar, GOONS, Box G, 14 Charterhouse Buildings, Goswell Road, London EC1M 7BA.

The meaning and origins of surnames
The custom of using surnames developed around the twelfth and thirteenth centuries in England, before which time our forebears would have carried only one personal name. As the number of men named Godfrey or Walter in a town

or village grew, further precise identification was needed to separate Godfrey (the) Wainwright from Godfrey (of) Morley, Walter (the) Redhead from Walter (who lived by the) Ford. From this period onwards, surnames gradually became hereditary, beginning with the nobility and gradually spreading to the common man in town and country during the next two centuries. In some settlements even to this day there is a need to distinguish individuals or family branches yet more precisely still. In a Scottish village full of James MacKays, in a Welsh settlement bristling with Hugh Williamses, nicknames will be employed in the interests of precision - hence Jones the coal or Evans the bread.

The regular use of surnames in Scotland and Ireland followed somewhat later than in England, and in Wales hereditary surnames were not finally adopted until well into the late eighteenth and early nineteenth centuries. Surnames fall into four broad categories, with many others of miscellaneous origin:

1. Surnames based on a first name, male or female, such as Johnson/Johnstone (meaning son of John); Emms, (son of Emma); Dickenson (son of Dicken - a pet name for Richard).

2. Surnames based on a place or locality from where an ancestor had originated. For example, Lydiard (places in Wiltshire and Somerset); Leicester/Lester/Lessiter (from Leicester); Coombe (from a small valley); Mudford (a dweller by the muddy ford); Park[e] (a dweller by the enclosure or park).

3. Surnames based on a nickname which described an ancestor in some way - his looks, figure, temperament, etc. Redhead (red haired); Tench (sleek, like the fish); Trueman (trusty and faithful); Bragge (proud, arrogant, brisk, brave).

4. Surnames which recorded the occupation or status of an ancestor. For example, Parmenter/Parminster (tailor); Dexter (dyer); Neate (ox-herd or cowherd); Cooper (barrel maker).

Surname aliases

When researching ancestral surnames in parish registers and in other records, you may have found two surnames yoked together: 'Smith, alias Jones' or 'Jones, alias Smith'. Eventually one of these alternatives will probably be abandoned entirely, or the two surnames may be fused permanently into a double-barrelled surname: 'Smith-Jones'.

These aliases, often shown as 'als' or 'otherwise', can have arisen due to a variety of circumstances. If a mother remarried, her children might take the surname of their new step-father, with their original surname as an alias - or vice-versa. Illegitimacy often gave rise to the use of two surnames; a child might bear the maiden surname of the mother and also that of the father. An early stage in this process can be seen in this example from the parish register of Halberton in Devon:

> *Baptism, 1803. John Hellier, son of Betty Hemburrow, maidservant, illegitimate.*

When a couple were not married, the common-law wife may be entered in records under her maiden name, with the surname of her partner as an alias. Any children born to the couple might bear a resultant double surname.

Some tenants who held copyhold land in more than one manor would be known by a different form of an alias in each, being referred to as 'James Batt, alias Boxall' in one manor, and 'James Boxall, alias Batt' in the other.

During the Interregnum period of the seventeenth century, all marriages consisted of a civil ceremony, and many took the view that couples were not married in the eyes of the church. In certain such cases the wife's maiden name would be kept and used as an alias (see D. Steel, *National index of parish registers*, vol. 1, 1968, pp. 92-96).

Variations of a surname spelling may appear on legal documents with 'alias' between the two: 'Philips alias Phelps'.

Members of the gentry or the nobility would not be averse to changing their surname completely if an inheritance was involved. The great Bedfordshire genealogist and antiquary, F.A.Blaydes, changed his surname to Page-Turner by Royal Licence in 1903, having succeeded to the estates and the baronetcy of his maternal uncle, Sir Edward Henry Page-Turner; the well-known herald, G.E. Cokayne, had started life as George Adams before assuming his mother's maiden name as his own surname in 1873 in accordance with a wish expressed in her will; and Florence Nightingale's father, William Edward Shore, abandoned his own surname in 1815 on inheriting the Derbyshire estates of his mother's uncle, Peter Nightingale.

Golden rules for research

- Never assume. Check all family stories against known facts.
- Always do your homework before visiting a record office.
- When working in a record office, write everything down in a notebook, never on odd scraps of paper - and never rely on your memory alone.
- Methodically record all your research, negative searches as well as positive ones.
- Always double-check your findings.
- Aim to arrive at an understanding of your family within the context of its historical period. 'Ancestor spotting' alone is a fairly arid activity, so try to take a broad view, not a narrow one. Plan, if you can, to be able to write a family history narrative once your research is well advanced.

Further reading

(General guides, manuals, bibliographies)

Backhurst, M.L. *Family history in Jersey.* 1992.

Barrow, G. *The genealogist's guide.* 1977.

Begley, D. *Handbook on Irish genealogy.* 1984.

Begley, D. *Irish genealogy: a record finder.* 1987. (Includes R.E. Matheson's 'Special report on surnames in Ireland', pp.195-232).

Begley, D. *The ancestor trail in Ireland.* 1987.

Bevan, A. *Tracing your ancestors in the Public Record Office.* (5th.Ed.) 1999.

Camp, A. *First steps in family history.* (3rd.Ed.) 1998.

Camp, A. *Tracing your ancestors.* 1970.

Camp, A. J. *Sources for Irish genealogy at the library of the Society of Genealogists* (2nd.Ed.) 1998.

Chapman, C. *Tracing your British ancestors.* (2nd.Ed.) 1996.

Cheney, C.R. *Handbook of dates for students of English history.* 1978.

Colwell, S. *The family history book.* 1980.

Currer-Briggs, N. and Gambier, R. *Debrett's Family Historian.* 1981.

Currer-Briggs, N. *Worldwide family history*. 1982.
Davis, B. *An introduction to Irish research: a beginner's guide*. (2nd.Ed.) 1994.
De Breffny, B. *A bibliography of Irish family history and genealogy*. 1974.
Family Records Centre, The. *Introduction to family history*. 1999.
Federation of Family History Societies. *The British Isles Genealogical Register (BIG R)*. 1994, 1997.
Ferguson, J. *Scottish family histories held in Scottish libraries*. 1960.
Filby, P.W. *American and British genealogy: a selected list of books*. (3rd.Ed.) 1983. Supplements appear from time to time.
Fitzhugh, T.V.H. (Ed. Lumas, S.) *Dictionary of genealogy*. (5th.Ed.) 1998.
Fitzhugh, T.V.H. *How to write a family history*. 1988.
Gandy, M. *Planning research: short cuts in family history*. 1994.
Gardner, D.E. and Smith, F. *Genealogical research in England and Wales*. 1956-1966.
Grenham, J. *Tracing your Irish ancestors*. (2nd.Ed.) 1999.
Guild of One-Name Studies. *Register of one-name studies*. Published at intervals.
Hamilton-Edwards, G. *In search of ancestry*. 1983.
Hamilton-Edwards, G. *In search of Scottish ancestry*. 1983.
Harvey, R. *Genealogy for librarians*. (2nd.Ed.) 1992.
Herber, M. *Ancestral trails: the complete guide to British genealogy and family history*. 1997.
Hoffman, M. *Genealogical & local history books in print: family history volume*. (5th.Ed.) 1996.
Humphery-Smith, C.R. *A genealogist's bibliography*. 1985.
Humphery-Smith, C.R. *The Phillimore atlas and index of parish registers: England, Wales and Scotland*. (2nd.Ed.) 1995.
Irvine, S. and Hickey, N.M. *Going to Ireland: a genealogical researcher's guide*. 1997.
Istance, J. and Cann, E.E. *Researching family history in Wales*. 1996.
James, A. *Scottish roots: a step by step guide for ancestor hunters in Scotland and overseas*. 1995.
Johnson, K.A and Sainty, M.R. *Genealogical Research Directory*. Annually from 1982.
Le Poidevin, D.W. *How to trace your ancestors in Guernsey*. 1978.
McLaughlin, E. *Interviewing elderly relatives*. (3rd.Ed.) 1993.
MacLysaght, E. *Bibliography of Irish family history*. 1982.
MacLysaght, E. *Irish families*. (3rd.Ed.) 1978.
MacLysaght, E. *More Irish families*. 1996.
Marshall, G.W. *The genealogist's guide*. 1903, several times reprinted.
Moulton, J.W. *Genealogical resources in English repositories*. 1988. Supplement, 1992.
Narasimham, J. *The Manx family tree; a beginner's guide to records in the Isle of Man*. (2nd.Ed.) 1996.
Neill, K. *How to trace your family history in Northern Ireland*. 1986.
Palgrave-Moore, P. *How to record your family tree*. 1979.
Pelling, G. *Beginning your family history*. (8th. Ed.) 2001.
PRO Pocket Guide. *Getting Started in family history*. 2000.
Rogers, C. *The family tree detective: tracing your ancestors in England and Wales*. (3rd.Ed.) 1997.

Rowlands, J, et al. *Welsh family history: a guide to research.*
 (2nd.Ed.) 1998.
Rowlands, J. & S. *Second stages in researching Welsh ancestry.* 1999.
Ryan, J.G. *Irish records: sources for family and local history.* 1999.
Ryan, J.G. and Smith, B. *Tracing Your Dublin Ancestors.* 2001.
Saul, P. *The family historian's Enquire Within.* (5th. Ed.) 1995.
Savin, A. *DNA For Family History.* 2001.
Sillers Floate, S. *My Ancestors Were Gypsies.* 1999.
Smith, B. *Tracing Your Mayo Ancestors.* 2001.
Society of Genealogists: *Note taking and keeping for genealogists.* Leaflet No.4.
Stuart, M. *Scottish family history: a guide to works of reference.* 1978.
Swinnerton, I. *Basic approach to keeping your family records.* 1995.
Thomson, T.R. *A catalogue of British family histories.* 1980.
Titford, D.G. *Moonrakers in my family.* 1995.
Titford, J. *Succeeding in family history: helpful hints and time-saving tips.* 2001.
 (With special attention paid to **names** and to **civil registration** and **census**
 records.)
Titford, J. *The Titford family 1547-1947.* 1989.
Titford, J. *Writing and publishing your family history.* 1996.
Todd, A. *Basic sources for family history: back to the early 1800s.* (3rd.Ed.) 1994.
Todd, A. *Basic record keeping for family historians.* 1991.
Webb, C. *Dates and calendars for the genealogist.* 1994.
Whitmore, J.B. *A genealogical guide.* 1953.
Willis, A.J. and Proudfoot, K. *Genealogy for beginners.* 1997.

(Surnames)
Bardsley, C.W. *A dictionary of English and Welsh surnames.* Originally
 published in 1901. Reprinted several times since.
Black, G.F. *The surnames of Scotland.* Originally published in 1946. Reprinted
 several times since.
Hanks, P. and Hodges, F. *A dictionary of surnames.* 1988.
MacLysaght, E. *The surnames of Ireland.* (6th. Ed.) 1985.
McKinley, R.A. *A history of British surnames.* 1990.
Morgan, T.J. and P. *Welsh surnames.* 1985.
Reaney, P.H. and Wilson, R.M. *A dictionary of English surnames.* (3rd.Ed.)
 1995.
Rogers, C.D. *The surname detective.* 1995.
Rowlands, J. and S. *The surnames of Wales.* 1996.

These lists of books - which have had to be highly selective - concentrate mainly on recently-published works which should be readily available for sale, or can be consulted on the shelves of larger reference libraries.

Many other short guides to family history research have been published by the Society of Genealogists, by the Federation of Family History Societies (including research guides by Jeremy Gibson, county genealogical bibliographies by Stuart Raymond and a 'Basic facts' series), by Colin Chapman, Eve McLaughlin and others.

CHAPTER 2

Civil Registration of Births, Marriages and Deaths

From 1 July 1837 all births, marriages and deaths taking place within England and Wales have been officially recorded by the civil authorities and certificates issued to the persons concerned. From the start the country was divided into a number of Registration Districts, each with its own Superintendent Registrar, based upon the existing Poor Law Unions. Within these Registration Districts lay Sub-Districts. The original records of births and deaths were to be kept at each registrar's office, with copies submitted every quarter to a central repository in London. This did not mean that the recording of events in churches and chapels would cease; baptisms and burials continued to be recorded in the usual way as and when they took place.

Clergy who conducted marriages in officially-authorised churches or chapels were responsible for submitting quarterly returns direct to the Registrar General in London. Local nonconformist congregations could request that their church or chapel be licensed to perform marriages. Until the Marriage Act of 1898, such ceremonies could only take place if the local registrar was present to note the details in his own register; from 1899 congregations were allowed to keep their own registers and thus dispense with the services of the registrar. The other alternative for a couple wishing to be married was a visit to the Register Office for a civil wedding, which had to be by notice of marriage or by licence.

In theory, all births, marriages and deaths should be found duly recorded; in fact, some are not, particularly in the case of births. Many people viewed the introduction of the system, as they did census enumeration, with a certain amount of suspicion, and were in no hurry to comply with its regulations if they could avoid doing so.

Until the Births and Deaths Registration Act of 1874, it was the responsibility of the registrar to search out and to record the fact that a birth or death had taken place; it has been estimated that up to 15% of births, for example, went unrecorded as a result. The 1874 Act shifted the onus onto the persons concerned to give due notification of a birth or death within specified time limits, with fines for those who failed to comply. By the same act the guess-work was to be taken out of the registration of cause of death; henceforward an official certificate was to be supplied, signed by a qualified medical practitioner.

Not all registration matters went smoothly or according to the rules. In one case a boy was born and baptised Edward, and promptly died. In the next few years a series of children was born until, ten years after the birth and death of the first Edward, the last boy of the family came along and he, too, was given the name Edward. Later in life, the second Edward had reason to obtain a copy of his birth certificate, but by this time both parents had died and he never even remembered seeing a copy of the certificate. The appropriate indexes were searched, and he was most puzzled to find there was no mention of his name at the time when there should have been. He later mentioned this to an older member of the family who informed him that he had an older brother named Edward who had died; when his parents chose to call him Edward, too, they decided that as they already had one Edward recorded, there would be no need to go through the same procedure again and register the boy. After learning of this, Edward went back and promptly found the record of his elder brother and obtained a certificate, using it whenever such a document was required for the rest of his life. Needless to say, he enjoyed a very long and happy retirement!

All the way along the road of ancestral research you must expect many pitfalls - mostly caused by human error, or even, at times, by sheer dishonesty. Don't despair: human beings have always been fallible, and it is happenings like this which help to make the hobby so fascinating.

General Register Office (GRO), London

You will have noticed, no doubt, that only England and Wales have been mentioned so far. Civil registration began later in other parts of Britain and more details of this are given later in this chapter. You will still hear people speak of records of birth, marriage and death being held at 'Somerset House'; that has not been true for many years now, and St Catherine's House in the Aldwych, the next resting place for such records, has been replaced by a new General Register Office (a central repository for all registered births, marriages and deaths in England and Wales), part of the Family Records Centre at 1 Myddelton Street, Islington, London EC1R 1UW. This is a large building off Rosebery Avenue, nearly opposite Sadler's Wells Theatre. It is close to the London Metropolitan Archives (formerly the Greater London Record Office) in Clerkenwell Road and not too far from the Society of Genealogists in Goswell Road. There is access for the disabled, and for those looking for records of adoption, the services of a counsellor will be available if required. The nearest underground stations are Angel and Farringdon. Opening hours are 9 am to 5 pm (Monday, Wednesday, Friday), 10 am to 7 pm (Tuesday), 9 am to 7 pm (Thursday) and 9.30 am to 5 pm (Saturday). The Centre is closed on Sunday and public holidays (including the relevant Saturdays).

You may consult the indexes to birth, marriage and death records held at Myddelton Street free of charge, but to obtain a certificate giving full details of any specific event copied from the registers you must find the appropriate reference to it in the indexes and fill in an application form. The completed form should then be taken to the cashier's desk and the statutory fee paid. Your copy of the certificate will then be sent through the post.

If, however, you are able to call back in person, you may collect your certificates, but this must be arranged at the time that you pay for them. The fee is revised from time to time. Details of charges may be obtained from the General Register Office by post or telephone. Staff will be happy to answer queries from researchers, and the GRO will supply general information leaflets by post.

Go prepared

Before even attempting to delve into either civil or any other officially-held records, it is wise to follow the well-trodden path of preliminary research within the family. It is so easy to pay good money for a certificate only to find that Great Aunt Maude had a copy of the same one hidden away in a 'safe place'.

When visiting the Family Records Centre try to avoid going loaded down with large bags or other luggage, although lockers are provided for your valuables. It is best not to take children unless they are old enough to do some useful research themselves, as they tend to get bored and cause a great deal of annoyance to other people. Don't take the dog either! The consumption of food or drink is not permitted in the search rooms.

Just before you launch into your research: remember to be flexible about those surname spellings!

The system at the Family Records Centre is as follows. The bound volumes of indexes are arranged in three sections: births (bound in red), marriages (bound in green) and deaths (bound in black). These are arranged in quarters, ending March, June, September and December each year. Forty-two days were allowed in which to register a birth, so if the entry is not in the quarter you think it should be, try the following one. More recent registers are in annual volumes.

Each quarter is arranged in alphabetical order of surname spelling. The early volumes were written in free-hand (though these are gradually being replaced by typescript substitutes) so there are usually more volumes in these sections. As typed indexes were introduced, more details could be condensed into each book, so the number of entries per volume is higher. When you are unsure of the exact quarter you need for the year in which you are searching, use a methodical approach. There may be other people looking for dates around the same time as yourself, so if you have looked first in March followed by June, you may then find that the September volume is missing. Instead of waiting for its return, it makes sense to go on to December and then back to September when the book is back in its place. This will save a lot of time in the long run. A very simple aid can be devised: all you need is a piece of notepaper and a pen or pencil, and draw something like this:

Year	M	J	S	D
1880				
1881				
1882				
1883				
1884				

It is a simple task then to tick off the period you have searched. After a while it is so easy to forget which book you have already looked at, so a system such as this is a 'must'.

Births

When you open an early birth index volume, you will see it set out in this fashion (though Roman numerals were used for volume numbers until the year 1851):

Surname	Forename(s)	Supt. Reg. District	Vol.	Page
JOHNSON	John R.	Basford	7b	251
JOHNSON	John S.	Birmingham	6d	314
JOHNSON	John T.	Huntingdon	3b	196

From September 1911 the maiden name of the mother is included in the indexes, so a list of births would look like this:

Surname	Forename(s)	Maiden name of mother	Supt.Reg. District	Vol.	Page
JOHNSON	John R.	MORGAN	Basford	7b	251
JOHNSON	John S.	SMITHURST	Birmingham	6d	314
JOHNSON	John T.	NEIL	Huntingdon	3b	196

There might, however, be twenty John Johnsons, some with a second Christian name, which is always seen as an initial in the indexes, and some without any second name. You may think that your particular John did not have a middle name, and that he was born in the Basford area of Nottingham. There is no point in applying for a certificate for 'John R. Johnson' - who has a middle initial - just because his birth is registered in Basford, given the fact that Basford Registration District encompasses not only part of Nottinghamshire but also places within south-east Derbyshire. Only when you are perfectly sure that there are no Johns without a middle name should you again focus your attention on the John R. Then you should begin to wonder just how well you did your homework in the first place. Unless you want to take the risk of wasting your time and money by applying for a wrong certificate, first try to find out from other sources if John did have a second Christian name.

Marriages

Searching for a marriage certificate will follow a similar pattern. When using the early indexes, if you are looking, for instance, for the marriage of Herbert Bowskill and Jean Summers, you will first have to look under 'B' for Bowskill, Herbert and then in the letter 'S' for Summers, Jean. Before March 1912, apart from the clues given by the use of identical reference numbers for both parties in the same quarter of the same year, there is no indication that these two people were married to each other. So, if the wedding took place in the Basford area you would first of all find: BOWSKILL, Herbert. Basford 7b 124 in the June quarter of 1900, and then: SUMMERS, Jean. Basford 7b 124 in the June quarter of 1900. Be sure that all reference numbers and the year and quarter tally in this way before you order a certificate. For all that, even if a couple share the same reference number, there is just the chance that they didn't marry each other, as the number refers to a whole page of entries!

After March 1912 things get a little easier, as the surname of the spouse appears alongside each main entry:

Surname	Forename(s)	Surname of Spouse	Supt.Reg. Dist.	Vol.	Page
BOWSKILL	Herbert	SUMMERS	Basford	7b	124

The corresponding entry in the 'S' part of the alphabet looks like this:

SUMMERS	Jean	BOWSKILL	Basford	7b	124

Deaths
When you open the pages of an early death index volume, a typical entry will look like this:

Surname	Forename(s)	Supt. Reg. Dist.	Vol.	Page
THOMAS	Herbert R.	Basford	7b	191

From March 1866 to March 1969 the age at death is added as given by the informant:

Surname	Forename(s)	Age	Supt. Reg. Dist.	Vol.	Page
THOMAS	Herbert R.	61	Basford	7b	191

From the June quarter of 1969 the date of birth, if known, is shown in the death indexes. Do double-check such information if you can.

When searching those indexes which contain an age at death, it is worth bearing in mind that the informant could have been anyone from a spouse to a person who only knew the deceased socially and who had a guess at the age - and even at the correct names. Be very careful not to take anything for granted, and always check with other sources if you are able to.

The Institute of Heraldic and Genealogical Studies has published two coloured maps of registration and census districts, 1837-1851 and 1852-1946, which show registration district boundaries and will help you make sense of the reference numbers which appear in the 'volume' column of the indexes.

Miscellaneous GRO records in the Family Records Centre
Before leaving the Family Records Centre, it is worth mentioning the miscellaneous collection of other GRO records and indexes held there, which include the following:

● Records of still-births registered in England and Wales since 1 July 1927, which may be seen by special permission of the Registrar General.
● Records of adoptions from 1927. Only short-form certificates with adoptive name, date of birth and adoption will be issued to the public. Full adoption certificates can only be issued to the adopted person and are obtainable from Adoptions Section, Office for National Statistics, General Register Office, Smedley Hydro, Trafalgar Road, Birkdale, Southport PR8 2HH.
● Records of births and deaths at sea on any ship registered in Great Britain and Northern Ireland from 1 July 1837. [Marine Register Book]

CERTIFIED COPY of an ENTRY
IN THE MARINE REGISTER

Application Number. 63908

Pursuant to the provisions of the Merchant Shipping Acts 1894 and 1970 and the Births and Deaths Registration Act 1953.

Return of Deaths at Sea, reported to the Registrar General of Shipping and Seamen under the provision of the the "Merchant Shipping Act,1894", during the Month of September 1902.

Name of Ship	Official Number	Date of Death	Place of Death	Name and Surname of deceased	Sex	Age	Rank or Profession or Occupation	Nationality	Last Place of Abode	Cause of Death	Passenger or Member of Crew
Dominion	109417	8.9.02	Lat 41.15. Long 10.57 W	Frederick George Cole	Male	41	Sergeant 3rd Wilts Regt.	English	Saint Helena	Rheumatism and Heart failure	Passenger

CERTIFIED to be a true copy of an entry in the MARINE REGISTER OF...DEATHS...........

Given at the GENERAL REGISTER OFFICE, LONDON, under the seal of the said Office, this 20th day of February , 19 80 .

The Births and Deaths Registration Act 1953 (sec. 34) provides that any certified copy of an entry purporting to be sealed or stamped with the seal of the General Register Office shall be received as evidence of the birth or death to which it relates without any further or other proof of the entry, and no certified copy purporting to be given in the said Office shall be of any force or effect unless it is sealed or stamped as aforesaid.

CAUTION:—Any person who (1) falsifies any of the above particulars on this certificate, or (2) uses a falsified certificate as true, knowing it to be false, is liable to prosecution.

NA   3341

Certified copy of a Marine Register entry, 1902. *The relevant latitude and longitude are given as 'Place of Death'.* (Crown copyright. HMSO)

- Records of births and deaths in any part of the world in any aircraft registered in Great Britain and Northern Ireland from 1949 or aboard any British-registered hovercraft. Records of deaths occurring on off-shore installations (i.e. oil rigs). [Air Register Book]
- Service records relating to births, marriages and deaths among members of HM Forces and certain other persons working for, or attached to, HM Forces, including registers of death of servicemen who died in the First and Second World Wars. Entries in the army registers date mainly from 1881, although some do extend as far back as 1761. RAF returns commenced in 1920 and Royal Navy returns in 1959.
- Returns relating to births, marriages and deaths of British subjects in most foreign countries registered by British Consuls, and births and deaths of British subjects in most Commonwealth countries registered by British High Commissioners.
- Certificates of marriage forwarded by the British High Commissioners in India, Bangladesh, Sri Lanka and Ghana from 1950 and foreign certificates of marriage forwarded by British Consuls.

Indexes to the above 'miscellaneous records' are also now sold on microfiche.

What information can be gleaned from certificates of birth, marriage and death?

Let us now consider what information can be gathered from the various civil registration certificates once you have obtained them. As with all family history research, you should begin from the present and work back in time. If you start with your own birth certificate, you will know that your name is, say, Robert John Holloway, and that you were born on 19 January 1954 at 12 Newton Street, Derby. Your father at the time of registration was a plumber's mate by the name of George Holloway, your mother's name was Mary and her maiden name was Ellison. Also included will be the date of registration and the name and address of the informant. It is easy to learn at this stage whether the informant could write or not; if this is not the case, a cross will appear at the side of the name. If your mother had been married before, her previous married name should also be included together with her maiden name, that is, if she had informed the registrar of this fact!

A birth certificate of an illegitimate child often has a blank space where the father's name should be. There was an understandable tendency to cover up an illegitimate birth. Before 1875 a mother was able to give the name of the reputed father, but after this date, the man in question either had to attend the registration of the birth in person, or supply an affidavit that he was the father.

From your birth certificate, then, you should now know the name of your father and your mother's maiden name. This information should, in most cases, enable you to search for their marriage certificate - unless, of course, your parents have one tucked away in an envelope somewhere.

Were you the eldest child? If not, when was your oldest brother or sister born? It is not uncommon for a child to arrive very soon after the marriage - or even before it! Once you have located the appropriate marriage certificate, you should learn the date of marriage; the name of the church, chapel or register office in which the ceremony took place; whether the wedding was by banns,

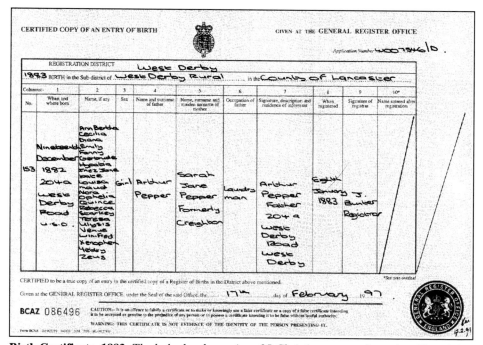

Birth Certificate, 1883. *The baby has been given 25 Christian names, from A to Z, omitting only the letter P which occurs in her surname of Pepper.* (Crown copyright. HMSO)

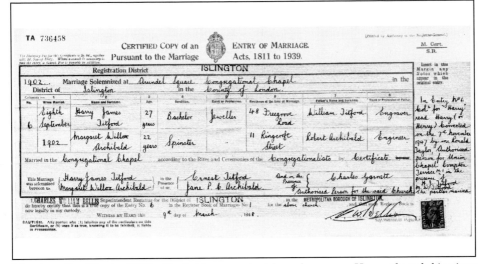

Marriage Certificate, 1902. *The bridegroom had been known as Harry, though his given name was Henry, and this 1948 duplicate certificate carries an official note of the distinction.* (Crown Copyright. HMSO)

notice or licence; the name of your father; his age at marriage (21 years and over is often shown simply as 'full age'); whether he was a bachelor, widower or divorcé; his occupation and where he lived at the time of the event. Also included is his father's name and occupation. Comparable information is given in the case of the bride. You can also establish whether the couple could write, the name of the officiating officer or minister, and - a very important point to note - the names of the witnesses. These could be relatives or friends. If the bride or groom was illegitimate, the appropriate space might be left blank, or the name of a fictitious father might be provided; a grandfather's name was often used for this purpose. If a father of either party was dead, the word 'deceased' could appear after his name - but the lack of such an annotation should not necessarily lead you to the conclusion that the father was alive at the time.

The information gained from this marriage certificate should be sufficient to enable you to obtain the birth certificates of your parents (be flexible about the ages given at time of marriage), after which you will require the marriage certificates of their parents - and so on.

Less information is gained from death certificates than from those for birth or marriage, but nevertheless it is important to use as many sources as possible in tracing a family history - even if only to corroborate what you already know. A death certificate gives us the name, sex and address of the deceased, the age as given by the informant, and the place of death. Also included is the occupation of a man or a single woman, or the name and occupation of a husband for a married woman, or of a father for a child. Also there is the cause of death, the date of registration and the name of the informant, the registrar's name and the district and sub-district. A coroner's inquest may have been held in the case of a sudden death and this fact will be recorded on the death certificate. Such a death will almost certainly have been reported in local newspapers.

Death Certificate, 1910. *Cause of death is given as 'blows on the head ... by Amos Peel and John Dugan.' Although they were subsequently acquitted for lack of evidence, the certificate stands as a permanent record of their 'guilt' of the murder of John Massey.* (Crown copyright. HMSO)

What to do if you cannot visit the Family Records Centre in London in person

If you cannot visit the GRO in person, or would rather spare yourself the time and expense of a visit to London for this purpose, other alternatives are open:

● Make a postal application to the GRO: Write to the Postal Application Office, Office for National Statistics, General Register Office, Smedley Hydro, Southport, Merseyside PR8 2HH, giving as many details as possible. A search made by staff in the indexes is restricted to a five-year period. In the event of an entry not being traced or not agreeing with the particulars you have supplied, a proportion of your fee will be returned. It should be noted that the fee for a postal application is much higher than that which is charged if you attend the Family Records Centre in person, but is reduced if you are able to supply a full reference from the GRO indexes.

● Use the services of a professional searcher: A professional genealogist or record agent will search for and obtain a certificate at little extra charge - and save you time and travel costs in the process. Look out for advertisements to this effect in *Family Tree Magazine*, the Society of Genealogists' *Genealogists' Magazine*, or various Family History Society journals.

● Obtain a certificate from a local superintendent registrar: Remember that original birth, death and some marriage certificates, with indexes, are still in the possession of superintendent registrars the length and breadth of the country. The certificates held by the GRO are only copies sent to London by local registrars and officiating clergy over the years.

It may be that you have visited the General Register Office and been unable to discover a particular birth, marriage or death in the indexes. It may just be the case, then, that the entry you seek has 'slipped through the net' between the local registrar and the returns made by him to the central repository. In this case, if you happen to know the district where the event took place, it could be a good idea to contact the district registrar and ask for a search to be made of the indexes. You must provide an approximate date to within a couple of years or so, and also supply names and places as far as you know them, for any search will be restricted to a five-year period. Each superintendent registrar's indexes and certificates relate only to events which took place in his or her own district.

In any case, if you do know the district in which an event took place and an approximate year, you could contact the relevant superintendent registrar by post, by telephone or in person in order to obtain a certificate - particularly if the surname you are seeking is quite a common one, for the indexes at the GRO may have literally hundreds of entries for that name from all over England and Wales. The local registrar's indexes may narrow the odds somewhat in this respect. In the case of a marriage, it is necessary to know exactly where and when the event took place - be it a specific church or chapel, or a register office - as all these registers are separate ones, and the registration and indexing of marriages has always been more complex than that of births and deaths.

If you decide you would like to make a personal search of the district registrar's indexes yourself, then for an affordable fee you may do so for up to six hours, which may be split into two or three visits. For this fee the registrar or his or her staff will check to see if the references you have chosen are the ones you require; this can be done up to a certain number of entries. If you decide from these references that you would like a certificate, the usual fee will apply, just as it does at the GRO for a personal search. If you need one specific certificate and you have the relevant details, it is possible to apply direct to the district registrar.

If you feel you would like to make a personal check, do telephone or write to the superintendent registrar of the office concerned first to make an appointment. Addresses will be found in a telephone directory of the area concerned under 'Registration of Births, Deaths and Marriages', or your own local superintendent registrar will be able to supply an address for you. Over the years various districts and sub-districts have been amalgamated or abolished, so vigilance is necessary.

Some church and chapel marriage registers dating from 1837 onwards are now being deposited in County Record Offices, and this practice may offer you the opportunity to seek a marriage you require in circumstances where you can make your own copy of the entry without paying the registrar's required fee. Many County Record Offices do not allow photocopying of their registers any more, but will be more than happy to give you a form stating that the entry you have found is a genuine one taken from the marriage register. You may also find that some marriage notice books (for marriages in a register office) have been deposited in the appropriate County Record Offices.

● Consult GRO indexes on microfiche: Purchasing these is an expensive proposition, but sets are held by the Society of Genealogists and at various major reference and local studies libraries. Dates covered will vary. Here you can browse at your leisure, away from the bustle of the Family Records Centre, and even steadily compile a full list of references to the surname you are researching, if it is a comparatively rare one. You will still have to order certificates by one of the means already stated, but it should be stressed that references from these microform indexes have no relevance to local registrars' holdings - they are specific to the GRO only.

Scotland

The Scottish civil registration system began on 1 January 1855, and the records for the whole of Scotland are kept at New Register House in Edinburgh. Conveniently enough, the same building also houses the Old Parish Registers (OPRs) for Scotland: New Register House is truly a one-stop repository.

Another advantage is that you can actually consult the 'statutory registers' of births, marriages and deaths whilst you are on the premises. You do have to pay to enter the building, but copying notes from the registers is then free. You must pay if you want to obtain official copies, but even then they are cheaper than those in England and Wales. For details of the search facilities and current charges, send a stamped addressed envelope to the General Register Office for Scotland, New Register House, Edinburgh EH1 3YT.

The indexes to the registers are computerised. Birth indexes give the child's names, the registration district and the register entry number. The mother's maiden surname is provided from 1929 onwards. There are separate marriage indexes for husbands and wives, and these give each party's name, the registration district and the register entry number. Death indexes give the name of the deceased, his or her age (from 1866 onwards), the registration district and

Scottish Marriage Certificate, 1870. *Note that the full names of both sets of parents are given.* (Crown copyright. HMSO)

the register entry number. From 1855 to 1865 married women are indexed under their married name with the maiden name added to the index entry. From 1866 there are separate entries under married name and maiden name. Ages are given - but do be aware that these may only be approximate, especially in the early years of registration. One further word of warning: Mac and Mc are indexed separately! Once you have found up to three entries which interest you in the indexes, you can order the appropriate registers on microfiche. You may make pencil notes from these of entries which specifically interest you.

There is a computer link between New Register House and the Family Records Centre in London, to enable visitors to the FRC to access the Scottish indexes - but not the microfiched registers. Users of the Internet are able, for a fee, to consult the Registrar General for Scotland's "Origins" at http://www.origins.net. Here you are able to access the indexes (only) to the Old Parochial Registers (baptisms and marriages 1553–1854) and to births, marriages and deaths 1855–1897, together with the 1881 and 1891 censuses for Scotland.

During the first year of registration in Scotland, 1855, the range of information provided - or asked for, at least - was exceptionally comprehensive. It was all too good to last, alas, and the amount of detail required was reduced in 1856, then further modified in 1861. Even after this date, however, the Scottish registers and the certificates made up from them are more informative than those for England and Wales. Birth registers give the name and then the date, time and place of birth; sex; father's name and rank or profession; mother's name and maiden name; date and place of the parents' marriage; residence if out of the house in which the birth occurred; signature and qualification of the informant. Marriage registers state when, where and how (e.g. by banns or proclamation) the marriage took place; the name, rank or profession, marital status, age and usual residence of the parties, together with the names of father and mother for both the bridegroom *and* the bride. For regular marriages the name of the officiating minister is stated and witnesses are recorded, while for irregular marriages the date of 'conviction' and the decree of the declarator or sheriff's warrant is given. A death entry gives the name, rank or profession and marital status of the deceased, along with his or her spouse's name, details of when and where the person died, sex, father's name and rank or profession, mother's name and maiden name, cause of death, signature and qualifications of the informant and the usual residence of the deceased if out of the house in which the death occurred.

Miscellaneous records at New Register House
Further records of genealogical value at New Register House include the following:

- Marine Register of births and deaths from 1855. Certified returns received from the Registrar General for Shipping and Seamen in respect of births and deaths on British-registered merchant vessels at sea if a child's father or the deceased person was a Scottish subject.
- Air Registers of births and deaths from 1948. Records of births and deaths in any part of the world in aircraft registered in the United Kingdom where it appears that a child's father or the deceased person was usually resident in Scotland.

- Service records from 1881. These include army returns of births, deaths and marriages of Scottish persons at military stations abroad during the period 1881 to 1959, and the Service Department Registers which, since 1 April 1959, have recorded births, marriages and deaths outside the UK relating to persons ordinarily resident in Scotland who are serving in or are employed by HM Forces. These include the families of members of the forces, also certified copies of entries relating to marriages solemnized outside the UK by army chaplains since 1892 where one of the parties to the marriage is described as being Scottish and at least one of the parties is serving in HM Forces.
- War Registers from 1899. There are three such registers: South African War (1899 to 1902) which records the deaths of Scottish soldiers; First World War (1914 to 1919) which records the deaths of Scottish persons serving as Warrant Officers, Non-commissioned Officers or men in the army or as Petty Officers or men in the Royal Navy; Second World War (1939 to 1945) which consists of incomplete returns of the deaths of Scottish members of the armed forces.
- Consular returns of births, marriages and deaths from 1914. Certified copies of registrations by British Consuls relating to persons of Scottish birth or descent. Records of births and deaths date from 1914 and marriages from 1917.
- High Commissioners' returns of births and deaths from 1964. These are returns from certain Commonwealth countries relating to persons of Scottish descent or birth. Some earlier returns are available for India, Pakistan, Bangladesh, Sri Lanka and Ghana, and some are extant for marriages in certain other countries.
- Registers of births, deaths and marriages in foreign countries from 1850 to 1965. Records compiled by the General Register Office until the end of 1965 relating to the births of children of Scottish parents and the marriages and deaths of Scottish subjects. The entries were made on the basis of information supplied by the parties concerned and after consideration of the evidence of each event.
- Foreign marriages from 1947. Certified copies of certificates (with translations) relating to marriages of persons from Scotland in certain foreign countries according to the laws of those countries without the presence of the British Consular Officer.
- Register of corrected entries. Where the letters 'RCE' appear in the margin of a register with a reference number, you are referred to the 'Register of Corrected Entries' - usually because there has been a change of name.
- Adopted children register, from 1930. Here are records of persons adopted under orders made by the Scottish courts. There are no entries relating to persons born before October 1909.
- Central register of divorce, from 1 May 1984. Extracts from the register show the names of the parties, the date and place of marriage and the date, place and details of any order made by the court regarding financial provision or custody of children.
- Register of neglected entries. Here are recorded births, marriages and deaths known to have occurred in Scotland between 1801 and 1854 which are not in the Old Parish Registers.

- The GRO holds a register of stillbirths recorded by district registrars from 1939, but this is not open to public scrutiny. Extracts will only be issued in exceptional circumstances - for legal purposes, for example.

You may obtain certificates by post from the GRO in Edinburgh, and the appropriate fees will apply. There is also limited provision for making searches in the duplicate records held by local registrars. You should telephone or write to the appropriate office for details. Some Family History Centres of the Church of Jesus Christ of Latter-day Saints (Mormons) hold filmed copies of Scottish birth, marriage and death indexes from 1855; the Society of Genealogists in London has microfilm copies of these indexes, 1855 to 1920, and the actual register entries for the year 1855 only.

Ireland

General registration in Ireland dates from 1864, though Protestant marriages were registered from 1845. Records for all of Ireland to 1922 and for southern Ireland only from that date are held at the General Register Office, Joyce House, 8-11 Lombard Street East, Dublin 2. Indexes have been microfilmed, and summaries of birth certificates, 1864-1867, are entered on the International Genealogical Index (see Chapter 6). The General Register Office for Northern Ireland is at 49-55 Chichester Street, Belfast BT1 4HL. Here you will find birth and death registers for the counties of Northern Ireland from 1864, but marriages from only 1922. To locate a death entry, 1864-1921, you need to know the registration district. In the event, then, it is more straightforward to make use of Joyce House in Dublin for Northern Ireland marriages and deaths, 1864 to 1922.

Miscellaneous records in the GRO for Northern Ireland

The General Register Office for Northern Ireland also holds the following records:

- Marine Registers of births and deaths from 1922.
- Consular returns of births, marriages and deaths abroad relating to individuals from Northern Ireland.
- High Commissioners' returns of births, deaths and marriages in Commonwealth countries relating to individuals from Northern Ireland.
- Service Department Registers: records of births, marriages and deaths registered according to the Army Act of 1879, but only those which date from 1 January 1927.
- Adopted Children Register, containing records of adoptions by court order from 1 January 1931.

You can consult birth, marriage and death indexes in both Eire and Northern Ireland; for full details you will have to order copy certificates, as in England. Copies of the indexes may be consulted at some LDS Family History Centres.

The Channel Islands, the Isle of Man, Lundy Island

Jersey

Civil registration of births, marriages and deaths began in 1842 and copies of all registers are with the Superintendent Registrar, States' Building, Royal Square, Saint Helier, Jersey.

Guernsey and neighbouring islands
Civil registration of births and deaths began in Guernsey, Jethou and Herm in 1840, and non-Anglican marriages are registered from 1841. Records are at the General Register Office, The Greffe, Royal Court House, St Peter Port, Guernsey GY1 2PD. The Greffe also holds deeds, wills, administrations and other records for Guernsey. Registration records for Alderney began in 1850; in Sark, death registers date from 1915, marriages from 1919 and births from 1925. From 1925, births, marriages and deaths for Alderney and Sark have been registered in Guernsey at The Greffe. Certain records of births, marriages and deaths for the Channel Islands are in the Public Record Office in London (RG32, indexed in RG43).

Isle of Man
Compulsory civil registration of births and deaths in the Isle of Man dates from 1878, with marriages being registered from 1884. Records are at the General Registry, Deemster's Walk, Bucks Road, Douglas, Isle of Man IMI 3AR. Copy certificates can be obtained in person or by post once relevant entries have been located in the indexes. The Registry also holds parish and nonconformist registers, wills, deeds, an Adopted Children Register (from 1928) and other records. A complete set of Manx baptisms and marriages appears on the International Genealogical Index. Some records for the Isle of Man will be found in the Public Record Office in London.

Lundy Island
Births on Lundy Island, off the coast of Devon, were treated as foreign registers and some appear in the records of the Registrar General in the Public Record Office (RG32-35, indexed in RG43).

For a succinct yet comprehensive study of civil registration records you are advised to read Tom Wood's *An introduction to civil registration* (1994).

General registration: hints and reminders

- Foundlings are located after the letter 'Z' at the end of the GRO birth indexes for each quarter.
- If the time of birth has been given on a certificate after 1839, it may be an indication of a multiple birth, such as twins. Before 1839 the time was commonly given for a single birth.
- A child may not always be given the same forenames on a baptismal certificate as on a birth certificate. Parents may have changed their minds between registration and baptism.
- There were penalties for non-registration or (after 1875) late registration of births. Sometimes parents fabricated a birth date to avoid having to pay a fine for late registration.
- A marriage could take place in a register office from 1 July 1837, and will either be by notice or by licence.
- Do not be adamant about occupations. Our ancestors were quite likely to

change their job, and sometimes the same occupation could be described using a different term. Also, a man who once worked as a silversmith, for example, but now ran a lodging house, might still appear as 'silversmith' on his marriage certificate or that of the birth of one or more of his children.

- Death indexes after 1866 give the age of deceased. An entry which reads simply 'O' will relate to an infant death.
- The last death index volume for each quarter is used to register unidentified bodies.
- Some children will be shown in the indexes at the end of each surname spelling simply as 'male' or 'female', with no forename given. In such a case, either the parents had not been able to decide upon a name, or the child had died before it could be given one.
- If you are unable to find a marriage, make a wider search using birth indexes to find children of the couple in question. A marriage may have taken place years before - or years after - the birth of the first child; it may never have taken place at all, or it may have been celebrated outside England and Wales.
- Our ancestors frequently lied about their ages, or were unable to remember just how old they were. Ages given on marriage certificates were often falsified, especially if a couple was under age. This was a crime punishable by law, but as long as a couple stated they were over 21 years and the registrar or minister was satisfied, the marriage could go ahead.
- If you are unable to locate a marriage using a woman's known maiden name, do consider the possibility that she had previously been married, and that her married surname, not her maiden name, will appear in the marriage indexes. Column five on a birth certificate should give a mother's maiden name as 'formerly...' and will also give any earlier married surname, prefixed by 'late...', if she has volunteered this information.
- In years gone by it was a very common practice to give a child the same name as an older brother or sister who had died. So if you find two children with the same Christian name in birth indexes, apparently born of the same parents, the chances are that you will find a death entry relating to the first one. Just to confuse matters, in earlier centuries it was by no means unknown for two or more children of the same parents to have the same Christian name; a man's will might refer to 'My son John...and my son John...'.
- Always obtain a full birth certificate, never a short-form one.
- Still can't find the entry you are looking for? Consider the various solutions recommended by Colin Rogers in his book, *Family Tree Detective*.

Adoption

Adoptions in England and Wales were made legal by the Adoption of Children Act 1926. The Legitimacy Act of 1926 amended the law relating to children born out of wedlock, allowing the legitimisation by the subsequent marriage of the parents, who were then able to re-register their child. Successive acts were passed, but the most important was the 1975 Children Act, when radical changes took place in the law. One clause in particular regards access to original birth records by an adopted person on reaching the age of eighteen years (seventeen years in Scotland) which is permitted after a simple process of gaining permission from the appropriate court. For adoptions which took place before 12 November 1975 counselling is necessary before the original birth certificate can be obtained (this does not apply in Scotland). Counselling is not mandatory for adoptions after 1975, but adoption agencies and social services departments may be able to provide further background details, thus making a search much easier.

Addresses for applications for information and birth requests forms:

For England and Wales: General Register Office (Adoption Section), Smedley Hydro, Trafalgar Road, Southport, Merseyside PR8 2HH. See 'Access to Birth Records. Information for people adopted in England and Wales' (ONS 1997).

For Scotland: General Register Office, New Register House, Edinburgh EH1 3YT.

For Northern Ireland: General Register Office, Oxford House, 49-55 Chichester Street, Belfast BT1 4HL.

For Eire: General Register Office, Joyce House, 8-11 Lombard Street East, Dublin 2.

Adoption records date from 1927 in England and Wales; 1930 in Scotland; 1953 in the Republic of Ireland and 1928 in the Isle of Man.

There are agencies which will provide assistance to adopted persons and natural parents:

- NORCAP (National Organisation for the Counselling of Adoptees and Parents), 112 Church Road, Wheatley, Oxon OX33 1LU. NORCAP will provide advice on the receipt of a stamped addressed envelope. They have produced a list of adoptees and natural parents who wish to contact parents and children. NORCAP advises against the use of profit-making enquiry agents or genealogists, and provides members with an experienced, specialised search service at a very reasonable cost.
- BAAF (British Agencies for Adoption and Fostering), 11 Southwark Street, London SE1 1RQ. BAAF produces a wide range of leaflets and books on adoption.
- Scotland: Adoption Advice Centre (Family Care), 21 Castle Street, Edinburgh EH2 3DN and Scottish Adoption Advice Services, 21 Elmbank Street, Glasgow G2 3PD.
- War Babes Association. Shirley McGlade, 17 Plough Avenue, Bartley Green, Birmingham B32 3TQ will help British children to find their Second World War American GI fathers. Send an SAE and all the information you can provide, please.
- TRACE (Transatlantic Children's Enterprise), 11 St. Tewdrick's Place, Mathem, Chepstow, Gwent NP6 6JW.
- The Child Migrants' Trust, West Bridgford, Nottingham, Notts. NG2 7PL. Helps put child migrants sent to distant parts of the Empire as 'orphans' in touch with their parents and relations.
- SKY Family Tree Message Service. SKY news text reaching the UK and Europe. Printed message of no more than 40 words including address to: Family Tree (SK/TT), PO Box 116, Swindon, Wilts SN3 6AZ.

Further reading

(Civil registration)

Blumson, C. *Civil registration of births, deaths and marriages in Ireland: a practical approach.* 1996.

Collins, A. *Basic facts about using the Family Records Centre.* 1997.

Cox, J. *Never been here before? A first time guide to the Family Records Centre.* 1997.

Dixon, B. *Birth and Death Certificates: England and Wales 1837–1969.* 1999.

Dixon, B. *Marriages and Certificates in England and Wales.* 2000.

East Yorks FHS. *District Register Offices in England and Wales.* (13th.Ed.) 1997.

Foster, M.W. *A Comedy of Errors: or the marriage records of England and Wales 1837–1899.* Wellington, New Zealand. 1999.

McLaughlin, E. *General Register Office.* 1997.

Matheson, R.E. *Surnames and Christian names in Ireland: for the guidance of registration officers and the public in searching the indexes of births, deaths and marriages.* 1901.

Nissel, M. *People count: a history of the General Register Office.* (2nd.Ed.) 1989.

PRO Pocket Guide. *Using Birth, Marriage and Death Records.* 2000.

Wiggins, R. *Registration Districts.* (2nd.Ed.) 1998.

Wood, T. *An introduction to British Civil Registration.* (2nd.Ed.) 2001.

(Adoption)

Howe, Hinnings and Sawbridge. *Half a million women.*

Humphreys, M. *Empty cradles.* 1996. Empire 'orphans'.

Leitch, D. *Family secrets* and *God stand up for bastards.*

Lifton, B.J. *Twice born.* 1975.

McGlade, S. and McCormack, M. *Daddy where are you?* 1992. GI interest.

Rogers, C. *Tracing missing persons.* 1986. Also an information leaflet, *Tracing the natural parents of adopted persons,* by the same author, from the Federation of Family History Societies.

Stafford, G. *Where to find adoption records: a guide for counsellors.* From BAAF.

Stafford, G. 'Adoption and its records', in *Genealogists' Magazine,* December 1995.

Toynbee, P. *Lost children.* 1983.

Verrier, N.N. *Searching for family connections* (essential first book for adoptees) and *The primal wound.* Both from NORCAP.

Wicks, B. *Yesterday they took my baby.* 1993.

Wingfield, P. *Bye-bye baby.* 1992. GI interest.

CHAPTER 3

National Census Returns

England and Wales

You will want to use national census returns to complement your discoveries in civil registration records, boxing and coxing between the two until a full picture of your ancestry emerges.

Censuses of population have been taken from ancient times, such as the one recorded in the Bible at the time of the birth of Jesus Christ, and in England the Normans lost little time in carrying out a census or survey of their own in 1086 - the famous Domesday Book. As the population of England grew, it was deemed necessary to take a census of the entire population - not just one which would include landowners or principal tenants. Although a census bill was introduced into Parliament in 1753, it failed because of the government's opposition to the whole idea. It was not until 10 March 1801 that the first official census of England and Wales, the Isle of Wight, the Scilly Isles, the Channel Islands and the Isle of Man was taken.

Statistics revealed that the total population of England and Wales in that year was just under nine million; by the 1851 census it had increased to nearly eighteen million, mainly as a result of an improvement in living conditions which had effected a significant decrease in the national death rate.

During this period many people left the countryside to work in industrial towns and cities. In 1801, 75% of the population lived in the country, but by 1851, 54% lived and worked in urban areas. The 1901 census statistics showed that by then only 30% of the population still lived in the countryside.

1801 was during the period of the Napoleonic Wars, with the ever-constant threat of invasion, and men were needed for the army and navy for the defence of the country. There were then more poor people than ever claiming relief from their parishes, and it was around this time that the first income tax was imposed and ordnance surveys of the country commenced, as well as an enumeration of the people being made. The national census has been taken every ten years from 1801 to the present day, with the single exception of the year 1941, when a national registration took place and national identity cards were issued. The returns for 1931 were destroyed by enemy action in the Second World War.

The 1801 census was placed in the hands of local overseers, who duly carried out the counting of persons within their own parish. These returns gave the number of people and of inhabited and uninhabited houses within a parish, and classified occupations within broad categories. When completed, the returns were sent to the government for statistical purposes and then destroyed. Certain parishes kept copies of these early censuses for their own purposes – some including the names of individuals, which were not asked for by central government – and these should be found amongst parochial papers, which are generally found in County Record Offices.

It was not until 1841 that more questions were asked of the population in general and that names of individuals were recorded. For the first time the returns were retained by the government, and would eventually be made accessible to the public for research purposes. It is interesting that the 1841 and 1851 censuses were made available in 1912 through the instigation of the then newly-formed Society of Genealogists. The censuses of 1861, 1871, 1881 and 1891 have now been duly released for public viewing after a one-hundred year period has elapsed in each case.

From 1841, census forms were distributed by enumerators to each household in their designated areas, just as happens today. The forms were collected, checked, and entered into a printed book of blank forms provided for the purpose, the originals then being destroyed. For those of the population unable to read or write - and there were many such - the enumerator or some other responsible person, such as the parish clerk or the schoolmaster, would fill in the census forms for them and assist others who were unsure as to exactly what was required.

All census returns are in the Public Record Office and come under the one-hundred-year closure rule. Those which are currently available to the public, with their Public Record Office class references, are:

HO 107	1841	6 June
HO 107	1851	30 March
RG 9	1861	7 April
RG 10	1871	2 April
RG 11	1881	3 April
RG 12	1891	5 April

(HO = Home Office: RG = Registrar General)

Each census includes all persons residing in a house or institution at midnight on these dates. So the 1841 census on 6 June covers midnight on 6/7 June, and so on.

The 1841 returns are not as informative as subsequent censuses, but are nevertheless of great value to the family historian, the following details having been required:

1841 Census. 6/7 June.

1 Place (street name, house number or house name).
2 Houses: inhabited, uninhabited or a building.
3 Names of each person who abode therein the night of the census, with surname and forename.
4 Age and sex of each person, males in one column, females in another. Ages up to 15 years are given precisely in years. Over 15 years the ages were reduced to the nearest 5 years. For example: 53 years would show on the census return as '50 years' and 39 years would show as '35 years'.

Page 14]				The undermentioned Houses are situate within the Boundaries of the					
Civil Parish [or Township] of	City or Municipal Borough of	Municipal Ward of	Parliamentary Borough of	Town or Village or Hamlet of	Urban Sanitary District of	Rural Sanitary District of	Ecclesiastical Parish or District of		
Berm'y	Southwark	2	Southw'k				St Mary Magdalen		

No. of Schedule	ROAD, STREET, &c. and No. or NAME of HOUSE	HOUSES In-habited	Un-inhabited or Building	NAME and Surname of each Person	RELATION to Head of Family	CON-DITION as to Marriage	AGE last Birthday Male / Female	Rank, Profession, or OCCUPATION	WHERE BORN	If (1) Deaf-and-Dumb (2) Blind (3) Imbecile or Idiot (4) Lunatic
				Lovelock	Son		12hrs	Baby Born 10 o'clk night of 3rd	Surrey Berm'y	
56				Ellen McSweeney	Head	W	44	Skin Culler	Ireland	
				Julia	Dau	Mar	28	B.M. Bdr	London	
				Margaret	"	Unm	24		"	
				Ellen	"		16		"	
				Daniel	Son		14	Errand Boy	"	
				Joanna	Dau		9	Schlr	"	
				Willie	Son		6	"	"	
57	38 Berm'y St	1		Charles Conway	Head	Mar	55	Retired Carter Builder	"	
				Elizabeth	Wife		52	Picture Dealer	"	
				James	Son		11	Schlr	"	
				Elizabeth	Dau		18	Asst in Picture Bnss	"	
				Charlotte	"		16	"	"	
58	37 " "	1		James H Codgrove	Head	Mar	26	Fishmonger	Essex Leigh	
				Emily	Wife		25		Middlesex	
				Emily	Dau		1		Surrey Berm'y	
				Margaret Bridgeman	Head		40	Charwoman	Devon	
				Dorothy	Dau		8		Surrey Berm'y	
				Sarah	"		5		" "	
				Eliza	"		3		" "	
59				William Smithers	Head	W	38	Railway Jr Porter	Camberwell	
60				John Shents		Mar	34	House Decorator	Northumberl'd Newcastle	
				Ann Davison			40	Charwoman	Surrey Berm'y	
				Thomas	Son		13		Lancashire Bolton	
				Benjamin	"		9		Surrey Berm'y	
5	Total of Houses...	2			Total of Males and Females...		10 / 15			

NOTE.—Draw the pen through such of the words of the headings as are inappropriate.

1881 census, Bermondsey, London: *Master Lovelock (top), as yet unnamed, was born at ten o'clock on the night of the 3rd April — so would have been two hours old, not twelve as shown, at midnight.* (Crown Copyright. HMSO)

5 Profession, trade, employment, or 'of independent means'.
6 Where born. Column to be marked 'Y' for 'Yes' if born in the county, 'N' for 'No'. In the next column the following letters would be entered where appropriate: 'S'- born in Scotland; 'I'- born in Ireland; 'F' - born in foreign parts.
7 The end of a building is indicated by the use of two oblique strokes: //
8 The end of each household within the building is indicated by the use of one oblique stroke: /

In this particular census, relationships to the head of the household were not given, though they can often be guessed at.

The 1851, 1861, 1871, 1881 and 1891 censuses gave much more information:

1851 Census. 30/31 March.
1 Number of schedule.
2 Name of street, place or road with name or number of the house.
3 Name and surname of each person who resided in the house at midnight on the 30/31 March.
4 Relation to the head of the family - including servants, lodgers, etc.
5 Condition - whether married, unmarried, widow or widower.
6 Age and sex. Actual age at the time of the census.
7 Rank, Profession or Occupation.
8 Where born. Place of birth.
9 Whether blind, deaf or dumb.

Nell Gwynne, 97 year old orange seller, *has intruded into the household of an orange dealer in the 1881 census for St James, Duke's Place, London. The entry is clearly in a different hand; someone was taking the enumerator for a ride, surely? There is no sign of King Charles II ...* (Crown copyright. HMSO)

In 1871, 1881 and 1891, additional questions were asked in the column, 'whether blind, deaf and dumb', which was sub-divided into: deaf and dumb; blind; imbecile or idiot; lunatic. In the 1881 census the question was asked: 'age last birthday?' All relationships from 1851 onwards were specified by reference to the head of the household; individuals were not asked for their relationship to each other.

Once again, it must be remembered that some people lied about their ages or were unable to remember exactly how old they were or exactly where they had been born; some gave false information about children born out of wedlock, their marital status, their lodgers. All census returns depended on the veracity and the memory of the person who provided the information, so it is always wise to keep an open mind and to be more than a little sceptical.

Where to find the census

The only place in England and Wales where the complete census returns for England and Wales can be found (and these are on microfilm) is The Family Records Centre, 1 Myddelton Street, Islington, London EC1R 1UW. A reader's ticket is not required. For opening hours see Chapter 2.

The Family Records Centre issues free leaflets on how to find and use the census; do avail yourself of these and study them carefully on your first visit in order to familiarise yourself with the procedure involved in finding the film reference you require for a particular place in a particular census year. Photocopies can be made, and are well worth the money; in this way you can add a copy of the census to your own family documentation – indeed, you may well spot something on the photocopy which you had overlooked while scanning the microfilm.

The census returns were arranged by enumeration districts, and if you can spare the time you could look at an entire parish or hamlet or even a small town, taking note of all families with the same surnames as the ones you are seeking. If you can, look at neighbouring districts for members of the family who may be employed on a night shift nearby or working away from home or in service. Don't ignore the workhouses, prisons, hospitals, barracks, asylums, ships - and even (to 1851) the prison hulks which had prisoners confined awaiting transportation to the colonies.

Large towns and cities were divided amongst a number of districts, and it is necessary to have some idea of an address of an ancestor before searching these, although it has been known for some determined researchers to have trawled methodically through a large town from beginning to end in an endeavour to find an ancestor when the address has not been known!

Details of the various enumeration districts and of the villages and towns which each contains are available in the census room, and there are street indexes for London and other cities and large towns.

The original census books are still in existence at the Public Record Office, but only microfilms of these are available to the searcher - so be prepared for a certain amount of eye-strain and a lot of winding of take-up spools!

If you cannot visit the Family Records Centre in London in person, all may not be lost: there are copies of censuses on microfilm in various local reference libraries and record offices, though most of these relate only to one particular locality or county.

Census indexes

Some Family History and Local History societies - and some individuals - have transcribed or indexed various censuses for their area or county, and these can be an excellent short-cut to finding out details for your family. Some indexes give the barest details; others give you all the essential information for each census entry. Many county census indexes produced by Family History Societies are on sale either as booklets or on microfiche.

Just a few years ago a project was inaugurated by the British Genealogical Record Users' Committee and the Genealogical Society of Utah, whereby the whole of the 1881 census for England, Wales and Scotland would be transcribed and indexed. This mammoth task was brought to completion thanks to the efforts of members of the Church of Jesus Christ of Latter-day Saints and volunteers from Family History Societies, and the results have been made available on microfiche (county by county, with a national index) and on a set of 25 CD ROMs. The LDS Church has also published a similar index on both microfiche and CD ROM for the 1851 census, covering the counties of Devon, Norfolk and Warwickshire only.

Census returns for 1901

Census returns for 1901 onwards are with the Registrar General, Office for National Statistics, 1 Myddelton Street, Islington, London EC1R 1UW, and are closed to the public for a hundred years. The ONS plans to make the returns for 1901 (containing 32 million names) available on the Internet in January 2002, but meanwhile a form may be obtained from the Registrar General at the above address to enable a direct descendant or next-of-kin to apply to be given limited information from the 1901 census. An exact address must be supplied, and the names required from the census; in return the enquirer will receive the surname, forename, age and place of birth of the persons named. This is an expensive service, but it may be worth the money on occasions when all other leads have dried up.

Scotland

Census returns were taken every ten years in Scotland, just as in England and Wales. Those for 1841, 1851, 1861, 1871, 1881 and 1891 can be seen at the General Register Office, New Register House, Edinburgh EH1 3YT, where a charge is payable. The Registrar General for Scotland's "Origins" at http://www.origins.net on the Internet will allow you to consult the indexes to the 1881 and 1891 censuses for Scotland for a fee.

Ireland

The first state-organised Irish census was taken in 1821. Tragically enough, these returns were destroyed in the disastrous fire at the Four Courts in Dublin in 1922, as were those for 1831, 1841 and 1851. A few fragments survive, and one or two transcripts were made. The returns for 1861 and 1871 were destroyed by government order, none was taken in 1881 and 1891, and so the earliest extant return for the whole country is for the year 1901. These may now be viewed (along with the 1911 census) at the National Archives of Ireland, Bishop Street, Dublin 8, the National Library of Ireland, Kildare Street, Dublin 2 and the Public Record Office of Northern Ireland, 66 Balmoral Avenue, Belfast BT9 6NY, Northern Ireland. Transcripts of a certain number of Irish census returns including some for 1901 are now in print, while for a county-by-county list of those census returns which have survived, you should refer to *Irish genealogy: a record finder* by D.F.Begley (1987).

There is at least some compensation for the researcher in Ireland, despite the disastrous loss of so many census returns, in that the invaluable Griffith's Valuation has survived. This was a survey of land and property carried out in each county between 1846 and 1865 in order that a tax could be calculated for the upkeep of the poor. It is arranged in order of county and lists names of landowners and tenants with the extent and valuation of their property. The Valuation may be consulted at the National Archives, Bishop Street, Dublin, and at other Irish repositories. A CD-ROM version has also been produced by EMS in conjunction with Irish Microfilms Ltd., and a CD-ROM index to the valuation was published by Heritage World and the Genealogical Publishing Company in 1998. Tithe applotments compiled between 1824 and 1828, arranged in volumes for each parish, give occupiers' names, quantity of land and amounts to be paid, but they do not list families or landless persons. Tithe applotment books for Ireland, south and north, may be seen at the National Archives, Dublin, and in the Public Record Office of Northern Ireland. The tithes records are also on microfiche. In 1970 the National Library of Ireland produced *An index of surnames of householders in Griffith's Primary Valuation and Tithe Applotment Books* in fourteen volumes.

Ireland, like England, has a number of surviving records for the seventeenth century which, like Griffith's Valuation, can be thought of as 'census substitutes', including muster rolls, books of survey and distribution, a census of landowners for 1659, hearth money rolls, subsidy rolls and poll tax rolls. Details are given in a leaflet numbered 14 in the 'Your family tree' series produced by the Public Record Office of Northern Ireland, under the title *Seventeenth century census substitutes*.

The Channel Islands and the Isle of Man

Guernsey, Jersey, Alderney, Sark and the Isle of Man appear at the end of the class of records that make up the census returns for England and Wales, and are featured in a separate section of the 1881 census index on microfiche. *The 1891 census of Jersey: an all-island listing* was published by the Channel Islands Family History Society in 1994.

Census returns: hints and reminders

- Do not accept all the information included in a census return as the absolute truth. Opportunities for error were legion, and you may find discrepancies between the returns for different years. It is a documented fact, for example, that some individuals gave a different place of birth in every census from 1841 to 1891!
- Although the usual rule in the 1841 census was to round down ages for adults to the nearest five years, this stipulation was not always followed. Sometimes exact ages were given, and it was not unknown for the ages of elderly people to be rounded down to the nearest ten years.
- Try to take all family details from every census year from 1841 through to 1891 so that a family pattern can be established and analysed and seen as a whole.
- To save time, make out your own census pro-forma to make recording easier.
- If you are using, for example, a civil registration birth certificate to determine a family's address in order to find them on a census, you may find that the certificate falls between census dates. In such a case, either look for other births in civil registration records for brothers or sisters, or consult trade or street directories to try and find the family and an address. This method can be more helpful if a forebear was a tradesman, in business, or in a profession, but it is always worth trying in any event.
- If you are unable to find a particular address on a census return, bear in mind that street names and numbers may have changed between the date on your records and the date of the census. Consult a local directory or street map of the locality around the date you are looking for. These should be available in a local reference library or record office.
- You will find explanations of many of the abbreviations used in census returns in the appropriate appendix at the end of this book. Note that the term 'Daughter in law' can sometimes indicate a step-daughter, as well as its more usual modern meaning of 'Son's wife'. The same applies to 'Son in law' and 'Mother in law'.
- Gazetteers have been published for every census year, showing all the places covered in that census for that year. Be aware that some of these places may subsequently have disappeared.
- Whenever you find a family that interests you on a particular census return, wind back the reel to the beginning of that section for a description of the area covered by the enumerator.
- Take your time in the census room - 'make haste slowly'. Don't rush and make mistakes which will cost you time and money in the long run. Learn to 'read' the census in the round, rather than just plucking out items of interest from it. Always take note of everyone, even servants, as they may just turn out to be 'family'!
- When using the census rooms and microfilm reels, remember to wind back the reel to the beginning when you have finished, so that it is ready for the next user. When not using the microfilm reader for a while, switch off the lamp to avoid over-heating and the risk of damage to the film.

The Ecclesiastical and Education Censuses of 1851

It is worth mentioning that in addition to the 1851 census of the population, another was taken in 1851 on the 30 March - this time a census of places of worship. It was arranged by registration district, as in the other census returns, and shows the name and denomination of all places of worship - be they Anglican churches, nonconformist or dissenting Protestant churches and chapels, or Roman Catholic churches.

The returns, now held by the Public Record Office, give the following details: the date of consecration or age of the building; the space available for public worship; the total number of attenders at services on 30 March 1851, and the average attendance during the previous year. This census often includes useful information regarding the buildings and any endowments, and may contain various comments by the minister.

Although this census is often ignored by the family historian, it can be of great help in establishing the location and nature of a nonconformist place of worship within a parish, and give a clue as to a possible starting date for any registers or records which may have survived. At times some of the comments and information supplied by the minister may even produce 'family' names!

Further information is provided by the PRO information leaflet no. 51, *The Ecclesiastical Census 1851*. A number of these ecclesiastical census returns are in print, such as those for Bedfordshire, Buckinghamshire, Lincolnshire and North and South Wales.

A voluntary Education Census was carried out at the same time as the Ecclesiastical Census but, unfortunately, was not undertaken by the majority of parishes.

Further reading

Bryant Rosier, M. *Index to census registration districts*. (6th.Ed.) 1998.

Chapman, C. *Pre-1841 censuses & population listings*. (4th.Ed.) 1994. Includes details of surviving name-list censuses, 1801-1831.

Churchill, E. *Census copies and indexes in the library of the Society of Genealogists*. (3rd.Ed.) 1997.

Gibson, J. *Census returns 1841-1891 in microform: a directory to local holdings.* (6th.Ed.) 1997.

Gibson, J. and Hampson, E. *Marriage and census indexes*. (7th.Ed.) 1998.

Higgs, E. *A clearer sense of the census*. 1996.

Higgs, E. *Making sense of the census: the manuscript returns for England and Wales 1801-1901*. 1989.

Johnson, G. *Census records for Scottish families at home and abroad*. 1994.

Lumas, S. *An introduction to census returns for England and Wales*. 1992.

Lumas, S. *Making use of the census*. (3rd.Ed.) 1997.

McLaughlin, E. *Census 1841 1891*. (6th.Ed.) 1995.

Mills, D. and Pearce, C. *People and places in the Victorian census, a review and bibliography 1841-1911*. 1989.

PRO Pocket Guide. *Using Census Returns*. 2000.

PRO Information Sheets: 1, 2, 3, 4 and 5 – '1901 Census Project'. Information available on www.pro.gov.uk

CHAPTER 4

Parish Registers, Bishops' Transcripts, Monumental Inscriptions

Parish registers

Just as the details given on a birth, marriage or death certificate can enable you to move on to census returns, so information from the census should eventually identify ancestors who were born before civil registration began in 1837. To proceed further with your quest you will probably now turn in the first instance to parish registers and bishops' transcripts.

As it happens, you may have known that your ancestors lived in one particular parish in the years after 1837, and have already chosen to consult the appropriate parish registers and collected details of baptisms, marriages and burials. At least that way you do not have to pay the cost of ordering certificates, but although parish marriage registers duplicate the record held by the civil authorities, birth and death certificates will contain further information not to be obtained from regular parish register entries of baptism and burial.

You may have established something like the following scenario from the 1871 census: John Smith was aged 45 years in 1871, living at King Street, Leighton, Yorkshire. He stated that he was born at Hungerford, Berkshire.

With John Smith's age deducted from the year of the census, the natural next step is to locate the parish registers for Hungerford, and look for a baptism in or about the year 1826, the time of John Smith's birth.

The beginnings of parish registers

By a mandate issued in 1538 Thomas Cromwell, Vicar General to Henry VIII, ordered the clergy to keep written records of baptisms, marriages and burials. The response in many cases was cool, to say the least, and an injunction of 1597 (given full approval in 1598) reinforced the original order and gave instructions that existing registers be copied onto parchment in the interests of more permanent preservation. In parishes where the original paper registers survive alongside the parchment copies, extra information may often be gained.

Take, for example, the parchment copy register of the parish of Steeple Ashton in Wiltshire, which records the fact that Thomas Titford and Margaret

Ferfield were married on 25 June 1598 (the very year, as it happens, in which the order to copy registers was becoming fully effective). This copied entry is not only incomplete, it is also misleading, since anyone reading it would assume that the couple were married in the parish church of Steeple Ashton - which they were not. A virulent pestilence had struck the village in 1597, carrying off Thomas Titford's first wife, Elizabeth. Survival dictated that he leave Steeple Ashton with all haste, which he did, making his way into Oxfordshire, where he married Margaret Ferfield. Only the original paper register for Steeple Ashton reveals the true facts concerning this marriage, one of several recorded on their return by parishioners who had fled, married while away, and then come back home. The paper register entry for Thomas tells the full story:

> *1598. June 25th. Thomas Titford and Margaret fferfield were married*
> *at Shypton Under Whichwood in the countie of Oxon.*

The parish register system eventually improved over the years, following further directives from the authorities, and most churches kept at least reasonable records of baptisms, marriages and burials.

Throughout the centuries many registers have been subject to damage caused by damp, gnawing rodents or the effects of general neglect. It must be said that only a comparatively small number of registers exist from as early as 1538; many were not even begun in accordance with the mandate of that year, a good number are incomplete, and others have been lost, stolen or destroyed - particularly during the years of the English Civil War.

Some clergymen were very conscientious about keeping records, others not so. Many made relevant notes in the margins, and some of these gems give us an insight into social conditions in the past. The following family reference was found in the Rose Ash, Devon, parish register and was written by the Reverend Mr Southcombe:

> *1733 Memorandum. This is so dry a summer and water so very scarce*
> *that this day, August 5th, the Parish Clark's wife, Sarah Nicols, came*
> *hither to the Parsonage to fetch water from our well. They live at Ash*
> *Town in the house adjoining to the Stile by the Churchyard call'd ye*
> *Church House.*

In some of the early registers the entries are in Latin, but do not let this deter you: this is usually Latin of a simple variety, and you can soon become adept at translating with the aid of a dictionary. A simple guide to palaeography (the study of older forms of handwriting) should take its place on your bookshelves alongside your Latin dictionary. Practice will make perfect! We will consider some of the problems and challenges posed by older forms of handwriting later in this chapter.

Bishops' transcripts

From the year 1598, the incumbent of each parish was obliged to send a full copy of the previous year's parish register entries annually to his Bishop. These copies are known as Bishops' Transcripts (BTs for short) or sometimes as 'register bills' or 'parish register transcripts'. In the event, some parishes had already been submitting such transcripts before the 1598 ruling - so the earliest BTs for the Berkshire parishes of Blewbury, Little Coxwell and Faringdon, for example, date from 1591, 1585 and 1589 respectively. In the Diocese of Canterbury the Archdeacons demanded their own copies of the registers; a series of 'Archdeacons' transcripts' for certain parishes in Kent was the result.

Bishop's transcript of baptisms, marriages and burials, Arborfield, Berks. 1580–82. *An order of 1597 specified that details from parish register entries were to be forwarded to the Bishop annually. This example from a Berkshire parish within the Diocese of Sarum is evidence that such a practice was well established in some parishes at an earlier date.* (Wiltshire Record Office)

As with any other copied record, the accuracy of the transcription depended on the capability of the transcriber. Some BTs were a true record of the parish registers and some were not, whilst some had more details added than appeared in the parish register; many have baptisms, marriages and burials entered in one chronological sequence, not separated out. You will frequently find that the value of these records lies in the fact that they may enable you to fill in gaps where parish registers are missing, and to check for any additional or corrected entries. Always double-check parish registers against the BT entries whenever you can; in theory these transcripts extend to the late nineteenth century, but the bad news is that their survival has been patchy. No BTs exist for cathedrals, nor for several areas of 'peculiar' jurisdiction; none was submitted during the period of the Civil War and the Interregnum, 1641 to 1660; in London it was not the normal practice to produce them at all, and in other dioceses the surviving transcripts for certain parishes, if there are any, may begin very late or be uneven in coverage.

The format of parish registers

In the years immediately following 1538, at the commencement of parish registers, entries were usually brief: 'John, son of John Smith, was baptised'. As time went on, more details would frequently be added: 'John, the son of John Smith and Mary his wife, was baptised'. In the early years baptism, marriage and burial entries were usually recorded in the same register, perhaps with baptisms in the first section, marriages in the middle and burials in the last section. Sometimes baptism, marriage and burial entries would be made in chronological order, all events being recorded in one continuous sequence. Gradually, as the years went by, separate registers were kept for each event.

By 1753 and Hardwicke's Marriage Act (for more details see below), much more standardised information than before was required for each marriage entry, and many parishes used printed register books for this purpose. Banns registers were also instituted.

From the late eighteenth century to 1812, some printed or manuscript baptism and burial registers, referred to as 'Dade registers' (after William Dade, a

Marriage register entry 1758, Beckington, Somerset. *Possibly unique, as every participant has the surname Sainsbury. A typical printed marriage register following Hardwicke's Marriage Act of 1753.* (Somerset Record Office)

Page 85.

BAPTISMS solemnized in the Parish of _Rickmansworth_ in the County of _Hertford_ in the Year 1818–19

When Baptized.	Child's Christian Name.	Parents Name.		Abode.	Quality, Trade, or Profession.	By whom the Ceremony was performed.
		Christian.	Surname.			
1818. Decem. 13th No. 673.	Mary Anne Dau. of	James & Lydia	Eames	Rickmansworth	Labourer	J. J. Cory
Decem. 16th No. 674.	Christopher Son of	Christopher & Hannah	Leach	Croxley Green Rickmansworth	Farmer	Edwd. Hodgson
Dec. 27th No. 675.	Louisa Dau. of	Joshua & Elizabeth	Smith	Rickmansworth	School-Master	J. J. Cory
1819. Jany. 3. No. 676.	Ann Dau. of	William & Hannah	Coster	Rickmansworth	Labourer	J. J. Cory
Jany. 10. No. 677.	Lucy Dau. of	William & Elizab.	Ashby	Rickmansworth	Wheelwright	Hodgson
Jany. 17. No. 678.	Henry Ramsay Son of	William Henry & Lydia	Weedon	Rickmansworth	Grocer	Hodgson
Jany. 24. No. 679.	William Son of	William & Elizabeth	Humphry	Rickmansworth	Labourer	J. J. Cory
Jany. 24. No. 680.	Caroline Dau. of	William & Elizab.	Austin	Rickmansworth	Labourer	J. J. Cory

Christopher Leach was born September 23. 1728 – therefore was in 91st year – when baptized. His mother was a Dissenter, which was the reason he was not christened when young. — Hodgson

Baptism of a man in his 91st year at St Mary the Virgin, Rickmansworth, Herts, 1818. The annotation reads: 'Christopher Leach was born September 23rd 1728... His mother was a Dissenter which was the reason he was not christened when young.' Printed baptism registers were in use after George Rose's Act, 1812. (Herts Record Office)

Yorkshire clergyman) contain exceptionally detailed entries. A baptismal entry would include the dates of birth and baptism, the position of a child in the family, the occupation and place of origin of the father and mother - and often details of the grandparents of the child. Some burial entries would record the age of the deceased, his or her parentage (no matter how old the dead person may have been), occupation, cause of death and the name of the husband in the case of the death of a married woman. The number of parishes using this or a similar recording system during this period (and it was voluntary rather than mandatory) was quite large, including a number in County Durham, Northumberland and parts of Yorkshire and Lancashire. Similarly detailed entries may be found in a few parishes in Berkshire, Devon, Essex, Surrey and Wiltshire.

An entry such as the following, from Yorkshire, would be a wonderful find for a genealogist:

1787. May 20. John son of William Moor of Thorpe Audlin, labourer, son of William Moor by Ann, daughter of John Sommersall of Hoot Green, farmer, by mother's descent Hannah his wife, daughter of William Minns of Carlton, labourer, by Betty daughter of William Wild of Carlton, labourer, born 3 April, bap. Badsworth.

For more information on this topic, see 'Dade registers' by Pauline Litton in *Family Tree Magazine*, vol.11, no.9 (July 1995).

From 1813, following George Rose's Act of 1812, new printed registers, arranged in columns, were introduced for baptisms, marriages and burials. From 1813 onwards most registers lack the occasional relevant and even idiosyncratic comments added by the compiler, but at least a basic minimum of information could be assured.

From 1 July 1837 and the introduction of civil registration, marriage registers were altered to include the information still found on marriage certificates today.

Note that there will be differences between the birth and death dates given on civil registration certificates and the baptism and burial details gleaned from parish registers. A birth certificate should give the precise date of birth, while the date in the church registers is that of baptism, though occasionally the date of birth will also have been added to the entry. The length of time that may have elapsed between a birth and a baptism can usually be reckoned to be a few days or weeks. However, many people were baptised as adults - sometimes just before they planned to be married in an Anglican church. At times a spate of late baptisms occurred, as on the eve of the tax on baptisms, marriages and burials, imposed from October 1783, or of the system of civil registration which came into effect on 1 July 1837. In some cases children were not christened at all, not in a church or chapel of any denomination. Many parents favoured what are often called 'batch baptisms', whereby a number of sons and daughters would be baptised all at one time in one ceremony, even though their ages might range from a few weeks to several years. So never assume that a child being baptised is necessarily a new-born baby, nor that two or more children baptised on the same day were twins, triplets or whatever.

Similarly, the date of death on a death certificate should be correct, but will probably differ from the date of burial as shown in a burial register. A date of marriage given on a marriage certificate, of course, should be the same date as that found in a church marriage register.

Civil marriage by a Justice of the Peace during the Protectorate, 1655. *Anthony Timson/Timpson of Cranoe, Leicestershire and Elizabeth Plauritt/Ploret of Braybrooke, Northamptonshire have each obtained a banns certificate from their local 'Parish Register'. John Maunsell, JP for Northamptonshire, married them and signed the bride's certificate; the witnesses also signed. Such certificates were either kept by the justice, as in this case, or have simply been lost or destroyed over the years.*

The Julian and Gregorian calendars

There is one vital piece of information you should know at this stage if you are to make full sense of some of the parish register entries you abstract. Until the year 1752, the English were using what is known as the Julian calendar, whereby each year began on 25 March, Lady Day. If you are reading through a parish register compiled prior to 1752, you will find that the year does not change until 25 March - so, for example, entries will run up to the month of December 1670, and then carry on into 'January 1670' without a break. Only on 25 March 1670 will the year change to 1671. A failure to understand this could give you all sorts of headaches; you could assume, for example, that a child was born before his parents were married, when this was not really the case. By an Act of Parliament known as Lord Chesterfield's Act (1751/2) the Julian calendar was abandoned in favour of the Gregorian calendar - with the year commencing on 1 January and ending on 31 December. This Act stated that the year 1752 would commence on 1 January (the year 1751 therefore being of only nine months' duration), but for that particular year of 1752 only, to adjust the calendar for all time, 2 September was to be followed by 14 September - thus omitting eleven days. Thereafter, of course, people had a problem about when to celebrate their exact birthdays! It is said that John Wesley, for example, was never quite sure on this point.

If you are noting a parish register entry which is dated 3 February 1669, the year is 1669, 'Old Style', but 1670, 'New Style'. In other words, it took place in the year 1669 in the dating of the time, but would be 1670, a year later, in our method of dating. How do you make this clear? You could write '1669 OS' or some such, but the usual convention is to write '1669/70', yoking both dates together. Some people simply 'update' the entry, calling it '1670', but this is potentially dangerous, as another researcher could come along and, assuming that the date was in Old Style, add yet another year onto it! Get into good habits here: whenever you come across any date from 1 January to 24 March inclusive in any year prior to 1752, stop and think. Let alarm bells ring.

Having said all this, it was not unknown for some individuals to refer to 1 January as 'New Year's Day' even before 1752, and Samuel Pepys begins each new year in his celebrated diary on 1 January, not 25 March - so exceptions will prove our general rule in certain isolated cases.

England lagged behind Scotland when it came to adopting the new calendar; north of the border the Gregorian system had been in operation since the year 1600.

The Civil War and the Interregnum

The period of the English Civil War and the Interregnum brought havoc to the orderly registering of baptisms, marriages and burials in the period 1641 to 1660. Many clergy were ejected from their livings; the Book of Common Prayer was abolished in 1645, and the so-called 'Directory' was to be the only legal service-book in England. Officials known (confusingly enough) as 'Parish Registers' - some barely literate - were appointed in 1653, charged with registering births (rather than baptisms), marriages and burials. In principle, such men were to be 'able and honest'; in the event, some possessed neither quality. Fees were paid - a shilling for every entry of marriage and fourpence for a birth or burial. In a number of parishes, the original parish clerk carried out his registering duties as before.

The Marriage Act of 1653 stipulated that only civil marriages were allowed. A Parish Register would ensure that banns were published on 'three several Lord's Days' or market days in the church porch or market place of the parish in which each of the parties lived. A signed written statement would then be made out to certify that this had happened; the couple could then present their certificate or certificates to a local Justice of the Peace who would conduct the marriage in the presence of two witnesses. Some marriages took place in churches, others did not. In any event, details of a marriage which had taken place will often be found in the register of the appropriate parish, theoretically in a new register book called for by the 1653 Act.

Here is a record of a civil marriage from the registers of St Martin in the Fields, London:

> *Upon certificate of Willm. Williams Register of the Parish of Martins in the ffields that hee had published three severall Market Dayes in three severall weekes the intention of marriage between Charles Titford and Rebekah Costin both of the said parish of Martins according to the Act of Parliament for marriage of the 24th of August, 1653, the Parties before named were married before mee the 15th of May 1654.*

Ralph Titford, brother of the above-named Charles Titford, was living within the parish of St Botolph Bishopsgate in the City of London at this period, and clearly felt that a civil marriage ceremony performed by Alderman Thomas Andrews would hardly feel like the real thing. Ralph and his new wife Hester arranged for a second ceremony to be performed in a proper church by a proper minister later the same day:

> *Raphe Titford and Hester Hollis. By Ald. Andrewes, and afterwards married by Mr.Stevens, Curate of Bishopsgate, the same day. Aug 18th, 1656.*

Not every Parish Register carried out his duties responsibly, and not all events were recorded; family historians whose researches have stalled during this fraught period will speak ruefully of a 'Commonwealth Gap'.

The insistence in the 1653 Marriage Act that only a civil ceremony was legal was not repeated in a later Act of 26 June 1657. Fully normal service was resumed, in theory, at the Restoration of Charles II in 1660, though some returning parish clergy destroyed 'hatch, match and despatch' registers kept during the years of the Interregnum which they had heartily despised. A number of adults underwent baptism in the 1660s, having been denied the chance earlier, and some couples remarried, possibly in a spirit of 'belt and braces'.

Foundlings

Babies would often be born out of wedlock, or to parents who were unable to afford to support yet another child. One time-honoured way to solve such a problem was to leave the baby in a place where it would easily be found, giving rise to the term 'foundling'. This practice was most prevalent in London and other large cities, although it did occur in smaller places and will merit a mention in parish baptismal registers:

William Trowbridge. Parents unknown, found in a garden in this parish 19 April 1832, supposed to be aged about six weeks. Sponsors: William Edgell, junr, W. Webb, junr, and Elizabeth Nightingale. [Trowbridge, St.James. Baptismal register. July 9, 1832].

A foundling would often be named after the place where he or she was first discovered. If a baby had been left in the porch of St Patrick's church, he may have been christened Patrick Church, whereas George Christmas may have been found on the steps near St George's church on Christmas day. The baptismal register for St Pancras in London contains the following entry:

(Page *1*) The YEAR 18 *24*

[No. *1*] **Banns of Marriage between**

William Bunter Widower

and *Hannah Mason Widow both of this Parish*

1st Time, Sunday, *24 Octr 1824* by

2nd Time, Sunday, *31st Octr* by *Thos Hardwicke*

3rd Time, Sunday, *7th Nov* by *Thos Hardwicke*

[No. *2*] **Banns of marriage between**

John Winter Bachelor of the Parish of St George the Martyr Southwark

and *Sarah Dance Spinster of this Parish*

1st Time, Sunday, *24 Octr 1824* by

2nd Time, Sunday, *31st Octr* by *Thos Hardwicke*

3rd Time, Sunday, *7 Nov* by *Thos Hardwicke*

Banns book, St Mary Rotherhithe, London, 1824.

Marriage licence, St Andrew, Holborn, London, 1847. *Survival of original licences is a matter of chance; they were handed to the incumbent at the time of marriage and most were subsequently lost or destroyed. A paper-covered seal is suspended from the licence.*

> *William Euston. Child found in a Box in a Railway Carriage at Euston Station. Baptised July 14, 1894. Arthur S.D.Peile, Off. Minister.*

Shades of Oscar Wilde's Lady Bracknell here, who was horrified to hear that a young man had been found on the Brighton Line of the railway, 'in a handbag...'.

Some foundlings were taken in by the Foundling Hospital in London or one of its various branches elsewhere, and you may find surviving records concerning that child. The Sonning, Berkshire, parish register records the burials of children from the Foundling Hospital there, such as:

> *1757 Ann Underwood, an infant from the Foundling Hospital.*

Many such children were left to be cared for by a parish, placed in a local workhouse or orphanage, put out to a foster home or passed on to a children's society. It may just be possible to trace births of such children in towns and cities from records of lying-in hospitals. *The Family Historian's Enquire Within* by Pauline Saul (5th.Ed.1995) lists a substantial number of children's societies and orphanages.

If you trace your ancestry back to a person who was a foundling, you may come across such documents as apprenticeship indentures concerning the child, but in general you would be extremely fortunate to be able to establish the identity of the natural parents of such a child.

Marriage: banns, licences, bonds and allegations

The 1753 Hardwicke Marriage Act, effective from 1754, stipulated that couples wishing to be married in church were to have banns of their intention to marry read on three occasions in the parish churches of both the bride and the groom; if they were not to be married after the calling of banns, then they would need a marriage licence. Banns do exist before 1754, in the event, and are an extremely useful source of information; look for them within parish registers, or in a separate banns book after 1754.

Banns may be especially vital in helping you to determine the parish in which a bride or groom was living, other than the one you are researching at the present time. Most marriages took place within the parish of the bride - but if the banns register informs you that the bridegroom lived elsewhere, you can then begin a new search in a new parish.

If a marriage entry in a register appears with the words 'by licence' against it, then a search should be made for the marriage licence allegation and bond; where these survive, they will, like bishops' transcripts, belong with diocesan archives as they were issued by ecclesiastical officials such as an Archdeacon, a Bishop or an Archbishop.

Licences were granted from the fourteenth century, but records of bonds and allegations usually only survive from around the sixteenth and seventeenth centuries onwards. No marriage licences were issued during the Protectorate from 1653 to 1660 when all marriage ceremonies were civil ones. An intending groom applying for a marriage licence would pay a visit to the appropriate church office; here an allegation and a bond would be required, after which the licence itself would be issued. The couple would hand the licence to the minister on the day of the wedding. Few original licences survive, though an impressive collection of those for certain London parishes, bound up into books for the genealogist F.A. Crisp, can be seen at the Institute of Heraldic and Genealogical Studies in Canterbury, other volumes in the series being at the Society of Genealogists in London.

The licence allegation or bond will give information of value which you would rarely find in the subsequent parish register entry of marriage.

Typical allegations would include the following range of information, these examples being taken from a printed collection of marriage allegations issued by the Commissary Court of Surrey, 1673–1770, transcribed by Alfred Ridley Bax and published in 1907:

15 May, 1675. John Nevell of Lingfield, husbandman, widower, 45, and Mary Winsett of Godstone, widow, 38; at Lyngfield. Alleged by

KNOW all Men by these Presents, That We *William Charles Titford of the Parish of Saint Ethelborga London Gentleman and John Doe*

are holden and firmly bound to the most Reverend Father in God, *John* by Divine Providence, Lord Archbishop of CANTERBURY, Primate of all ENGLAND, and Metropolitan, in the Sum of *Two Hundred Pounds* of good and lawful Money of GREAT-BRITAIN, to be paid to the said most Reverend Father, or his certain Attorney, Successors or Assigns: To which Payment, well and truly to be made, we bind ourselves, and each of us by himself for the Whole, our Heirs, Executors and Administrators, firmly by these Presents. Sealed with our Seals, Dated the *Eighteenth* Day of *June* in the *Thirty nine* ———— Year of the Reign of our Sovereign Lord *George the third* ———— by the Grace of God of Great-Britain, France, and Ireland, King, Defender of the Faith, and in the Year of our Lord One Thousand Seven Hundred and *ninety nine*.

THE Condition of this Obligation is such, That if hereafter there shall not appear any lawful Let or Impediment, by Reason of any Pre-Contract entered into before the Twenty-fifth Day of *March*, One Thousand Seven Hundred and Fifty-four, Consanguinity, Affinity, or any other lawful Means whatsoever; but that the above bounden

William Charles Titford a Batchelor and Ann Odgar Spinster

———————————————— may lawfully solemnize Marriage together, and in the same afterwards lawfully remain and continue for Man and Wife, according to the Laws in that Behalf provided: And moreover, if there be not at this present Time any Action, Suit, Plaint, Quarrel, or Demand, moved or depending before any Judge Ecclesiastical or Temporal, for or concerning any such lawful Impediment between the said Parties: Nor that either of them be of any other Parish, or of better Estate or Degree, than to the Judge at granting of the Licence is suggested, and by *him* sworn to ————

————————————————

And lastly, if the same Marriage shall be openly solemnized in the Church or Chapel in the Licence specified, between the Hours appointed in Constitutions Ecclesiastical confirmed, and according to the Form of the Book of Common Prayer, now by Law established, and if the above bounden *William Charles Titford*

do save harmless the above-mentioned Most Reverend Father, his Commissary of the Faculties, his Surrogates, and all other his Officers whatsoever, by Reason of the Premises; then this Obligation to be void, or else to remain in full Force and Virtue.

Sealed and Delivered in the Presence of

Marriage bond, Faculty Office, 1799. *William Charles Titford and his fictitious partner, John Doe, are bound in the sum of £200.* (Lambeth Palace Library)

A Fleet Register 1749–50. *Peter Symson, 'educated at the University of Cambridge, and late Chaplain to the Earl of Rothes', performed marriages at the Fleet and also assisted Rev Alexander Keith at the May Fair Chapel. He was tried for bigamy in 1751. Bridegrooms shown here include a peruke maker, a weaver, a pauper, two labourers and a guardsman. Note the baptism entry for 'Thos. Wilson, a Black'.* (Crown copyright. HMSO.)

Edward Staplehurst of Lingfield, mercer.
15 Oct., 1768. George Johnson of Chobham, abode 4 weeks, tallow chandler, bachelor, 21, and Sarah Thatcher of Godalming, a minor, 19; at Chobham or Godalming. With consent of Thomas Woods, clothier, her guardian legally appointed by the marriage deed of Sarah Hedger, the mother of the said Sarah T. Both sign.

Just consider the range of information you have here: the ages of the parties, their parishes of abode, their status as bachelor, spinster, widower or widow, the occupation of the man and the name of a friend or relation 'alleging'. Parents or guardians should be named in the case of a minor. Note that a licence was often issued for use in more than one church ('Chobham or Godalming'). Where printed collections like this exist, usually with indexes, they can be a wonderful short-cut if you're not sure exactly where or when your ancestors married.

'Bonds' represent a very common legal device used in centuries past; by entering into a bond, a person would agree that he would perform some act or other (make an inventory of the goods of a deceased person, for example) or that a statement made was true. If the act wasn't carried out, or a statement said to be true was proved to be false, then a sum of money would have to be paid as a forfeit. Thus it was with a marriage bond. The bridegroom-to-be and a fellow bondsman would declare that there was no 'lawful let or impediment' to the proposed marriage; if such proved not to be the case, a penalty would be due to the church dignitary concerned. By the late eighteenth century such a penalty would commonly be £200. Benjamin Titford (1786-1816) needed to get married in a hurry in 1807 - his bride-to-be being heavily pregnant at the time - and he entered into a bond with the Archbishop of Canterbury's Faculty Office in Doctors' Commons in London, his fellow bondsman being 'John Thomas'. Who was this Mr Thomas? A friend? A relation? No, nothing more than a legal fiction: beware the assumption that a bondsman called 'John Thomas' or a 'John Doe' were part of your family!

It was quite usual for dissenters and for gentry and the yeoman class to marry by licence - after all, they did not particularly want the 'world and his wife' to know their affairs by virtue of banns being called in the parish church. If an ordinary labouring-class couple wished to marry on a fast day, holy day, or during Lent, then they, too, had to apply for a licence. If a woman was expecting an illegitimate child and the man responsible, if single, could be 'persuaded' by the parish authorities or justices of the peace to marry her, then it was quite usual for the parish to pay the man, or to pay for a marriage licence, as in this reference found with the Diocese of Exeter marriage licences and bonds now held in the Devon Record Office, Exeter:

Dear Sir,
By this post i have sent you Five and Twenty shillings for a Licence to marry John Greet of this parish, & Grace Hill of the parish of St. Neot in Cornwall. They are both of age, and of an inferier Rank; so there is no need of a Bond; The woman is big with child, and doubts whether shee shall hold out till Easter. I demise therefore you will send me the Licence by the return of this post, or the wont at furthest, my service to your spouse, I am, Yrs heartily, Tho: Burnaford. Bridestowe 29: March 1726. The woman is here & waits for the Licence.

Marriage: clandestine and irregular marriages

In the year 1754 Lord Hardwicke's act 'for the better preventing of clandestine marriages' in England and Wales (but not Scotland) came into effect. Prior to this landmark legislation, all that was required for a marriage to be valid in the British Isles was a declaration of mutual consent by the parties in the presence of witnesses or by public repute. If a marriage was celebrated in the parish of the

David Lang's Gretna Green Marriage Register, *showing the famous entry for 12 October 1818 - the marriage of Thomas, Lord Erskine, aged 68 and a former Lord Chancellor, to Sarah Buck, his housekeeper. Erskine escaped from his sons, who wanted the marriage stopped, by dressing as a woman.* (Institute of Heraldic and Genealogical Studies)

bride or the groom and by banns or licence, it was 'regular'. If it took place in the parish of one of them without banns or licence, or in the parish of neither party by banns or by licence, it was 'irregular', though usually considered to be regular enough if the name of the 'neutral' church was specified on a licence. If there were no banns and no licence and the parish was foreign to both bride and groom, the marriage was 'clandestine'. Having said that, various marriages at the Fleet and at the May Fair Chapel in London, both notorious clandestine marriage centres, were often described in the registers as being by licence - even if such a licence was issued by the same man who was conducting the marriage. Some original licences for marriages at the May Fair Chapel are still in existence, issued by 'The Ordinary of the said chapel'.

From the 1670s, many couples in London who were in a hurry, who might have had something to hide or who wanted a cut-price ceremony would take themselves off to the precincts of the Fleet Prison, where 'marriage mongers' would be only too happy to oblige them for a fee. A priest would be found and a ceremony performed in some local hostelry or other convenient room. Approximately three hundred Fleet Marriage Registers and five hundred or more rough notebooks have survived and are to be found at the Public Record Office, class RG7. Many are very full in the detail they provide, some less so; a certain number have been shown to be forgeries, but most are not. The number of weddings celebrated at the Fleet during the first half of the eighteenth century in particular was vast: in the 1740s over half of all London weddings took place there or at the May Fair Chapel, and there were 217 Fleet weddings on the day before Hardwicke's Act came into force. A certain number of Fleet register abstracts can be found at the Society of Genealogists, and some are featured in J.S. Burn's book (see 'Further reading', below). The first two volumes in a projected series of annotated transcripts of original Fleet registers entitled *Clandestine marriages in the Chapel and Rules of the Fleet Prison 1680–1754* by Mark Herber were published by Francis Boutle in 1998–9.

Other notorious clandestine or irregular marriage centres in London included St James, Duke's Place, various registers of which are in print, and Holy Trinity, Minories, for which a number of transcripts are available on microfiche from the East of London Family History Society.

Rural churches where clandestine marriages were celebrated include Peak Forest Chapel in Derbyshire, and a book by A.B. Clarke includes references to clandestine marriages taken from the records of the Archdeaconry of Leicester.

Following Hardwicke's Act (which excluded only Jews and Quakers from its stringent regulations), many couples of all social classes who wished to marry anonymously or secretly would head north to the Scottish borders, to Gretna Green or to other similar locations, where various self-appointed 'priests' would witness their marriage vows in exchange for appropriate payment. Show-business trappings such as a blacksmith's anvil only came much later, after Gretna Green marriages had become illegal. Many original Gretna Green registers survive; some are still with solicitors, some in private hands, others in the Ewart Library in Dumfries and the University of Durham Library. The most significant collection, that of the Lang family, 1783-1895, is held by the Institute of Heraldic and Genealogical Studies in Canterbury. For border marriage registers in print, see the bibliography below.

Marriage settlements

It often suited wealthier families to arrange for marriage settlements to be drawn up. A father might settle land or personal property on his son or on his daughter and new son-in-law at the time of their marriage, sometimes to be held in trust for them, in order to ensure that they could live in a style suitable to their station in life. Settlement deeds on vellum, which can provide a great deal of information as to property holdings and relationships, may frequently be seen in the collections of manuscript dealers, but others have found their way into County Record Offices, the British Library or other repositories. Volume 11 of F.A. Crisp's *Fragmenta genealogica* consists of a series of transcripts of marriage settlements then in his possession. A typical example follows:

> *Indenture made 26 May 1704, between (1) Thomas Andrew of Newcastle-upon-Tyne, gent, (2) John Thompson and John Bradley of Gateshead, co.Durham, gents, (3) Robert Andrew of Newcastle-upon-Tyne, merchant, eldest son of Thomas Andrew, and (4) Grace Thompson, the younger, of Gateshead, spinster, sister of John Thompson.*
>
> *In consideration of an intended marriage between Robert Andrew and Grace Thompson, Thomas and Robert Andrew agree before 1st June next ensuing to convey their copyhold in Morton, co.Northumberland, to John Thompson and John Bradley, to the use of the said Robert and Grace and their issue.* [Signed and witnessed]

Robert Andrew and Grace Thompson were married on 30 July 1704 in Gateshead.

Where are parish registers and bishops' transcripts now?

The 1978 Parochial Registers and Records Measure stated that although parish registers are the property of the Parochial Church Council of the particular parish, they should be deposited in a local record office if over a hundred years old. Such registers can be kept at the church only under strict conditions regarding the correct environment to aid preservation. This act has ensured that the vast majority of parish registers are now in the safe keeping of County Record Offices and other officially-recognised repositories. Those that still remain in churches can be viewed by arrangement with the minister, who is entitled to charge the appropriate fees as laid down in the Parochial Fees Order, which is adjusted from time to time.

Once you have found an ancestral parish which interests you, turn to *The Phillimore atlas and index of parish registers* by Cecil Humphery-Smith (2nd.Ed. 1995). The map section of the book will indicate the boundaries of the parish, its place within the county, the date of the earliest surviving parish register and the ecclesiastical jurisdiction within which it lay. The accompanying text section will provide further information on the parish in question under the following headings: overall dates of deposited original registers; overall dates of coverage in the International Genealogical Index; local marriage indexes; copies of registers at the Society of Genealogists; Boyd's Marriage Index; copies of registers not at the Society of Genealogists; Pallot's Marriage Index; nonconformist registers at the Public Record Office.

The *Phillimore Atlas* will give you an overall picture, then; for more detail about surviving registers and copies, you should consult the appropriate volume in the *National Index of Parish Registers*, published by the Society of Genealogists. A list of county volumes already published appears in 'Further reading', below.

A visit to the appropriate County Record Office will probably be necessary, then, if you are to consult the parish registers which interest you. In a very few cases it is still possible to see the original registers in a CRO, but nearly all are now available on microform (that is, microfilm or microfiche), many with a self-service system operating. Do make arrangements in advance and book a microfilm reader for a certain length of time. Microform copies are also often available for consultation in local studies libraries.

Extracting entries from an original parish register can be a long and painstaking job, so do check to see whether the relevant record office, a local studies library or the Society of Genealogists' Library in London has copies, photocopies, transcriptions or indexes available for consultation or for sale. Local historians and antiquaries have long been fascinated by the idea of producing a printed transcript of a parish register, and we can now benefit from their endeavours. Several Family History Societies have since carried on where the Victorian and Edwardian antiquaries left off. Printed parish register transcripts were published from the second half of the nineteenth century onwards, and at least two series of volumes are national in scope - namely, the publications of the Parish Register Society and the invaluable set of printed marriage entries produced by W.P.W. Phillimore and his associates. 'Phillimore' is arranged by counties, and many volumes contain details of marriage entries up to 1812 or 1837. Most are unindexed, but several have been incorporated into Family History Society county marriage indexes. Relevant Phillimore volumes should be found in County Record Offices and local studies libraries. Never expect total accuracy from any printed transcript; always check with the original source wherever possible.

The Federation of Family History Societies, ever active in the field of genealogical publishing, produced its *National Burial Index* in 2001, the result of several years' work by constituent societies and members up and down the country. The index is available on two CD-ROMs (burials 1538-1825 and 1826-2000), and features over five million names taken from parish, nonconformist, Roman Catholic and cemetery registers throughout England and Wales. Each entry provides the following information (if known): forename(s) and surname of the deceased; date of burial; age; parish or cemetery where the event was recorded; pre-1974 county of the parish or cemetery; society or group which transcribed the record. This is an ongoing project, and it is hoped that many more entries will be made available in future editions of the index.

The greatest single collection of parish register transcripts is available for consultation at the library of the Society of Genealogists in London; here you will find the famous Boyd's Marriage Index and much else.

Bishops' transcripts, where they survive, will form part of the records of the diocese to which they were submitted. They should be available for consultation either at the appropriate Diocesan Record Office, or at a County Record Office in cases where diocesan and county records have been combined in one place under the care of one county and diocesan archivist.

How should parish registers be consulted?

Parish registers (and bishops' transcripts) need to be searched in a methodical manner. You may have to travel a great distance to reach a record office and only have a limited number of hours in which to do your research, so it follows that no time should be wasted. Before your visit, do your homework. What family are you looking for? What parish? What dates and time-span? Go armed with a good supply of A4 lined paper - and pencils, as the use of pens is not allowed in any archive office.

If you begin with the latest relevant records available and work backwards, copying every entry of the surname(s) you are looking for, this will ensure that no stone is left unturned. We make no apology for reminding you again at this stage that you should be sensitive to possible variations in the spelling of surnames. Another important point to remember is that you should make a complete copy of the entry, exactly as written, no matter how many seemingly superfluous words there are connected with it. If an entry states 'eodem die' or 'same day', look at the entries above for the date in question; the word 'ibid' will suggest that at least some wording already used (a date, for example) is now applicable again in the present entry, but is not being repeated. You should note the title or description of each volume you consult, together with its catalogue number and the years it covers; make a similar note for any printed or typescript books you have used. You will feel most annoyed if in two years' time you wish to check an entry and have no idea where you found it in the first place.

If you have a relatively uncommon surname you may be able to complete your search of the registers comparatively quickly. For all that, it is important not to hurry your research, for to do so is a recipe for disaster. Even if it means making several return visits in the future, take your time and carry the task out thoroughly.

Divorce

In the days when England was a Roman Catholic country, the ecclesiastical courts dealt with matters relating to marriage and its dissolution, and an appeal could be made to the Pope. This state of affairs continued until the reign of Henry VIII; following the Act of Supremacy and the Statute of Appeals the Crown became the supreme authority in all matters appertaining to the Church and its affairs, and the right of appeal to Rome was abolished.

After the Reformation, church courts dealt with all business concerning annulment, separation and divorce. From 1668 to 1857 full divorce (as opposed to a mere separation) could only be brought about by a Private Act of Parliament. This was an option open only to the wealthy; up to the year 1858, only a total of 330 divorces had ever taken place in the whole of England and Wales. From 1669 onwards records of divorce bills are in the House of Lords Record Office, and are indexed in Part 13 of the *Index to local and personal acts*, accounts of the proceedings being in the published *Journals* of the House.

The Court for Divorce and Matrimonial Causes was established following the 1857 Matrimonial Causes Act, which allowed for divorce on the grounds of adultery by the wife and various 'offences' by the husband. Cruelty could also be cited as a reason for dissolution in a petition by the wife. The grounds for divorce remained much the same up to 1937.

Divorce records from 1858 to 1937 are kept at the Public Record Office (J77) with indexes to matrimonial causes, 1858-1958 (J78). Files are mostly closed to the public for seventy-five years, and the indexes are subject to a thirty-year closure rule. Divorce records from 1938 to the present day are at the Principal Registry of the Family Division, 1st Avenue House, 42-49 High Holborn, London WC1V 6NP. The index to these is not open to the general public, but searches can be made for a fee. You should also contact the Principal Registry for permission to look at the papers of a closed case.

One solution to the problem of finding more information about a specific divorce case where the files are closed is to look for one or more newspaper reports where these exist. Indexes of divorces reported in *The Times*, 1788 to 1910, have been published on microfiche by Mrs Annie Weare and Brian Wall, who will also supply copies of the reports in question. Write to: PO Box 123, Limerick, Ireland or 40 Ela Street, Leeming 6155, Western Australia.

Of course, couples who wanted to separate and who did not have the means to resort to church or civil courts would often simply decide to go their different ways, occasionally marrying bigamously until the law caught up with them or living with a new partner without the sanctity of marriage. It was not unknown for some men to sell their unwanted wives in the market place!

In **Scotland**, divorce was only possible in cases of adultery and desertion until acts of 1938, 1964 and 1976 added other grounds. Divorce cases up to 1830 were heard in the Commissary Court of Edinburgh, and thereafter at the Court of Session. Records are at the National Archives of Scotland. A catalogue of cases, 1658 to 1800, was published by the Scottish Record Society in 1909.

Divorce in **Ireland** could originally be granted only by the ecclesiastical courts or following a Private Act of Parliament, as in England and Wales. The English Matrimonial Causes Acts of 1857 and 1884 did not apply in Ireland, however, and the church courts continued to exercise jurisdiction until 1870, when the High Court assumed responsibility. The High Court would only grant a degree of nullity (by which it was declared that a marriage had never come into being), not one of dissolution as such. Only in 1995, following a narrow majority in a referendum, was civil divorce allowed in the Republic of Ireland.

Major Acts of Parliament relating to parish registers

Burial in Woollen Acts of 1667 and 1678
These acts, passed in an attempt to protect the English wool trade, stated that all corpses should be buried in wool, except those who had died from the plague. The 1678 Act in particular stated that 'no corpse of any person shall be buried in any shirt, shift, sheet or shroud or anything whatsoever made or mingled with flax, hemp, silk, hair, gold or silver, or in any stuff or thing other than what is made of sheep's wool only'. An affidavit was required to be sworn within a few days of the burial that the deceased had indeed been buried in woollen only, and this was usually recorded in the burial register, sometimes in full with names of witnesses and a magistrate, or just with the notation 'aff'd' or 'aff't'. If a burial in woollen had not taken place, a fine of five pounds was imposed. The practice gradually fell into disuse, and by 1814 the acts were repealed. Always look for affidavits for extra family information. A typical full entry in a parish register would read as follows:

> *Elizabeth Paterson of the Parish of Walmer in the County of Kent*
> *maketh Oath that Robert Upton of the same Parish deceased was not*

put in wrapt or wound up or buried in any Shirt Shift Sheet or Shroud made or mingled with Flax Hemp Silk Hair Gold or Silver or other than what is made of Sheeps Wool only or in any Coffin lined or faced with any Cloth Stuff or any other Thing whatsoever made or mingled with Flax Hemp Silk Hair Gold or Silver or any other Material but Sheeps Wool only.
Sworn before me April 7, 1747. Nicolas Carter, Rector of Ham. The mark (x) of Elizabeth Paterson. Witnesses: Mary Carter, Margt. Carter.

Note, incidentally, that it was common practice at this period to begin every noun with a capital letter - a custom still used in the German language to this day.

An Act to impose a tax on births, marriages and burials, 1694
This Act of 1694, effective from 1695, is sometimes referred to as the 'Marriage Act', and followed quickly on the heels of the defunct hearth tax in an attempt to help finance the war against France. A tax was levied on all births, marriages and burials, charged at two shillings, two shillings and sixpence and four shillings respectively. Parents were required to notify the parish of a birth in the family and to pay the fee, a fine being levied in cases of default. Occasionally parish registers will include the names of unbaptised but 'notified' children at this period. Bachelors over 25 years of age and childless widowers were required to pay one shilling annually. The nobility were charged at higher rates, but paupers were exempt. Avoidance was not uncommon, and several so-called 'paupers' may not have been so poor, after all. The Act remained in force until 1706, though very few records survive. Relevant publications in print, giving lists of names, are: *The inhabitants of Bristol in 1696* (Bristol Record Society, 1968), *London inhabitants within the walls 1695* (London Record Society, 1966), and two volumes of *Surviving North Wiltshire 1695 tax censuses*, published by the Wiltshire Family History Society.

Hardwicke's Marriage Act 1753
Hardwicke's Marriage Act of June 1753 (coming into effect on 25 June 1754) was designed to end marriages in prison chapels, public houses and other such places around the country by genuine or charlatan ministers. The Act stipulated that all marriages had to be by banns or by marriage licence, and were to be performed in a parish church by a Church of England minister; Quakers and Jews, but not Roman Catholics, were the only exceptions.
Many parishes kept separate marriage registers from this date, very often using printed books with spaces for handwritten insertions. Entries had to show the place of residence of both parties and their marital status, and the bride, groom and two or more witnesses had to sign or make their marks. If the marriage was by licence and either party was below the age of 21, parental consent had to be obtained.

Stamp Duty Act of 1783
By this Act, a duty of 3d was imposed on all baptism, marriage and burial entries in the parish registers, the minister receiving a 10% fee. Paupers were exempt from this tax, and parish register entries will be annotated with the letter 'p' or the word 'pauper' beside the entry in such cases. By 1785 the tax was extended

to nonconformists. This was a most unpopular tax and was repealed in 1794. During its operation, parents who could not claim exemption as paupers but who were really unable to afford the tax, would be very reluctant to have their children baptised. Sometimes the local incumbent would catch up with a family in which a number of unbaptised children were lurking, and a multiple ceremony would follow. If a baptismal entry seems to be missing at this time, it is worth looking for records of adult baptism in the years after the Act was repealed.

George Rose's Act (the Parochial Registers Act) 1812-13

In 1813 George Rose's Act was introduced. This ensured that the parish register entries for baptisms, marriages and burials were laid out in a formal fashion in all parish registers. From this date each group of entries was to have its own printed register, to be completed in manuscript to provide the following details:

Baptisms: Date of baptism, Christian name of child or person, parents' Christian names and surname, abode, father's occupation.

Marriages: Names of bride and bridegroom, their parishes, date of the marriage, names and signatures or marks of bride and groom, whether married by banns or licence, names and signatures or marks of witnesses. If one or both parties to the marriage was a minor, the entry should also indicate the fact that the consent of parents or guardians had been given.

Burials: Name of deceased, abode, date of burial, age.

Parish Registers: hints and reminders

- Remember that no parish registers were kept systematically before 1538, and that many do not begin until the early 1600s or later. Check to see whether any bishops' transcripts pre-date the earliest surviving register.
- Most parish registers are now deposited in County Record Offices, although a few are still with the parish church. Check the present whereabouts with the record office concerned before making any journeys.
- Establish whether the parish registers which interest you have been transcribed and are available in handwritten, typescript or printed form. Never trust a transcript totally - it will only be as good as the transcriber. Always check a transcript with the original register where possible.
- Use bishops' transcripts to double-check parish register entries and to fill any gaps in the registers.
- Always be on the look-out for different spellings of the same surname - take into consideration the dialect of the area concerned.
- A date on a baptism entry is not the date of birth. Baptisms could have taken place several weeks, months or years after the child was born. If a new-born baby was sickly and its chances of survival seemed slim, it might have been privately baptised (or 'half baptised') at home - by the midwife or by any other 'competent person' if necessary. If such a child survived, it might have been publicly baptised in the church at a later date. Also check for adult baptisms and multiple baptisms.
- Sometimes a child may have been baptised more than once - in an Anglican church and in a nonconformist chapel.
- Birth certificates and baptismal entries may not always agree exactly, as parents may have changed their minds about given forenames between

Baptisms recorded in Welsh, 1755. *From the parish register of Llanegwad, Carmarthen. The use of the Welsh language in parish registers was very much the exception rather than the rule.* (The Representative Body of the Church in Wales; the National Library of Wales)

registration and baptism.

- The marriage age was 14 years for a male and 12 years for a female, providing that the consent of parents or guardians was obtained for those below the age of majority (21 years). These 'marriage ages' continued even after the 1753 Hardwicke Marriage Act, until the age for both parties was established at 16 years by an act of 1929. Parents' or guardians' consent was still needed for those below 21 until 1969 when the age was lowered to 18.
- Check for the existence of banns books.
- Do not just look for baptisms, but always search for burials as well. If you can, search through the entire parish register from beginning to end for other information which may have been entered out of sequence.
- A date given in a burial entry is not necessarily the date of death.
- Some civil registration certificates and parish register entries may reveal a surname given by way of a Christian name. This can be advantageous to you: it may be the surname of a mother, grandmother, godparent or even a close friend of the family, and can be a clue to further research. Do proceed with caution here, nevertheless: some families sought to ingratiate themselves with prominent members of the local community by using the surname of the local clergy or gentry for their children.
- If you are unable to find a family in parish registers, consider the fact that they may have been nonconformists.

Scotland

Most Scottish Old Parish Registers up to 1855, known as 'OPRs' for short, are to be found at the National Archives of Scotland in Edinburgh. These are the records of the Presbyterian Church of Scotland, and most begin in the 1690s. County-by-county indexes to all the baptismal and marriage entries in these registers are available on microfiche in a certain number of research centres; they give more detail than the equivalent entries in the International Genealogical Index. The Registrar General for Scotland's "Origins" at http://www.origins.net on the Internet allows you, for a fee, to access the indexes to the Old Parochial Registers (baptisms and marriages 1553–1854).

The quality of record-keeping in the OPRs varies significantly: some ministers were barely literate, some not very conscientious.

One baptism register may simply give the child's name and the father's name, while another will feature christening date, birth date, full name, father's full name with his occupation and residence, mother's full name including maiden name, name of minister and the name, occupation and residence of witnesses, sponsors or godparents.

Marriage registers may only give date, place and both parties' names, but extra information could include the full names of both the bride and groom, their parents' names and residences and occupations. Sometimes only a 'proclamation' of marriage is recorded - that is, the intention to marry as read out in church for three consecutive weeks by the minister.

Scottish burial registers are disappointing for the genealogist, where they were kept at all. They usually give no more than a name and a date.

In 1872 a very useful *Detailed list of the Old Parochial Registers of Scotland* was published in Edinburgh. Parishes are named, coverage dates are given and relevant annotations are added. *The parishes, registers and registrars of Scotland*, published by the Scottish Association of Family History Societies in 1993, includes baptism, marriage and burial dates for each parish to 1854, together with maps.

Using Scottish OPRs can present difficulties: there was a lot of under-recording of baptisms and burials; late baptisms are not uncommon - and these may not occur in the parish of residence; handwriting can be difficult to decipher, and dialect often affects spelling. The good news, however, is that Scottish women never totally lose their maiden names on marriage, and may often be identified more precisely as a result. It is also helpful to know that Scots have long favoured a logical pattern of Christian names for their children, whereby the first son is named after the paternal grandfather, the second after the maternal grandfather, the third after the father; daughters in order are named after the maternal grandmother, the paternal grandmother and the mother. Such a system was once very common amongst English families, too; see if it applies in your own case. Twentieth century parents may choose to pluck a child's name out of a book or use one from a television soap opera; Scots - and others, including Jews - are more likely to name their children in honour of ancestors.

Ireland

Many Church of Ireland parish registers were destroyed by fire at the Four Courts in Dublin in 1922, but several have survived. Some have been deposited with the National Archives, others are with the Representative Church Body Library, Braemore Park, Dublin, and some remain with individual parishes. The Public Record Office of Northern Ireland in Belfast has a large number of microfilm and photostat copies of Church of Ireland registers for Northern Ireland.

To give some perspective at this stage, it is perhaps worth mentioning the fact that in 1834, just over ten years before the great Irish famine with its resultant deaths and emigration, 81% of the population of Ireland was Roman Catholic. Few Catholic parish registers begin before the end of the eighteenth century, and they have always been retained within individual parishes. The National Library of Ireland has microfilm copies of the Catholic registers to 1880, but a letter of authorisation from the parish priest is required before those for certain dioceses may be consulted.

Presbyterian worship in Ireland was very much associated with the nine counties of the Province of Ulster, though the eighteenth century saw a massive emigration of Presbyterian ministers and their congregations to North America. Presbyterian parish registers are still in the possession of the local clergy, but some are with the Presbyterian Historical Society, Fishwick Place, Belfast, Northern Ireland.

Brian Mitchell's *A guide to Irish parish registers* (1988) should be consulted if you have Irish ancestors, since he gives tabulated lists of civil parishes together with starting dates of related Church of Ireland, Roman Catholic, Presbyterian and other registers.

Heritage Centres throughout Ireland, sponsored by the government, now have the task of transcribing and indexing parish registers. Each county has such a centre except Louth, which is covered by neighbouring County Meath.

General alphabet of the old Law Hands, *from Andrew Wright's* 'Court-hand Restored' (10th. Ed. 1912).

Monumental inscriptions, Ramsey, Cambs. *Three generations are featured on this monument – Stephen Whittome had a son John and grandchildren Alfred and Emily; William Vawser of March had a daughter Mary Ann, who married John. We can calculate, for instance, an approximate date of birth for John, and know where he died and that, as the eldest son, he must have had at least one other sibling.* (Michael Armstrong FSG)

The Channel Islands and the Isle of Man

Jersey
The old parochial registers for the twelve parishes of Jersey are generally written in French, and some date back to the sixteenth century. The originals are in the care of the incumbent of each parish, and all are in the process of being indexed. You will find these indexes in the research room of the Channel Islands Family History Society (Hilgrove Street, Saint Helier, Jersey) and in the library of the Société Jersiaise.

Guernsey and neighbouring islands
All old parochial registers for the ten parishes of Guernsey and its two island dependencies are with the incumbents concerned.

The Isle of Man
The Manx Museum holds copies of all the old parochial registers for the Isle of Man up to the year 1883 on microfilm. The earliest date from the early seventeenth century.

Old handwriting
It may be that your first attempt to read an entry in an old parish register will bring forcibly home to you the fact that styles of handwriting have changed

considerably during the centuries. The study of older forms of writing is known as palaeography; while some scholars make this a lifetime study, you may be surprised at how fast you can acclimatise yourself to reading what appeared at first to be an illegible scrawl. There is no substitute for practice, but a number of useful books have been published which will help you by explaining the ways in which letter-forms have changed, with worked examples.

You may find little difficulty with documents written from the seventeenth century onwards (though some writers have always been untidy or eccentric), but you will certainly need to pay close attention when you confront the so-called 'secretary hand' of Tudor times as used for parish register entries, wills and so on. With practice, everyone should be able to read the ordinary hand of the parish clerk during the sixteenth and seventeenth centuries, but it must be stressed that spelling was not uniform and the same word or name could be spelt in a variety of ways within one document. Many of our forebears were unable to read or write, and when a parish clerk wrote a name in the parish register, he would often spell it phonetically, dialect pronunciation and all, as he heard it spoken. The next time the same family turned up at church for a baptism, wedding or funeral, the same clerk (or a different one) might spell the names given to him in an entirely different way.

Here is a not untypical example of variation which can exist within one parish register:

> *Married 1636/7 February 20. George Rudall and Sarah Willsone.*
> *Baptised 1637 December 1. Henery son of Gorge Ruddle and Sarah his wife.*
> *Buried 1638 March 26. Henry son of George Ridall.*
> *Baptised 1640 June 4. Marie daughter of George Ruddle.*
> *Buried 1641 Dec 3. Mary daughter of George and Sarey Redall.*
> *Buried 1641 Dec 31. Sarah wife of Geo: Rudal in childbirth.*

With perseverance, a magnifying glass and a little help from your friends, you should make great progress in this field. Archivists will usually be happy to help you out with the occasional obscure or poorly-written word, but in any case it might be worth your while attending a class on how to read and interpret old handwriting. Some County Record Offices, Family History Societies, the Society of Genealogists and the Institute of Heraldic and Genealogical Studies hold the occasional series of day or evening classes for beginners.

A number of registers and documents will have been written in Latin up to the year 1733, except for the period of the Protectorate from 1653 to 1660. From 1733 all official documents should be written in English, though in many cases Latin had been abandoned long before this date. Again, practice and some background reading will make perfect - or at least prevent you from being intimidated by the kind of simple Latin phrases used in parish registers.

Monumental inscriptions

Many of the burial places of our ancestors are marked by gravestones or other memorials, and if you strike lucky, details given on a monumental inscription ('MI' for short) can establish facts and relationships which you might have discovered nowhere else. Many MIs give details of a husband or wife of the deceased, the names of children and places of residence; sometimes they include grandchildren, parents, nephews and nieces, an indication of previous or subsequent marriages and so on, at the whim of the bereaved relatives. In general, the grander the family, the grander the inscription, and you will find elaborate memorials to prominent local families inside as well as outside most parish churches - look on the walls and the floor.

Not all gravestones necessarily mark a burial place, however; some are memorials to those who have died in some distant location where they may have been buried. In the days of the British Empire, many men and women lived and served abroad in various capacities, and their lives and deaths may be commemorated on a stone back in their home parish church or churchyard.

Most Family History Societies have an on-going project to record their local monumental inscriptions, whether they be in churchyards, churches, non-conformist burial grounds or cemeteries. In addition, any inscriptions appearing in memorial books or on memorial windows, plaques, and war cenotaphs are recorded. Not all burials were marked with a monumental inscription of some kind, and even where a stone exists, the ravages of time may have rendered its inscription illegible.

More and more churchyards are being cleared of gravestones and the ground levelled and landscaped. Very often only a small notice of intent will appear in a local newspaper, hidden away in some obscure corner. If family historians are interested in preserving monumental inscriptions for posterity, they can either obtain permission from the authority concerned and record the inscriptions themselves, or contact the local Family History Society concerned, to see whether its members can record or even photograph the inscriptions before the stones are removed and the information on them is lost forever.

The Society of Genealogists in London has a magnificent collection of monumental inscription transcripts and abstracts, and a catalogue to these has been published in two volumes.

Further reading

(Parish registers and bishops' transcripts)

Begley, D. *Irish genealogy: a record finder.* 1981.

Bellingham, R. 'Dade Parish Registers' in *Family history news and digest.* September 1995.

Bourne, S. and Chicken, A. *Records of the Church of England.* (2nd.Ed.) 1991.

Bryant Rosier, M.E. *Index to parishes in Phillimore's Marriages.* 1988.

Chapman, C. and Litton, P. *Marriage laws, rites, records and customs: was your ancestor really married?* 1996.

Cole, J. and Church, R. *In and around record repositories in Great Britain and Ireland.* (4th.Ed.) 1998.

Cox, J. C. *The parish registers of England.* 1910. Reprinted 1974.

General index to the townlands and towns, parishes and baronies of Ireland. 1851. Reprinted 1984.

Gibbens, L. *An introduction to ... church registers.* 1994.

Gibbens, L. *Basic facts about using death and burial records for family historians.* (2nd.Ed.) 1999.

Gibson, J. *Bishops' transcripts and marriage licences, bonds and allegations; a guide to their location and indexes.* (4th.Ed.) 1997.

Gibson, J. and Peskett, P. *Record offices: how to find them.* (8th.Ed.) 1998.

Humphery-Smith, C. *The Phillimore atlas and index of parish registers.* (2nd.Ed.) 1995.

Litton, P. *Basic facts about using baptism records for family historians.* 1996.

Litton, P. 'Dade Registers' in *Family Tree Magazine.* July 1995.

Litton, P. 'The Foundling Hospital and its children' in *Family Tree Magazine.* Vol.2, no.4. (May/June 1986).

Litton, P. and Chapman, C. *Basic facts about using marriage records for family historians.* 1996.

McLaughlin, E. *Parish registers.* (3rd.Ed.) 1994.

National Library of Wales. *Cofrestri Plwyf Cymru/Parish Registers of Wales.* 1985.

Nichols, R.H. and Wray, F.A. *The history of the Foundling Hospital.* 1935.

Owen, D.M. *The records of the established church in England, excluding parochial records.* 1970.

PRONI. *Guide to the Public Record Office of Northern Ireland.* 1991.

Sinclair, C. *Tracing your Scottish ancestors in the Scottish Record Office.* (Revised Ed.) 1997.

Society of Genealogists. *List of parishes in Boyd's Marriage Index* (6th.Ed.) 1993.

Society of Genealogists. *National Index of Parish Registers.* An ongoing series of county volumes, the following having been published to date: Bedfordshire and Huntingdonshire; Berkshire; Buckinghamshire; Cambridgeshire; Cheshire; Cornwall; Cumberland and Westmorland; Derbyshire; Devon; Durham and Northumberland; Essex; Lancashire; Leicestershire and Rutland; Lincolnshire; London and Middlesex; Norfolk and Suffolk; Northamptonshire; Nottinghamshire; Somerset; Staffordshire; Surrey; Wiltshire; Yorkshire. There are also separate volumes for the parish and nonconformist registers of Wales.

Society of Genealogists. *Parish register copies in the library of the Society of Genealogists.* (11th.Ed.) 1995. (This printed listing, and other related Society publications, are now being superseded by a series of smaller volumes which feature parish register copies and other source material on a county-by-county basis.)

Society of Genealogists. *Parish register copies other than the Society of Genealogists' collection.* 1974.

Steel, D.G.(Ed.) *National index of parish registers, vol.1: introduction to parish registers before 1837.* 3rd (corrected) impression, 1976.

Steel, D.G.(Ed.) *National index of parish registers, vol.12: sources for Scottish genealogy and family history.* 1970.

(Clandestine and irregular marriages)

Benton, T. *Irregular marriages in London before 1754.* 1993.

Brack, A. *Irregular marriages: Annan, Dumfriesshire 1797-1854.* Dumfries and Galloway Family History Society. 1997.

Brack, A. *Irregular marriages: Portpatrick, Wigtownshire 1759-1826.* Dumfries and Galloway Family History Society. 1997.

Brack, A. *The registers of Henry Collins: marriages at Lamberton Toll, 1833-1849.* 1995. This is the first volume in a planned series of irregular border marriage transcripts published by the Northumberland and Durham Family History Society.

Burn, J.S. *History of the Fleet marriages.* (2nd.Ed.) 1834.

Clarke, A.B. *Some Leicestershire clandestine marriages.* 1955.

'Claverhouse' [Meliora Smith]. *Irregular border marriages.* 1934.

Herber, M. *Clandestine marriages in the Chapel and Rules of the Fleet Prison 1680–1754.* 3 vols. 1998–2001.

McConnel, E.W.J. (Ed.) *Marriages at Gretna Hall, 1829-April 30, 1855.* Scottish Record Society. Old series 80. 1949.

Marshall, G.W. *The marriage registers of Peak Forest Chapel, Derbyshire* [1727-1764]. 1901.

Nicholson, R. *Irregular Border and Scottish runaway marriages: A list of custodians and owners of all existing records.* (3rd.Ed.) 1997.

Outhwaite, R.B. *Clandestine marriage in England 1500-1850.* 1995.

Steel, D. *National index of Parish Registers.* Vol.1, pp.319-320, contains a list of London churches and chapels at which marriages were performed before 1754 without banns.

(Divorce)

Gillis, J.R. *For better, for worse - British marriages, 1600 to the present.* 1985.

Horstman, A. *Victorian divorce.* 1985.

McGregor, O.R. *Divorce in England.* 1957.

Menefee, S.P. *Wives for sale.* 1981.

Stone, L. *Broken lives, separation and divorce in England 1660-1857.* 1993.

Stone, L. *Road to divorce - England 1530-1837.* 1990.

Stone, L. *Uncertain unions, marriage in England 1660-1753.* 1992.

(Palaeography)

Buck, W.S. *Examples of handwriting 1550-1650.* 1996.

Emmison, F.G. *How to read local archives 1550-1700.* 1988.

Gandy, M. *Basic approach to Latin for family historians.* 1995.

Gooder, E. *Latin for local history.* (2nd.Ed.) 1990.

Grieve, H.E.P. *Examples of English handwriting 1150-1750.* 1981.

Ison, A. *A Secretary Hand.* 1990.

McLaughlin, E. *Reading old handwriting.* (3rd.Ed.) 1994.

McLaughlin, E. *Simple Latin for family historians.* (5th.Ed.) 1994.

Markwell, F.C. and Saul, P. *Facsimiles of documents of use to family historians.* 1987.

Morris, J.A. *Latin glossary for family and local historians.* 1995.

Munby, L. *Reading Tudor and Stuart handwriting.* 1988.

Simpson, G.G. *Scottish handwriting 1150-1650.* 1973.

Stuart, D. *Latin for local and family historians.* 1995.

(Monumental inscriptions)

Monumental inscriptions in the library of the Society of Genealogists. 2 Parts. 1987.

Rayment, J.(revised Pattinson, P.) *Notes on recording monumental inscriptions.* (4th.Ed.) 1992.

White, J.L. *Monuments and their inscriptions: a practical guide.* (2nd. Ed.) 1987.

CHAPTER 5

Nonconformists, Roman Catholics, Huguenots and Jews

Nonconformists

Maybe you have searched the parish registers for the town or village which was home to your ancestors, and have drawn a blank? Of all the explanations for the absence of individuals from such registers, the most likely is that they were nonconformists.

The term 'nonconformist' is normally used to refer to those Christian believers who did not conform to the doctrines of the Church of England. Quakers, Methodists, Baptists and members of a wide variety of different sects would come into this category - and, in a sense, so would Roman Catholics. The term 'recusant' is often used synonymously with 'Roman Catholic', though strictly speaking it could be applied to anyone who refused to attend his or her parish church, while the word 'dissenter' is often used in place of 'nonconformist'.

If members of your family seem to vanish suddenly from parish registers in the area you are researching, it is most likely to be for one of two reasons: either they had moved to live elsewhere, or they were nonconformists, in which case your task will be to determine which group of believers was involved and to locate the appropriate registers, if they exist. Before we consider registers as such, however, it will be well to take a closer look at the evolution of nonconformity in Britain, which has been a complex matter but has had a great impact on the lives of ordinary people and on the recording - or the non-recording - of vital events in their lives.

Do be aware at the outset that it is quite likely that a family worshipped and had their children christened and buried in the churches or chapels of more than one denomination, also returning to the Church of England at certain periods in their lives. Many families and individuals came and went, in and out of various nonconformist denominations. They might have discovered that certain sects held more attraction in the way they preached the Christian message than the Established Church; many relished the idea of running their own affairs, casting off the shackles of Anglicanism. Once they had gained the independence of worship they craved, many dissenters then fell out among themselves, and splinter groups proliferated.

In any event, do not always assume that your ancestors became nonconformist for good theological reasons. In the eighteenth century in particular, when many Anglican clergy were at least as interested in huntin', shootin', fishin' and socialising with the local gentry of the 'box pews' class as in tending their flocks, a good number of parishioners may have found the entertainment at the local chapel more to their liking, with provocative sermons and plenty of local gossip on offer with people of the same social class as themselves.

Do keep an open mind when researching your family history; never assume that your ancestors did not have at the least a mild flirtation with nonconformity of one sort or another.

A history of nonconformity

The Church of England itself began life as a nonconformist or dissenting institution, riding on the wave of European protestantism following the protest made by Martin Luther in 1517 against what he and his followers considered to be the intolerant practices and decisions of the Roman Catholic Church. Gradually, the name 'Protestant' came to describe the churches and people who severed their connections with Rome at the time of the Reformation.

The religious revolution spread, in varying degrees, throughout Europe. In England at this time Henry VIII decided to refute Luther's heresies, and in return was rewarded with the title of Defender of the Faith by the Pope. However, by 1533, Henry had been excommunicated because of his continued defiance in trying to annul his marriage to his unwanted wife, Catherine of Aragon, in order to marry Anne Boleyn - and to beget, he hoped, a male heir for the throne of England to continue the Tudor dynasty.

In 1534 Henry VIII declared himself Supreme Head of the Church in England by the Act of Supremacy, and the rift with the Catholic Church and Rome was finally complete. This resulted in considerable disunity within the Church, and factions were at odds with each other. Many parish priests decided to accept Henry as Supreme Head of the Church, and performed the ceremonies of christening, marriage and burial as usual. These eventually formed the nucleus of the Church of England as we know it today. On the other hand, there were the parish priests - and many of their parishioners - who refused to accept Henry as the Supreme Head, and who still followed the teachings and rites of the Church of Rome.

Gradually, around 1563, Roman Catholics started to keep their own records of baptisms, marriages and burials, although many of these were lost or destroyed through the various harassments of the seventeenth and eighteenth centuries. As the seventeenth century progressed, groups referred to as 'Puritans' or 'Dissenters' achieved an increasingly high profile, eventually gaining political and religious power under Cromwell. The Restoration of Charles II saw a reversal in their fortunes. The Act of Uniformity of 1662 required all ministers to accept the Book of Common Prayer and to assent to the Thirty-nine Articles, part of the doctrine of the Church of England. Some two thousand ministers who did not agree were ejected from their livings. In 1664 the Conventicle Act effectively made it a penal offence for anyone to attend nonconformist services held by these ejected ministers, and the Five Mile Act of 1665 prohibited such ministers from coming within five miles of any corporate town.

Despite all these tribulations, meetings were held in secret and the numbers of nonconformists gradually increased. Conventicles still took place whatever the law might say, and those who attended them were held in great suspicion, as an example from the Episcopal returns of 1669 makes clear:

Conventicles. Sarum Diocese. Archdeaconry of Berks.
Hinton Walridge [now Hinton Waldrist]. In ye house of Wm Brookman. Fanatiques. About 40 or 50. Meane & poore tradesmen. Women most. Teacher: Wm Brookman afores^d, Cordwayner.
[From: *Original records of early nonconformity under persecution and indulgence.* G.Lyon Turner. 1911. Vol.1, p.116]

One can almost sense the ecclesiastical authorities gasping in amazement at the temerity of a mere 'cordwayner' (a shoemaker) setting himself up as a religious teacher!

The 'Glorious Revolution' of 1688 ejected the Roman Catholic James II and sent him into exile. William of Orange and his wife, Mary, acceded to the throne early in 1689. The Toleration Act of that year gave religious freedom to all who accepted thirty-six out of the Thirty-nine Articles of religion, and from this time relief came to nonconformist churches, as the act enabled Protestant dissenters to practise their own forms of worship in premises licensed for that purpose and did away with penalties for disobedience. These provisions for registering religious houses by the Toleration Act of 1689 remained until 1812. From 1689 many nonconformists, including Roman Catholics, established their own burial grounds. A new Toleration Act, passed in 1812, made many alterations to the procedures for registering meeting houses, and registration became compulsory for any religious assembly 'at which there shall be present more than 20 persons', besides the immediate family and servants of the person in whose house or upon whose premises meetings took place. Certificates of meeting houses dating from 1689 to 1852, and dissenting ministers' or teachers' oaths and declarations from 1689 to 1829 are to be found in the records of the Clerk of the Peace in County Record Offices. In 1828 nonconformists were allowed into Parliament. From 1791 Roman Catholics were, at last, allowed to have their own places of worship.

Nonconformist records in the Family Records Centre

In 1836, at the same time that civil registration of births, marriages and deaths was about to be introduced into England and Wales, a Royal Commission was established; in 1840 non-Anglican churches were invited to send their registers to the Registrar General so that they could be authenticated. Many registers, but not all, were submitted, and a list of these was published in 1841. In 1857 a second request was made for registers to be sent in, and a new list was published in 1859. Since augmented and with Quaker registers added, it was made available again as volume 42 of the publications of the List and Index Society in 1969, and makes fascinating reading, being a catalogue of the non-parochial registers which found their way into the Public Record Office as classes RG4, RG6 and RG8, the Non-Parochial Registers or 'NPRs' for short.

Please note that a considerable number of records from Public Record Office classes RG4, RG6 and RG8 have been microfilmed and may now be consulted at the Family Records Centre in Myddelton Street. It would be wise to check whether the ones you wish to examine are at Myddelton Street or at the Public Record

Congregational Church baptismal register, *Old George Yard, Kimbolton, Huntingdon, 1809. The bottom entry notes a birth in 1799. Note the name Bethiah, precisely the kind of Christian name favoured by nonconformists.* (Huntingdon Record Office)

Office in Kew before paying a visit.

The Non-Parochial Registers include those of the main nonconformist sects from 1567 onwards for England and Wales, including just under a hundred Catholic registers and a few for foreign churches in England, including the register of the Independent Church at St Petersburg in Russia from 1818 to 1840. Many other lesser-known sects are also represented here: the Bible Christians; the Inghamites; the Irvingites (the Catholic Apostolic Church); the

New Jerusalemites or Swedenborgians - and the Sandemanians or Glasites. If you have determined that your ancestors came from a certain county, do look carefully at the appropriate county list of NPRs.

In all, several thousand registers are in RG4, RG6 and RG8, but many selected transcripts or microform copies may be consulted at the relevant County Record Offices or local studies libraries. In addition, many registers which have come to light in more recent years are still finding their way into various record offices, and a great many births, baptisms and marriages, but not deaths or burials, have been extracted from NPRs and are in the International Genealogical Index (IGI), for details of which see information in our next chapter.

Other vital sources for nonconformist genealogy in class RG4 are the registers for the major dissenters' burial ground at Bunhill Fields in City Road, London (1713 to 1854), and the series of birth registers once held in Dr Williams's Library. Dr Daniel Williams, who died in 1716, was a Presbyterian minister who developed Unitarian views in later years and whose major collection of books and manuscripts formed the basis of a library dedicated to his memory which opened in 1729. It was becoming increasingly clear at this time that nonconformists in London and elsewhere would welcome the chance to have the births of their offspring registered in a formal fashion, and it was arranged with the trustees of the library that it would house a proposed register of such births. This was begun in 1742, and slowly gained in popularity; parents would obtain a birth certificate which included not only the usual details but also the exact date of their child's birth and the name of the mother's father. Some births were entered retrospectively from as far back as 1713. Registration cost sixpence, and a copy certificate was kept in the library as an official record. The registry was used by others as well as nonconformists, and includes many entries from outside London. In 1837 the certificates held in the library itself were bound into books and handed to the Registrar General. In all 48,975 births are featured - a happy hunting ground for present-day researchers in class RG4, especially since indexes are also available. Dr Williams's Library, meanwhile, is still alive and well; situated in Gordon Square in London, it carries a very significant collection of books and manuscripts covering the history of nonconformity, including an index of Congregationalist ministers and much else.

What nonconformist group might my ancestors have belonged to?

Puritans

A general term for dissenting believers whose activities in the sixteenth century formed the essence of what would become the Presbyterians, the Independents (or Congregationalists) and the Baptists. Puritan parents were particularly fond of giving their children Old Testament forenames - so don't be surprised to find a Bezaleell Nichollson or an Aholiab Nicholson baptised at St Peter's, Cornhill, London, in 1589 and 1599. To the amazement of a scoffing world, many Puritan children would also be burdened with compound names full of theological zeal, most famous of which were those borne by Praise-God Barebone and his brothers, Jesus-Christ-came-into-the-world-to-save Barebone and If-Christ-had-not-died-for-thee-thou-hadst-been-damned Barebone. The latter was referred to by acquaintances weary of using his full name, simply as 'Damned Barebones', and it didn't take contemporary comic dramatists long to realise that a useful, if cruel, anagram of 'Puritan' was 'A turnip' - a singularly appropriate term, they thought, for their cropped-haired fellow men.

Presbyterians
Dissenters who followed in the footsteps of Thomas Cartwright (1535-1603) who maintained that episcopacy (that is, government of the church by bishops) had no basis in scripture. The majority of Puritans adopted this creed. Many Presbyterian church records - the earliest dating from 1650 for York - have been deposited in the Public Record Office. Dr Williams's Library also has records of Presbyterian chapels. You should refer to the Society of Genealogists' publication *My ancestors were English Presbyterians/Unitarians* by Alan Ruston for more information.

Separatists
Presbyterians were happy enough to work for change from within Anglicanism, but the Separatists rejected the close connection between church and the state on scriptural grounds, and held that only committed Christians should be counted as members of the church.

Independents
The Separatists developed into Independents, holding that only congregation-alism was an acceptable basis for a church. Independents began establishing their own churches in the late sixteenth century. Oliver Cromwell was an Independent, and so were members of the London contingent of passengers aboard the *Mayflower* when she sailed for America.

Congregationalists
The Independents were later known as Congregationalists. In 1972 the United Reformed Church was founded as a successor to the Presbyterian and Congregational churches. The United Reformed Church History Society is at 86 Tavistock Place, Hampstead, London WC1H 9RT, but its collection of denominational records relating to the Presbyterian Church of England and the Congregational Church of England and Wales, together with some baptismal registers, biographical information on former ministers and a collection of 17th-century pamphlets, has now been deposited at Westminster College, Madingley Road, Cambridge CB3 0AA. Some Congregational churches chose not to join the United Reformed Church in 1972, and have remained independent from this organisation since. They are the Congregational Federation based at Notting-ham, the Evangelical Federation of Congregational Churches at Beverley and the Union of Welsh Independent Churches at Swansea. See *My ancestors were Congregationalists in England and Wales* by D.J.H. Clifford for more detail and a list of registers.

Baptists
The Baptists were Independents who rejected the idea of infant baptism. Baptists trace their origins back to the year 1611, but in 1633 a splinter group which adopted Calvinistic doctrines of predestination formed its own church. If your ancestors were Baptists, then, they might be General Baptists (believing

that salvation is available to all) or Particular Baptists (believing that only those elected or chosen can be saved). These two branches of the Baptist movement operated independently of each other and generated separate records until the creation of the Baptist Union in 1891. There is a certain regional dimension to all this: if you have Kent ancestors, for example, they would probably have joined a 'General' congregation, whilst in Somerset the 'Particular' chapels were in the ascendancy. Records relating to Baptist ancestors would include church registers and minute books, and the proceedings of regional meetings of Baptist believers. Relevant records are at Regent's Park College, Angus Library, Pusey Street, Oxford CX1 2LB. The Society of Genealogists' publication, *My ancestors were Baptists* by Geoffrey R. Breed is recommended reading.

Quakers (the Society of Friends)

The society was founded by George Fox (1624-1691) in 1647; the term 'Quaker' began to be used after he once exhorted a judge to 'Quake ... before the Lord'. Radical in their thinking and relentlessly persecuted for many years, members of the Society of Friends avoided all ritual in their worship and believed that every individual had the power of direct communication with God. Friends have no appointed ministers, their worship being maintained in silence until someone is moved by the Holy Spirit to utter his or her message.

In the 1650s the Society of Friends in London started keeping records; in due course, Quakers would become renowned as the most conscientious and thorough of all record-keepers. They were exempt from Hardwicke's Marriage Act of 1753 and were still allowed to marry according to the tenets of their own faith, whereby a couple pledge themselves to each other in front of witnesses. In 1840 and in 1857 all known Quaker registers were copied into digests; the originals were then handed over to the Public Record Office. The digests are held - along with many other Quaker records - by the library at Friends' House in Euston Road, London, and may also be consulted on microfilm at the Society of Genealogists. You will find a county-by-county catalogue of the originals in volume 42 of the List and Index Society, *General Register Office list of non-parochial registers: main series and Society of Friends' series* (1969). Some Society of Friends records have also been deposited in County Record Offices. The Society of Genealogists' publication *My ancestors were Quakers* by E.H. Milligan and M.J.Thomas will be useful for you to read and refer to.

Unitarians

From the beginning of the eighteenth century Unitarian belief, which rejected the doctrine of the Trinity, began to influence Presbyterian and Congregationalist assemblies, often splitting them asunder. Worshippers from many nonconformist congregations would 'drift' into Unitarianism as the years went by; sometimes separate Unitarian chapels were formed, but most Unitarian records deposited at the Public Record Office were classed as Presbyterian. The Unitarian Historical Society may be found at 6 Ventnor Terrace, Edinburgh EH9 2BL. See the Society of Genealogists' publication *My ancestors were English Presbyterians/Unitarians* by Alan Ruston for more information.

Methodists

This religious movement originated in the impassioned and dedicated Christian activities of John and Charles Wesley. It was not their intention to break away from the Anglican church as such, but their followers did precisely that, forming Methodist churches the length and breadth of the country. Eventually Methodism, like many another nonconformist sect, split into various factions: Wesleyan, Bible Christian, Primitive, New Connection and Tent Methodists. The Countess of Huntingdon founded the Calvinistic Methodists known as The Countess of Huntingdon's Connection. Her Christian name of 'Selina' was subsequently much favoured by Methodists when baptising a daughter. By 1932 most of these factions had joined together to become the Methodist Church. The earliest Methodist registers date from around 1779 for London, from 1780 for Somerset and from 1784 for Lancashire. In 1818 a Metropolitan Registry was established in London for the registration of births and baptisms from Methodist congregations. Look for Methodist registers in classes RG4 to RG8. The Methodist Archives and Research Centre, University of Manchester, John Rylands Library, Deansgate, Manchester M3 3EH, will respond to written enquiries, while further details of Methodist records can be obtained from the Methodist Church Liaison Officer, Methodist Church Archives, 34 Spiceland Road, Northfield, Birmingham B31 1NJ. The Society of Genealogists' publication *My ancestors were Methodists* by William Leary is recommended reading.

Moravians
Moravian missionaries from mainland Europe brought their mode of worship to London and Oxford in 1728. Ten years later John and Charles Wesley originally joined the movement and became its leaders, but left in 1740. In 1742 the congregation of the Unity of the Brethren was founded. The earliest registers date from 1741 for London, 1742 for Yorkshire and 1743 for Bedfordshire, and you will also find Moravians in Derbyshire, Cheshire, Lancashire and Wiltshire. After Hardwicke's Marriage Act of 1753, Moravians had to be married in an Anglican church, but details were also kept in their own registers. Surrendered registers are in class RG4, others are with local congregations. Records from defunct congregations are held at Moravian Church House, 5 Muswell Hill, London N10 3TH.

Other nonconformist sects
In Britain these include the Plymouth Brethren and many others, often regional in their membership, while of all the many religious groupings in America, the Church of Jesus Christ of Latter-day Saints (Mormons) is one of the best known in family history circles. The Salvation Army, founded by William Booth, is a world-wide Christian organisation, and its history and records are dealt with by Ray Wiggins in a title featured in the Society of Genealogists' *My ancestors* series of books.

A number of nonconformist burial grounds were eventually established, especially in London, of which those at Bethnal Green (Gibraltar) and Bunhill Fields, City Road, London, are the best known. Records will be found in class RG4, and Bunhill Fields' indexed series of thirty-three registers, 1718 to 1854, contains in excess of 100,000 interment entries.

Wales
Nonconformity took hold very firmly in Wales, and in some areas few towns, villages or rural settlements were without a chapel - and often many more than

Irish Quaker births 1789 *from a register kept by Hannah Pettigrew, who seemed to have intimate knowledge of Friends throughout Ireland. Her register of births, marriages and deaths begins in 1771 and additions were made up to 1848. Note the Quaker manner of referring to the month of January as '1 mo' and so on.*

one. This makes the two-volume *Religious census of 1851: a calendar of the returns relating to Wales* (1976-1981) particularly useful for determining which chapels existed at that period. Many have since closed, changed their use or been pulled down. For a comprehensive account county-by-county of registers, see *Nonconformist registers of Wales* by D. Ifans (1994), a companion volume to *Parish registers of Wales* by C.J. Williams and J. Watts-Williams (1986).

Scotland

The Church of Scotland itself is Presbyterian; details of its ministers from 1560 to 1954 may be found in *Fasti Ecclesiae Scoticanae*, published in nine volumes between 1915 and 1961, with addenda and corrigenda for the period 1560-1949 appearing in 1950.

You are strongly recommended to refer to Don Steel's *National index of parish registers*, vol 12, *Sources for Scottish genealogy and family history* (first published 1970), pp. 185-248, for a comprehensive account of Scottish nonconformity, covering the following groups of believers: Episcopalians, Seceding Presbyterian churches, Independents, Baptists, the Society of Friends, Methodists, Roman Catholics, Huguenots, Moravians, Bereans, Universalists, Unitarians, The New Church (New Jerusalemites or Swedenborgians) and Jews.

Ireland

Only a few nonconformist registers for Northern Ireland have survived, of which a small number date from before 1800. All Presbyterian registers and Roman Catholic registers 1830-1880 covering the Province of Ulster are on microfilm in the Public Record Office of Northern Ireland, Belfast. Here also are records for the Methodist Church, the Moravian Church and the Society of Friends. The Presbyterian Historical Society, Church House, Fisherwick Place, Belfast, is able to supply information about Presbyterian registers, some of which are held by them and some by local ministers. The Society of Friends had a significant presence in Ireland; do read *Guide to Irish Quaker Records 1654-1860* by O.C. Goodbody (1967), which is a catalogue of manuscript collections mainly housed at the Society of Friends Historical Society, Swanbrook House, Morehampton Road, Dublin 4.

In general, if you wish to find addresses of various nonconformist archive repositories, refer to *British archives: a guide to archive resources in the United Kingdom* by J. Foster and J. Sheppard (3rd.Ed.,1995).

Nonconformist records: hints and reminders

- Although some nonconformist registers commenced around 1660, the majority do not start until the eighteenth century. These records are generally of births, baptisms, deaths and burials, with some marriages before Hardwicke's Marriage Act of 1753. Some have been transcribed and will be found in record offices in print, in typescript or on microform.
- Many nonconformist groups (especially the Baptists) did not believe in infant baptism, and Quakers didn't believe in baptism at all.
- Before the passing of Hardwicke's Marriage Act of 1753, it was possible to contract a common-law marriage by making a declaration before witnesses or in the presence of an unlicensed minister. This kind of marriage was frowned on as being 'irregular', but was still accepted as valid by both church and state. Nonconformists could be married in this way in their own meeting houses, but after Hardwicke's Marriage Act all marriages had to be solemnized in the Church of England by a minister of that church. The only exceptions were Jews and Quakers, who were still allowed to marry within their own faiths. If marriage registers of nonconformist churches or chapels from 1754 to 1898 are discovered which were not submitted for

Church of the Sacred Heart
Tunstall

Henry Green, son of Henry & Catharine Green was born on 23rd of February & Baptised on 19th March 1893. Margaret and James Murphy being Sponsors.
I certify this to be a true & correct copy taken from the Register of births & baptisms kept at this church

Signed P. J. Lynch

29 / " / 35

Certified 1935 copy of a Catholic baptism, *Tunstall, Staffs, in 1893.* (Terry Green)

authentification to the Registrar General and are not now in classes RG4, RG6 or RG8, then they were not strictly official records in the eyes of the law.
- As many nonconformist sects did not have their own burial grounds, burials often took place in Church of England graveyards and the event should be recorded in parish registers.
- Anglican parish registers often record early nonconformist events such as a

birth or death, sometimes adding derogatory annotations such as: 'anabaptists'.

- Many sects 'came and went' from the seventeenth century onwards, and any records which did exist may have completely disappeared. Some sects did not believe in keeping records at all.
- Many nonconformist ministers considered chapel or church registers to be their own private property. When the minister moved on, the register(s) would often move with him. Sometimes very careful research into the family connections of a minister or the history of chapels that closed or merged can lead you to an otherwise-forgotten register.
- In a County Record Office you may find 'meeting house certificates' issued when places of worship were licensed by a bishop; these will date from the period 1698 to 1852 and may be the only surviving record of the existence of a meeting house. You should also look at the 1851 ecclesiastical census for evidence of nonconformist chapels in an ancestral parish.
- When researching Irish ancestry, always consider the records of Protestant nonconformist denominations.

Roman Catholics

Roman Catholics take the understandable view that it was the Anglican church which was nonconformist, not they themselves, yet it was that very Anglican church which repressed its Roman Catholic fellow-Christians for hundreds of years. Catholics were subject to double payment of Land Tax; they were fined for not attending Anglican services and for attending Catholic ones.

'Recusant' was the term used to describe anyone who failed to attend his or her parish church. From the mid sixteenth century onwards, considerable fines and forfeiture of goods could be the punishment for such absence, and details are given in the Recusant Rolls. Most, but not all, recusants were Roman Catholics, and many Recusant Rolls have been published by the Catholic Record Society. Annual rolls of the county sheriffs, 1592 to 1691, are at the Public Record Office (E376 and E377/1-82).

Faced with oppression and punishment, the Roman Catholic church became something of an underground society for many years, and baptisms and marriages continued in secret; very often the services were repeated in the Anglican church to keep within the law.

From Hardwicke's Marriage Act of 1753, only marriages in the Church of England by a Church of England minister and those celebrated by Jews and Quakers were legal. In 1778 the more stringent laws against Roman Catholics were relaxed, and in 1791 they were, at last, officially allowed to worship in their own churches. Very few Roman Catholic registers were deposited in the Public Record Office, and those which were submitted refer mainly to the north of England. Many Roman Catholic registers and records are in the custody of the 'priest in charge' of a parish. For a comprehensive listing of surviving registers, see *Catholic missions and registers 1700-1880* by Michael Gandy. The Catholic Record Society has published a great number of registers and other historical records dating from the sixteenth century. You might also like to contact or to join the Catholic Family History Society.

Huguenots

The Huguenots, like the Jews, fled in large numbers to England and to other friendly countries as a result of religious persecution at home. The impact of Huguenot refugees upon the life, the culture and the financial health of England can hardly be overestimated. Their arrival in force in the 1680s (though many had arrived long before then) constituted what the Duke of Buccleuch and Queensbury refers to in his foreword to *Huguenot ancestry* by Noel Currer-Briggs and Royston Gambier (1985) as 'the greatest "brain drain" in history'.

The name 'Huguenot' was given to French Protestants who adopted the Calvinistic form of the reformed religion. They suffered persecution for heresy and from around 1560 to 1598 were engaged in a series of religious wars with the French Crown. The Edict of Nantes of 1598 gave the Huguenots freedom of worship; it was the revocation of this edict by Louis XIV in 1685 that drove many Huguenots to seek refuge in other Protestant countries, including England. Europe's loss was Britain's gain, and the Huguenot contribution to Britain's life and wealth has been enormous. Huguenot immigrants of all social classes settled in such places as London, Norwich, Plymouth and Canterbury. Expect to find many Huguenot immigrants later working as silk weavers in the Spitalfields area of London. Many Huguenot records from the sixteenth century onwards, including church registers written in French, have been published by the Huguenot Society; particularly useful are *Letters of Denization and Acts of Naturalization for aliens in England 1509-1800* (Vols.8, 18, 27 and 35), *Return of aliens in London, 1523-1603* (Vol.10), *The French Protestant Hospital: extracts from the archives of 'La Providence' relating to inmates and applicants for admission 1718-1957 and to recipients of and applicants for the Coqueau Charity 1745-1901* (Vols.52 and 53) and *Returns of strangers in the Metropolis 1593,1627,1635,1639* (Vol.57).

Also of interest, containing thousands of names with comprehensive indexes, is *Protestant exiles from France in the reign of Louis XIV; or, the Huguenot refugees and their descendants in Great Britain and Ireland* by D.C.A. Agnew (3 vols., 1871-1874).

Many Huguenots were rapidly absorbed into the English community, often anglicising their surnames. There may be a tradition in your family that 'we came over with the Huguenots', and this may well be true; but beware - such a legend is fairly commonplace, and may well have no foundation in reality. Not all French immigrants to England were Huguenots. Some were emigrés from the French Revolution during the period 1789 to 1795.

You will find the Huguenot Society of London at the Huguenot Library, University College, Gower Street, London WC1E 6BT.

Jews

Jews were banished from England in 1290 and only during the Commonwealth period in 1655 did a number of wealthier Sephardic Jews begin to arrive from Portugal, Italy and Spain. A large number of Ashkenazi Jews fled the pogroms in the Russian Empire during the period 1881-1914, and more came to England as refugees in the 1930s to escape from Germany and other countries controlled by the Nazis. As with the Huguenots, Europe's loss was Britain's gain, and many Jews have made an enormous contribution to British life and culture over the years.

Jewish records were never deposited with the Registrar General but should be still with the synagogues or, possibly, in certain record offices. After 1837, of course, Jewish births, marriages and deaths were to be officially registered along with those of all other English and Welsh subjects.

Bevis Marks Hall, 2 Heneage Lane, London EC3A 5DQ, has several Jewish registers covering the period 1687 to 1837, the Society of Genealogists has substantial collections, and the Jewish Historical Society of Great Britain has published a considerable amount of relevant material. The chairman of the Birmingham branch of this society is Dr Anthony Joseph, 25 Westbourne Road, Edgbaston, Birmingham B15 3TX, who also kindly acts as an agent for those wishing to communicate with overseas Jewish societies. The Jewish Genealogical Society of Great Britain, formed in 1992, can be contacted at 32 Tavistock Street, London WC2E 7PD and publishes a journal called *Shemot*. The Anglo-Jewish Association may be found at Woburn House, Upper Woburn Place, London WC1H OEZ, and there is a Jewish Museum at the same address.

Records held at the Office of the Chief Rabbi, Adler House, Tavistock Square, London WC1H 9HP are not available for public consultation, but paid researches may be carried out in certain circumstances. The Jewish Genealogical Society of Great Britain, formed in 1992, can be contacted at 32 Tavistock Street, London WC2E 7PD and publishes a journal called *Shemot*. The Anglo-Jewish Association may be found at Woburn House, Upper Woburn Place, London WC1H OEZ, and there is a Jewish Museum at the same address.

Do be aware that many Jews became assimilated into the gentile communities in which they found themselves, and sometimes you will find Jews in Anglican records of baptism, marriage and burial, especially in London.

The Register of Births at the College of Arms

A little-known register of births was commenced by the College of Arms in 1747/8. The number of entries it contains is fairly small (less than three hundred in all), but each includes exceptionally useful genealogical information. The register was used mainly by Roman Catholics, Moravians and Jews. For information from this register you will need to contact the College of Arms, Queen Victoria Street, London EC4 4BT. Further details on its contents are given in the third volume of *National index of parish registers: sources for Roman Catholic and Jewish genealogy and family history* (Ed.D.G. Steel, 1974).

Further reading

(Nonconformists)

Bate, F. *The Declaration of Indulgence 1672: a study in the rise of organised dissent.* 1908.

Breed, G. *My ancestors were Baptists.* (3rd.Ed.) 1995.

Clifford, D.J.H. *My ancestors were Congregationalists in England and Wales.* (2nd.Ed.) 1997.

Gandy, M. *Basic facts about English Nonconformity for family historians.* 1998.

Gordon, A. *Freedom after ejection: a review (1690-1692) of Presbyterian and Congregational nonconformity in England and Wales.* 1917.

Ifans, D.(Ed.) *Cofrestri anghydffurfiol Cymru/ Nonconformist registers of Wales.* 1994.

Kendall, H.B. *The history of the Primitive Methodist Church.* No date.

Leary, W. *My ancestors were Methodists.* (3rd Ed.) 1999.

Livingstone, E.A. *The concise history of the Christian Church.* 1977.

Lyon Turner, G. *Original records of early nonconformity under persecution and indulgence.* 3 vols. 1911-1914.

McLaughlin, E. *Nonconformist ancestors.* 1995.

Milligan, E. and Thomas, M. *My ancestors were Quakers.* (2nd.Ed.) 1999.

Palgrave-Moore, P. *Understanding the history and records of nonconformity.* 1987.
Ruston, A. *My ancestors were English Presbyterians/Unitarians.* 1993.
Steel, D.G.(Ed.) *National index of parish registers, vol.2: Sources for nonconformist genealogy and family history.* 1973.
Wiggins, R. *My ancestors were in the Salvation Army.* (2nd Ed.) 1999.

(Roman Catholics)
Gandy, M. *Catholic missions and registers 1700-1880.* 6 regional volumes + atlas volume. 1993.
Gandy, M. *Catholic family history: general sources.* 1996.
Gandy, M. *Basic facts about tracing your Catholic Ancestry in England.* 1998.
Lannon, D. *The directory of Roman Catholic archives.* 1994.
Shorney, D. *Protestant nonconformity and Roman Catholicism.* 1996.
Steel, D.G.(Ed.) *National index of parish registers, vol.3: Sources for Roman Catholic and Jewish genealogy and family history.* 1974.

(Huguenots)
Currer-Briggs, N and Gambier, R. *Huguenot ancestry.* 1985.
Gwynn, R. *Huguenot heritage.* 1985.
Smiles, S. *Huguenots, their settlements, churches and industries in England and Ireland.* 1867.

(Jews)
Emden, P.H. *Jews of Britain: a series of biographies.* 1943.
Jewish Genealogical Society of Great Britain. *Jewish Ancestors: A Guide to Jewish Genealogy in Germany and Austria.* 2001.
Jewish Genealogical Society of Great Britain. *Jewish Ancestors: A Guide to Jewish Genealogy in Latvia and Estonia.* 2001.
Jewish Historical Society of England. 1949. *Anglo-Jewish notabilities: their arms and testamentary dispositions.*
Joseph, A.P. 'Jewish records' in *Family History* (IHGS), vol.12, 87/88 (Jan.1982).
Mordy, I. *My ancestors were Jewish.* 1995.
Rottenburg. *Finding our fathers: a guidebook to Jewish genealogy.* New York. 1977.
Samuel, W.S. *Sources of Anglo-Jewish genealogy.* Jewish Museum Publication no.2. 1933.
Steel, D.G.(Ed.) *National index of parish registers, vol.3: Sources for Roman Catholic and Jewish genealogy and family history.* 1974.
Wenzerul, R. *Jewish ancestors? A beginner's guide to Jewish genealogy in Great Britain.* 2000.

CHAPTER 6

The International Genealogical Index (IGI)

Luckily for us all, there is one especially useful general name index to millions of parish register and bishops' transcript entries of birth, baptism and marriage: the International Genealogical Index of The Church of Jesus Christ of Latter-day Saints (the Mormons).

The Church of Jesus Christ of Latter-day Saints was founded in New York State in 1830 by Joseph Smith, who claimed that he had had a vision from God with instructions to find some golden plates which were to be the basis of 'The Book of Mormon', now used by members of the church together with the Bible and other scriptures in their worship. After the death of Joseph Smith another leader emerged, Brigham Young, who was to take his people on the arduous journey to their new spiritual home, Salt Lake City in Utah. The Church encourages its members to trace their genealogy, which is of great importance to them and their beliefs.

One of the greatest achievements of the Mormon Church in the field of genealogy has been the compilation of the International Genealogical Index (IGI) which has proved to be an invaluable aid to family historians.

What is the IGI?

The International Genealogical Index (formerly known as the 'Computer File Index' or CFI) is one of the most useful 'finding aids' available for the genealogical researcher and has been formed from parish and nonconformist register entries, together with information provided by church members and others. Available to Mormons and non-Mormons alike, it contains millions of references to births, baptisms and marriages. This index was first published in 1969, and has been regularly updated every few years since. Initially produced on microfiche up to 1992, it now forms part of the LDS 'Family Search' package, which is available on the Internet and (to institutions only) on CD-ROM. You may submit your own information for inclusion in the Ancestral File by writing to Salt Lake City. The IGI covers not only British records, but also those of many other countries all over the world. So far as the British Isles is concerned, the Index is subdivided into counties for England, Wales and Scotland, and also includes Ireland, the Channel Islands and the Isle of Man. It contains births, baptisms and marriages, but practically no deaths or burials are included except for deaths of infants (shown as such) who died under the age of eight years. This does not include any illegitimate infants who died before the age of eight. When details of relevant entries have been noted from the IGI, it is essential then to search the original records (together with those of deaths and burials) in order to verify your findings. It cannot be emphasised too strongly that the IGI is only a finding aid; it is the beginning of your journey, not the end of it.

A Parish and Vital Records Listing has been produced which covers each county, and it is wise to consult this to discover exactly which parishes and nonconformist congregations have been covered, for what period and from what source. It is by no means rare to find that an ancestral parish has not been covered from beginning to end in the IGI (sometimes because entries have been taken from bishops' transcripts, not parish registers), and this needs to be taken into account.

It is part of Mormon belief that families should be joined together into one genealogical unit, and church members trace their ancestors who are then baptised into the faith. Mormon missionaries have been despatched to archive repositories in a great number of countries to film vital records of birth, baptism and marriage for inclusion in the IGI. Not all the entries on the Index are taken from parish registers; many are drawn from bishops' transcripts or from nonconformist registers, and others from miscellaneous notes taken from wills, census, parish chest and other records gathered by the church from its members or from family historians who have transcribed or indexed local records and made them available.

Family historians owe an incalculable debt to the Church of Jesus Christ of Latter-day Saints for the opportunity of using the IGI, and its existence has revolutionised research in recent years. To give you an idea of the magnitude of the IGI, reflect upon the fact that the 1988 edition listed the names of no fewer than 121,000,000 deceased persons world-wide.

The IGI is available for consultation in the Family History Centres of the Church of Latter-day Saints, and the microfiche version, at least, has been purchased by various record offices, local studies libraries and by most Family History Societies. The world-wide version on CD-ROM may be seen at the Society of Genealogists and elsewhere.

There is no fee for using the LDS Family History Centres, but a small charge is made for photocopies of the IGI frames, or for any other records which need to be ordered from the Family History Library in Salt Lake City. Look at a current issue of *Family Tree Magazine* to find details of advertisers who will provide frames from the IGI for a reasonable fee.

How to interpret the IGI

The IGI on CD-ROM will allow you to search for names which interest you on a nationwide basis; with a little practice you will be able to use the program effectively, and will probably choose to store various entries in a holding file before printing them all out together or downloading the information onto a floppy disk. For all the sophistication of the software, the searcher is not yet able to get an answer to one very common kind of query, namely: 'I know that a man with the surname "Carpenter" married a woman with the surname "Bradford" somewhere in England; can you locate this marriage for me?' The CD-ROM - and the Internet version of the IGI - are a delight to use, for all that. One of the

COUNTRY: ENGLAND — COUNTY: DERBY	AS OF JUL 1984				PAGE 392			
NAME / FATHER MOTHER OR SPOUSE	SEX / T Y P E·C	EVENT DATE	TOWN, PARISH	B	E	S	BATCH	SERIAL SHEET
ARMSTRONG, THOMAS								
ARMSTRONG, THOMAS — THOMAS ARMSTRONG/HANNAH	M C	24AUG1823	ALFRETON	D6MAR1976NZ	13MAR1976NZ	14APR1976NZ	C046271	1294
ARMSTRONG, THOMAS — RICHARD ARMSTRONG/HANNAH	M C	31OCT1824	DERBY,SAINT ALKMUND KING STREET-WESLEYAN METHODIST					
		14JAN1978AL		09MAR1978AL	29MAR1978AL		C066661	0489
ARMSTRONG, THOMAS — THOMAS ARMSTRONG/HANNAH	M C	26FEB1832	ALFRETON	D6MAR1976NZ	18MAR1976NZ	16APR1976NZ	C046271	2574
ARMSTRONG, THOMAS — GEORGE ARMSTRONG/JANE	M C	12FEB1833	DERBY,SAINT WERBURGH	24JUN1976OG	07SEP1976OG	21OCT1976OG	C049861	7538
ARMSTRONG, THOMAS	M C	04MAR1836	GLOSSOP,NEW MILLS-WESLEYAN	D2NOV1977SL	26NOV1977SL	17FEB1978SL	C066751	0090
SAMUEL ARMSTRONG/MARIA WOOLEY								
ARMSTRONG, THOMAS — CHARLOTTE RAINS	H M	11OCT1841	NORTH WINGFIELD			22AUG1978SL	M058751	0554
ARMSTRONG, THOMS — MARTHA LOW	H M	10JAN1771	NORTH WINGFIELD			02NOV1978OG	M058752	0681
ARMSTRONG, THOS. — RUTH CUTT	H M	19OCT1704	BLACKWELL BY ALFRETON			04JAN1972SG	7106033	76
ARMSTRONG, WALTER	M C	28NOV1869	HEATH	20MAY1981SE	30JUL1981SE	15SEP1981SE	C055091	0665
GEORGE ARMSTRONG/ELIZABETH								
ARMSTRONG, WALTON — /AMY ARMSTRONG	M C	27MAR1844	CHESTERFIELD	29APR1977PV	15JUN1977PV	UNCLEARED	C035862	9869
ARMSTRONG, WILLIAM	M C	11FEB1731	BOLSOVER	15MAR1979OG	18MAY1979OG	01JUN1979OG	C060972	0992
WILLIAM ARMSTRONG/BRIDGET								
ARMSTRONG, WILLIAM — MARY LOWE	H M	01JUN1734	CHAPEL EN LE FRITH			09APR1948SL	A184796	4780
ARMSTRONG, WILLIAM — MARY LOWE	H M	01JUN1734	CHAPEL EN LE FRITH			18JUN1973LG	7230730	32
ARMSTRONG, WILLIAM — ELIZABETH BEANE	H M	29NOV1748	SUTTON CUM DUCKMANTON			21JAN1982LG	M059402	0147
ARMSTRONG, WILLIAM — MARTHA BOULSOVER	H M	09AUG1756	BOLSOVER			22JAN1981OK	M060972	0174
ARMSTRONG, WILLIAM — SARAH YEOMANS	H M	12AUG1762	CHESTERFIELD			10NOV1978LA	M035863	3040
ARMSTRONG, WILLIAM — WM ARMSTRONG/MARTHA	M C	06FEB1768	BOLSOVER	15MAR1979OG	18MAY1979OG	05JUN1979OG	C060972	1709
ARMSTRONG, WILLIAM — WM ARMSTRONG/MARY	M C	07MAR1768	BOLSOVER	15MAR1979OG	18MAY1979OG	05JUN1979OG	C060972	1710
ARMSTRONG, WILLIAM — CATHERINE JACKSON	H M	14APR1789	BOLSOVER			22JAN1981OK	M060972	0447
ARMSTRONG, WILLIAM — BENJM ARMSTRONG/MARY	M C	21OCT1795	BOLSOVER	15MAR1979OG	19MAY1979OG	01JUN1979OG	C060972	2812
ARMSTRONG, WILLIAM — RUTH MITCHEL	H M	18APR1814	BOLSOVER			19OCT1977PV	M060971	0017
ARMSTRONG, WILLIAM — MARGARET CHAPMAN	H M	07OCT1823	CHESTERFIELD			23AUG1977WA	M035862	0923
ARMSTRONG, WILLIAM	M C	19OCT1824	BOLSOVER	24AUG1977WA	26OCT1977WA	12NOV1977WA	C060971	0490
WILLIAM ARMSTRONG/MARGARET								
ARMSTRONG, WILLIAM — WILLIAM ARMSTRONG/ANN	M C	09APR1827	CRICH	22MAY1976MT	14AUG1976MT	31AUG1976MT	C049781	1456
ARMSTRONG, WILLIAM — THOMAS ARMSTRONG/HANNAH	M C	03JAN1830	ALFRETON	06MAR1976NZ	17MAR1976NZ	16APR1976NZ	C046271	2269
ARMSTRONG, WILLIAM — WILLIAM ARMSTRONG/RUTH	M C	16MAY1831	HEATH	17JUL1976LA	07OCT1976LA	13OCT1976LA	C055091	0245
ARMSTRONG, WILLIAM — SARAH ADAMS	H M	12AUG1833	MELBOURNE			13OCT1977SL	M055591	0863
ARMSTRONG, WILLIAM	M C	29JUN1850	BOLSOVER	24AUG1977WA	27OCT1977WA	15NOV1977WA	C060971	1569
BENJAMIN ARMSTRONG/ELIZA								
ARMSTRONG, WILLIAM # — ELIZABETH RATCLIFFE	M C	09JUN1851	ALFRETON			CLEARED	M046273	085A
ARMSTRONG, WILLIAM HENRY	M C	16NOV1862	STAVELEY	15SEP1976AZ	18DEC1976AZ	03FEB1977AZ	C055751	5654
MATTHEW ARMSTRONG/MARY								
ARMSTRONG, WILLIAM JOHN	M C	20JUL1862	BOLSOVER	24AUG1977WA	27OCT1977WA	17NOV1977WA	C060971	2004
JAMES ARMSTRONG/MARY								
ARMSTRONG, WM — BENJ ARMSTRONG/ANN	M C	18MAR1748	BOLSOVER	15MAR1979OG	18MAY1979OG	01JUN1979OG	C060972	1206
ARMSTRONG, WM — JOHN ARMSTRONG/MARY	M A	18MAY1789	AULT HUCKNALL	20JUN1974SL	17SEP1974SL	22NOV1974SL	7405302	47
ARMSTRONG, WM — WM ARMSTRONG/CATHARINE	M C	13JUN1800	BOLSOVER	15MAR1979OG	19MAY1979OG	01JUN1979OG	C060972	3032
ARMSTRONG, WM. — JOHN ARMSTRONG/MARY	M C	18MAY1789	AULT HUCKNALL	26FEB1976PV	08APR1976PV	20MAY1976PV	C048271	0714
*ARMSTRONGE , ** SEE ARMSTRONG								
*ARMSWORTH								
ARMSWORTH, WM. — HANNAH WILSON	H M	08FEB1751	EYAM			03MAR1976LG	7518115	22
=ARNALL , ** SEE ARNOLD								
=ARNAT , ** SEE ARNOT								
=ARNATT , ** SEE ARNOT								
*ARNAUD								
ARNAUD, BENJAMIN — BENJAMIN ARNAUD/ELIZA	M C	10OCT1824	THORPE BY ASHBOURNE	04FEB1977MT	06APR1977MT	10MAY1977MT	C058991	0082
=ARNAULD , ** SEE ARNOLD								
*ARNE , ** SEE ARNEY								
=ARNEFIELD , ** SEE ARNFIELD								

A page from the IGI (1984 edition), *for the county of Derbyshire.* (Church of Jesus Christ of Latter-day Saints)

many improved features is that alternatives for the same Christian name ('Thomas' and 'Thos', 'William' and 'Wm') now appear together in the listed records, not separated as on the microfiche version.

Many users of the IGI, however, will be referring to the original microfiche, and a few words of explanation will not come amiss. Entries for England, Wales and Scotland are arranged under counties (though earlier versions have Scotland in one continuous alphabet), then within counties under surnames in alphabetical order - usually under one standard surname spelling containing variants of that surname. Within the surnames come Christian names, also in strict alphabetical order, entries for each name being listed in date order, the earliest first. Rob, Robert, Robt, Rbt, etc are entered separately, and 'Wm' is followed by 'Wm.' (with a full-stop). If you are searching for the surname of Voss or Volkes, for example, relevant entries may appear under such spellings as Voss/Vosse or Volke(s) and also possibly under Foss/Fosse or Folke(s). The Welsh IGI has the addition of a 'given name' arrangement in alphabetical order within Welsh counties.

At the top of each microfiche frame appears the name of the country, state or county, the date of the particular IGI edition and the page number. We then see the surname and Christian name of the recorded person. To the right of this comes the name of the father, mother or spouse, and then two narrow columns. In the first of these you will see the letter 'M' for 'male' or 'F' for 'female', 'H' for 'husband' or 'W' for 'wife'. In the second of the two narrow columns you will see another letter: 'A' for 'adult christening', 'B' for 'birth', 'C' for 'christening',

'D' for 'death or burial', 'F' for 'birth or christening of first-known child', 'M' for 'marriage', 'N' for 'census' or 'W' for 'will'. Any others are miscellaneous entries. These columns are followed by the date of each event, and then comes the town or parish. The contents of the final five columns consist of LDS church information, much of which will be unintelligible or irrelevant to most researchers. However, do note the source numbers (batch and serial/sheet numbers) from the two columns on the right of the frame, as these numbers can, on occasion, lead you to the original documents which may contain additional information.

Be careful when it comes to entries which pre-date the adoption of the Gregorian calendar in 1752: the IGI does not use double-dating, and moves the date forward by one year. An event which happened on 3 February 1714 (Old Style dating), which most family historians would represent as '1714/5' would appear on the IGI as simply '1715'.

Here is an example of one line taken from the July 1984 IGI for Derbyshire:

Armstrong, Thomas. Thomas Armstrong/Hannah. M.C. 24 Aug 1823. Alfreton.

This tells us that a male child named Thomas was christened on 24 August 1823 at Alfreton, Derbyshire, and was the son of Thomas and Hannah Armstrong.

Two entries before the above example comes a related one:

Armstrong, Thomas. Hannah Parkin. H.M. 17 May 1819.

Here we have Thomas Armstrong marrying Hannah Parkin at Alfreton on 17 May 1819. We can assume for now, if we like, that these are probably the parents of the Thomas baptised in 1823. 'Probably', but not definitely; we'll still need to refer to the original parish register entries and maybe other records, too, before feeling more confident about this hypothesis.

The IGI is, in a way, the tip of the Mormon Church iceberg. Salt Lake City, Utah, USA, is home to the largest genealogical library in the world, and houses the Family Group Records Collection which consists of some eight million record forms based upon international research. The library in Salt Lake City has thousands of family histories - mostly books, although some are on microfilm or microfiche - and the Family Registry which, with luck, can help you identify other researchers who have already worked on branches of your own ancestry and may perhaps be contacted to your mutual benefit.

If you cannot get to Salt Lake City in person, there is a pedigree referral service; if you send in a family surname with details of places and dates, it may be possible to supply information about others researching your particular family. It is necessary to write beforehand, as there may be a charge for this service. Write to: The Genealogical Society of Utah, The Church of Jesus Christ of Latter-day Saints, Family History Library, 35 North West Temple, Salt Lake City, Utah 84150, USA, and include three international reply coupons (IRCs), obtainable from your local post office, to pay for the reply.

Each Church of Jesus Christ of Latter-day Saints' Family History Centre has the Family History Library Catalogue (FHLC) which is on microfiche and compact disk, and which guides you through a locality search for the place where an ancestor lived. From this you can then choose the type of record you wish to search; your local Family History Centre can order microfilms from Salt Lake City and make them available for you to consult near to home. Volunteers at the Family History Centres are always willing to assist with these various areas of research. For a list of LDS Family History Centres in the British Isles, see Appendix II to Tom Wood's *An introduction to civil registration* (2000) or *The Family Historian's Enquire Within* by Pauline Saul (5th.Ed. 1995) pp.51-53 or send a stamped addressed envelope to The Area Manager, The Genealogical Society of Utah, 185 Penns Lane, Sutton Coldfield, West Midlands B76 1JU.

Further reading

McLaughlin, E. *Making the most of the IGI.* (5th.Ed.) 1999.
Nichols, E.L. *The International Genealogical Index: 1992 edition.* 1995.

CHAPTER 7

Probate Records

We now move from records of birth or baptism, marriage and death or burial to those associated with the granting of probate or Letters of Administration. Here, with luck, you will be able to establish some far-reaching family relationships and even gain an insight into the character of your ancestors.

Not everyone left a will in the past - or leaves one today - and Letters of Administration are not always taken out if someone has died intestate, but where probate documents have survived, they can bring our ancestors to life and help to untangle family relationships in an extraordinarily effective way.

Last will and testament

The Statute of Wills of 1540 provided that a *will* should deal with real estate ('realty'), land and buildings, and that a *testament* should deal with movable personal property ('personalty') such as goods, chattels, personal belongings, money, tools, crops and furniture. As time went on these two terms became interchangeable, although strictly speaking land or buildings given by a will are referred to as a 'devise', while goods and chattels bequeathed are termed a 'legacy'. A person generally had to have goods to the value of £5 or more, known as *bona notabilia*, in one area of ecclesiastical jurisdiction for the will to go to probate or for Letters of Administration to be granted in the case of a person who died intestate.

From 1540 until 1837 a will could be made by any male over the age of fourteen years and by a female over the age of twelve years. After 1837 a testator had to be of full age, that is to say, twenty-one years or over.

Following the 1540 Statute of Wills, very few married women made a will, except with the express approval of their husbands, though spinsters and widows with property were not subject to any impediment. Only with the Married Women's Property Act of 1882 was a married woman allowed to own property in her own right, and therefore to dispose of it in any way she chose; previously a married woman and everything she owned had been regarded in law as being the property of her husband.

Other persons unable to make a will were lunatics (whose estates were usually a subject of litigation and were dealt with in the Prerogative Court of Canterbury or in Chancery), prisoners, apostates, deserters, renegades and traitors.

A will constituted the final statement and desire of a person as to what would happen to his or her property once death had done its worst. In such important documents will be found statements as to the last bequests and wishes of the deceased.

For the family historian a will is an invaluable document, often pre-dating parish registers, even going back to the fourteenth century. It can provide evidence and proof of a family structure, can authenticate family relationships and corroborate your working hypotheses. No other document gives quite the same information as a will and it is this record which speaks to us from the past as the testator itemises in detail the way in which he or she wants the estate settled. It can give an indication as to how affairs stood within the family, and may name a spouse, children, godchildren, grandchildren, nephews, nieces, kinsfolk, 'cousins' (often a very vague term), friends, creditors, debtors.

If you are exceptionally lucky, a will might even take you *back* a generation - to the testator's father or mother - or even beyond. So the brief Prerogative Court of Canterbury will of Richard Tidford, mariner of Shoreditch, who died aboard HMS *St Michael* in 1691, mentions his mother Joanne, 'wife of Roger Tidford of London, victualler'. Here are the names of both parents, with the father's place of abode and occupation thrown in for good measure.

Expect a will to be signed by the testator, if he or she were literate, and to name beneficiaries, executors or executrixes and witnesses (who were not allowed to benefit from the will from 1752 onwards). The names of those appointed as 'overseers' of the will may also be mentioned, as may the desired place of burial. Early wills usually begin with the solemn preamble, 'In the name of God amen...'. If this is lacking, the testator might be a nonconformist. Then, normally, will come the testator's name, his place of abode and, very often, his occupation.

A will might be made years in advance of death, when the person was still healthy, but more often during a serious and life-threatening illness, almost as if the individual knew that his or her days were numbered.

Verbal death-bed utterances were acceptable in law provided that they were attested to by three witnesses and that the testator had been resident in the place where he or she died for ten days or more. Usually these death-bed wills begin with the words 'memorandum quod' or even just 'memorandum'. Verbal death-bed utterances, or 'nuncupative' wills as they were known, were different from a dictated will signed by a testator. Nuncupative wills are still legally acceptable when a person is on active military service. A will written entirely by the testator in his or her own handwriting is a 'holograph' will.

In the days when England was wholly Roman Catholic, a man would often leave money for prayers and masses to be said in his parish church. Sometimes a sum of money or other bequests for food and clothing would be left for the poor of the parish. A man may have moved to London to seek his fortune and have died there, making a will which included bequests to the poor of his home parish many miles away in the provinces. Thus you have a vital clue as to his origins. A husband would normally leave his wife his personal estate, often with the proviso that it was for her lifetime only or until her re-marriage, in which event her portion would revert to the family and not pass to her new husband. Often a will stipulates that a property left to a son or daughter must be available for the testator's widow to live in during her life. Sometimes the children honoured this stipulation, but often they did not, and an acrid case in the Court of Chancery could be the result.

Occasionally the wording of a will can give you an insight into the character or opinions of the testator. John Redman of Upminster, Essex, who died in 1798, was a bit of a revolutionary:

> '*To Mr. French of Harpur Street...a set of Tom Paine's 'Rights of Man', bound with common sense, with the answers intended by the longheads of the law, fatheads of the church, and wiseheads of an indolent usurping aristocracy...*'

David Davis of Clapham died in 1788, and was thoughtful enough to leave Mary Davis, daughter of Peter Delaport, '*the sum of five shillings, which is sufficient to enable her to get drunk for the last time at my expense*'.

Philip Thicknesse, soldier, author and discoverer of the painter Gainsborough, died near Boulogne in 1793, leaving instructions that his right hand be cut off and sent to his son, Lord Audley, '*in hopes that such a sight may remind him of his duty to God, after having so long abandoned the duty he owed to a father who once affectionately loved him.*'

A last will and testament was clearly regarded by some as a last chance to vent their spleen on an ungrateful relation or friend.

Letters of Administration

In many cases a person died 'intestate' - that is, having made no will. Very often matters could then be settled quite amicably by the relatives concerned without any need for legal process of any kind. If there was considerable property or if dissension broke out within the family, however, then Letters of Administration (very often referred to as an 'admon') would be required. These, once granted to the next-of-kin or other suitable adult over the age of 21 years, would confer the legal power necessary for the deceased's affairs to be administered. In cases where a will had been made but did not specify an executor or an executrix, or where an executor was unwilling to act, then Letters of Administration would be granted to allow the next-of-kin or other suitable person to administer the estate.

Probate jurisdictions pre-1858

For the genealogist, wills fall into two periods of time: up to and including 1857, and from 1858 onwards, in the January of which year civil district probate registries were set up in England and Wales. The power of granting probate was removed from the jurisdiction of the Church of England and passed to the state. Before this time, wills and administrations had been handled by various ecclesiastical courts up and down the country. During the Middle Ages the complex system of granting probate and administration in the church courts was based on the ecclesiastical court hierarchy, and this is how it continued until the state take-over on 11 January 1858.

In theory, at least, there were established rules which determined which ecclesiastical court of probate should be used in any given case.

The Archdeacon's Court would normally prove a will or grant letters of administration if the testator's property fell only within the area covered by the archdeaconry in question.

Suppose that Henry Jones, deceased, had held property only in the parish of West Grinstead in West Sussex. This parish comes under the jurisdiction of the Archdeacon of Chichester, so his will would have been proved in that Archdeacon's Court.

In the name of God Amen I William Read
of Lyme Regis in the County of Dorset Mariner being at present
as well in good bodily health as of a sound and perfect
mind and memory Praised be Almighty God therefore
and being (by Gods permission) outward bound on a voyage
at sea and well knowing the dangers thereof as also that it
is appointed for all men once to dye and the uncertainty of
that time and for the better setling my worldly affairs in case
of Death Do make and ordain this my last Will and Testament
in maner following That is to say I Give unto my Children
Elizabeth Mary Sarah and William twenty shillings unto Each
and whom I leave (next under God) unto the tuition of my
Wife Elizabeth Read Item All the Rest of my Lands Tenements
Goods Chattels and Credits whatsoever and wheresoever I Give
and bequeath unto my Loving wife Elizabeth Read whom I
Doe hereby constitute and appoint Sole Executrix of this my last
Will hereby Ratifying and confirming this and no other to be
my last Will and Testament In Witnesse whereof I have
hereunto sett my hand and Seal the twenty sixth day of January
in the thirteenth year of the Reign of our Soveroign Lord George
the second by the Grace of God of Great Britain France & Ireland
King Defender of the Faith &c and in the year of our Lord one
thousand seven hundred and thirty nine

Signed Sealed published pronounced
and declared by the Testator William
Read as and for his last Will and
Testament in the presence of us who
sett our names as wittnesses hereto
in his psesence

William Read

Rog: Crastey

Hannah Torr

Will of William Read, mariner, of Lyme Regis, Dorset, 1739. *He was 'outward bound on a voyage at sea ... well knowing the danger thereof.' The will was proved in the Court of the Peculiar of Lyme & Halstock in 1747.* (Wiltshire Record Office)

The Bishop's Diocesan Court, known as the **Consistory Court**, had jurisdiction if property was held in more than one archdeaconry. A Bishop's **Commissary Court** would operate under delegated powers in a particular part of the diocese only, such as an archdeaconry.

So taking once more our mythical Henry Jones: if he had held some property in West Grinstead within the Archdeaconry of Chichester's jurisdiction but also other property in the neighbouring parish of Cowfold, which came under the Archdeaconry of Lewes, then his will should have been proved in the Bishop of Chichester's Consistory Court and not in either of the two Archdeacons' Courts at all.

If the testator's property was held in more than one diocese, then the will would be proved in the appropriate Archbishop's Court, either the **Prerogative Court of Canterbury** or the **Prerogative Court of York**. Each Archbishop's area of jurisdiction is referred to as a 'Province'. If the property in question was held within both provinces, then probate should have been handled by the Prerogative Court of Canterbury, the senior court of the two. The Prerogative Court of York covered the counties of Cheshire, Cumberland, Durham, part of Flintshire, Lancashire, Northumberland, Nottinghamshire, Westmorland, Yorkshire and the Isle of Man. All other counties fell within the Province of Canterbury. There was no need for an executor to travel to London for a will to be proved in the Prerogative Court of Canterbury, as there were local surrogates (deputies appointed by the ecclesiastical courts) to perform this task. A considerable number of testators whose wills were proved in the PCC had died abroad; in such cases you will find the annotation 'parts' or 'pts' against the person's name in the probate calendars. Many sailors or soldiers would lodge their wills with the PCC before setting off abroad on a potentially hazardous military expedition.

Turning again, then, to our example of Henry Jones: if he had been a reasonably wealthy man and had owned property in more than one diocese, such as that of the Bishop of Chichester and also that of the Bishop of Exeter, then his will would not have been proved in either of these two Bishops' Consistory Courts but would have been dealt with by the appropriate Archbishop's Court - in this case, that of the Prerogative Court of Canterbury. Had his property been extensive enough and situated within both Sussex and Devon but also within Nottinghamshire, the first two being in the Province of Canterbury and the last in the Province of York, then Canterbury should have taken precedence.

Last, there were the so-called '**Peculiars**', the smallest jurisdictions or courts of all. Some peculiars came under the control of various ecclesiastical dignitaries from the cathedral such as a prebendary, a dean or the dean and chapter. Others were more secular in nature, coming within the jurisdiction of a manor, a liberty, a city, a town or a university. A little book by G.W. Marshall, *A handbook to the ancient courts of probate and depositories of wills*, published in 1895, contains a fascinating series of entries including such obscure jurisdictions as the Royal Peculiar Court of St Buryan in Cornwall, the Manor Court of Dale Abbey in Derbyshire and the Peculiar Court of Masham in North Yorkshire, still commemorated in the strong ale brewed by Theakston's and known as 'Old Peculier'. Peculiars had the privilege, often jealously guarded and dating back many centuries, of being exempt from normal ecclesiastical control. Some counties or dioceses contain very few if any peculiars. Others - like Yorkshire, for example - contain a great many. In the event, several peculiars had effectively ceased to function long before 1858.

Here, then, is the theory. There were exceptions to the rule - so most Yorkshire wills, for example, were proved within the Deaneries and registered with the Exchequer Court of York. Not only that, but some seemingly hard-and-fast rules were frequently ignored, and we find people apparently choosing a court almost as the whim took them. It was certainly the habit of better-off people to have their probate matters handled by the provincial courts of Canterbury and York, wherever their property was situated, partly for reasons of social prestige and partly out of a feeling that the PCC and the PCY offered more security. From the beginning of the nineteenth century, the PCC was the only probate court recognised by the Bank of England, which concerned itself with testators who held monies in the public funds. An impressive series of Bank of England will abstracts is held by the Society of Genealogists, and indexes to these are in the course of publication.

Yet it wasn't only wealthy people, as it happens, who used the Prerogative Court of Canterbury for probate purposes. Here you will find wills of seamen, of soldiers, of anyone who had died abroad and who had property in this country and of a person living in this country with property overseas. Do be sure to search the indexes of printed calendars of PCC wills and administrations in case your ancestors are featured.

Occasionally the word 'inhibition' crops up with regard to probate of wills, especially during the period of the Bishop's routine 'visitation' to a particular archdeaconry, during which time the Archdeacon's Court would be closed ('inhibited') and the Bishop's Commissary Court would take over its business. Visitations would generally last for a period of a few months or less, but some peculiars were exempt from both visitation and inhibition.

Following the death or translation of an archbishop, a bishop or another chief official, his court might be 'closed' and its business carried on in another court - often that of the Dean and Chapter. Wills proved during such a hiatus are known as 'sede vacante' or 'vacancy' wills.

From 1653 to 1660, at the time of the Protectorate, virtually all wills and administrations for the whole country (with the exception of those handled by a few manorial courts) were proved centrally in the Court of Civil Commission, power of probate being given to judges appointed by Parliament. These records will be found with those of the Prerogative Court of Canterbury.

How to determine probate jurisdiction pre-1858
The matter of probate within the ecclesiastical courts may seem complicated, but luckily help is at hand.

If your ancestors followed the general guidelines for probate affairs outlined above, it should be no very difficult matter to find a will, if one was left, or details of a grant of Letters of Administration if an individual died intestate.

First you must determine where your ancestor lived or owned land. You would be well advised to refer first to the excellent series of county maps published by the Institute of Heraldic and Genealogical Studies in Canterbury (IHGS). Find your county and look at the map; this will show you which archdeaconry or other ecclesiastical authority had jurisdiction over a particular parish, or whether it formed part of a peculiar. All IHGS maps for England, Wales and Scotland are available in one publication, *The Phillimore atlas and*

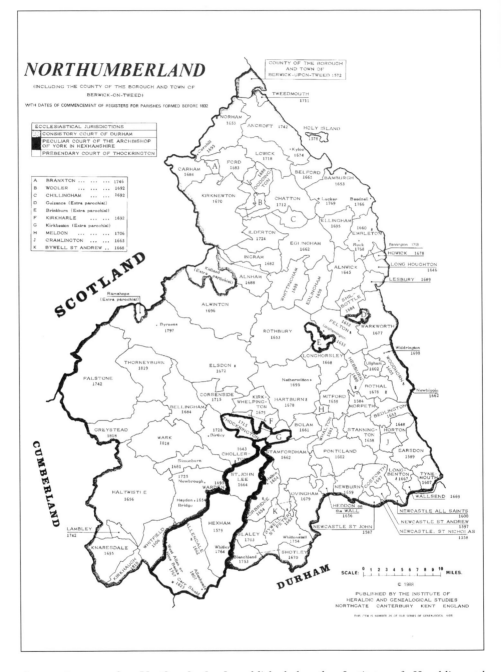

A county map for Northumberland *published by the Institute of Heraldic and Genealogical Studies, showing the network of parishes and ecclesiastical jurisdictions within the county. The year for which the earliest parish register survives is given in each case, and coloured boundary lines are used in the original to separate jurisdictions.* (Institute of Heraldic and Genealogical Studies)

index of parish registers by Cecil Humphery-Smith (2nd. Ed., 1995). You may notice that certain counties are very simple when it comes to probate matters: so the Palatine and Episcopal Consistory of Durham had jurisdiction for the whole of County Durham; Wiltshire and parts of Yorkshire, by contrast, are very complex, with more than one archdeaconry and several peculiars. Some dioceses bear little if any relation to county boundaries. So Buckinghamshire was mostly within the Archdeaconry of Buckingham, which formed part of the Diocese of Lincoln, and if you are interested in the wills of Derbyshire people you will need to search the records of the Diocese of Lichfield in Staffordshire.

An alternative method of approach is to find the place(s) which interest you in the 1833 edition of *A topographical dictionary of England* by Samuel Lewis. A typical entry would read as follows:

> *MINDTOWN (St John the Baptist). A parish in the hundred of Purslow, county of Salop, 5 miles (E.N.E.) from Bishop's Castle, containing 36 inhabitants. The living is a discharged rectory in the archdeaconry of Salop, and diocese of Hereford, rated in the King's books at £4.13.4, endowed with £200 private benefaction, and £200 royal bounty, and in the patronage of the Earl of Powis.*

Now you know the probate courts that might be relevant: that of the Archdeacon of Salop and that of the Bishop of Hereford.

To supplement the information you have gleaned from IHGS maps or Lewis's *Dictionary* you are advised to refer to a book which goes into more detail on pre-1858 wills and letters of administration. *Wills and their whereabouts* by Anthony J. Camp (4th.Ed., 1974) would be an excellent starting point, as would *Wills and where to find them* by Jeremy Gibson (1974). An affordable and very comprehensive modern guide to these matters is Jeremy Gibson's *Probate jurisdictions: where to look for wills*, first published in 1980 and reissued in updated editions since then.

The proving of wills

We need first of all to be clear what happened after the death of a person who had left a will. If the deceased was a person of limited means and there was no dispute regarding the estate, the will may never have been put through the formal probate system at all, in which case the survival of documentary evidence will be a matter of chance.

Most wills, however, were proved by the church courts in an official fashion. An executor or executrix should have been named, and he or she would take the will to the appropriate court - except in cases when the local rector was able to handle matters by commission from the bishop. If the court found the will satisfactory, it would be endorsed with a Probate Act then filed away, details of the act being entered in a Probate Act Book. Before 1733 probate acts will be in Latin, sometimes abbreviated, but the wording is usually in standard form and should present few difficulties. Here is a Latin example, with translation:

> *Probatum erat hujus modi Testamentum apud Herefordiam parvam secundo die mensis Novemberis Anno domini 1696 Coram Reuerendo viro Joseph Harvey Artium Magistro Cancellario Chori &c., per Elizabetham Coundley Relictam et Executricem &c. Cui &c. primitus*

de bene &c. ac de pleno &c. Necnon de vero &c. Coram discreto viro Thoa Marston Artium Magistro Surrogato &c. Juratam (salvo Jure cujuscunque).

[This will was proved at Little Hereford the second day of November in the year of our Lord 1696 before the Reverend Joseph Harvey, Master of Arts, Chancellor of the Choir (of the Cathedral Church of Hereford) &c., by Elizabeth Coundley relict and executrix &c. to whom (administration was granted) &c., she being first sworn well and (truly to administer the same and to exhibit the inventory of all and singular the goods chattels and credits of the said deceased) before Thomas Marston, Master of Arts, Surrogate &c. (saving the right of all).]

The court would then make a probate copy of the will, which it would hand to the executors by way of official authorisation; often a further copy of the will would be made in a volume of registered wills for future reference. You will sometimes find a number of wills which have been proved but unregistered; it may be that the registration fee was too high or unwelcome.

All wills - original, registered and unregistered - would be filed in bundles or boxes. Some may not have since survived the ravages of time, of course. To help the court (and therefore the present-day researcher, as it happens...) locate a will at some later date, there will be an entry in the probate act book, from which calendars were usually compiled annually. Expect these to be chronological and only loosely alphabetical within each year - that is, all surnames beginning with the letter H for any given year will be entered in chronological, not strictly alphabetical, sequence. You may find indexes if you're lucky.

You will sometimes read in a calendar of wills that the relevant documents consist of an 'administration with will annexed'. In such a case an executor or executors have not been able or willing to prove the will, and administration has had to be granted to the next-of-kin to act as executor in their stead.

If a minor had been left fatherless, the court was able to appoint a guardian who would enter into a Tuition or Guardianship Bond; these would usually be filed with the other relevant documentation.

The granting of Letters of Administration
We have already seen, when talking about marriage licences, that a very popular legal device in times past was the use of a 'bond'. You will find bonds amongst probate records, too, and some courts required the executor(s) of a will to enter into a Testamentary Bond, with an obligation 'well and truly to execute' the will.

When Letters of Administration were granted, the administrator(s) entered into an Administration Bond, 'well and truly to administer according to law' the goods, chattels, credits, etc of the deceased. The Administration Act would be entered in an Act Book and also usually endorsed on the Administration Bond, which was then filed away. Both Testamentary and Administration Bonds would usually require that an inventory be made of the deceased's goods. An inventory would normally be attached to the Administration Bond or original will and filed with it.

Do not be intimidated if you find a bond. Each will follow a similar pattern and have a similar structure. Many are printed, with manuscript insertions made

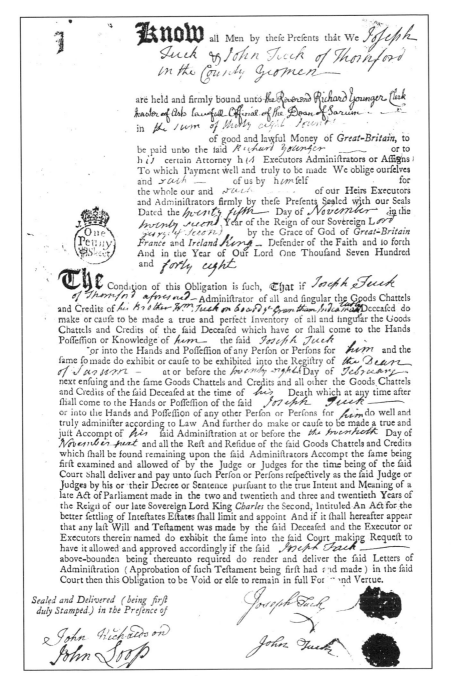

𝕶𝖓𝖔𝖜 all Men by these Presents that We *Joseph Tuck & John Tuck of Thornford in the County Yeomen*

are held and firmly bound unto *the Reverend Richard Younger Clerk master of Arts lawfull Official of the Dean of Sarum* in *the sum of thirty eight pounds* of good and lawful Money of *Great-Britain*, to be paid unto the said *Richard Younger* _____ or to h*is* certain Attorney h*is* Executors Administrators or Assigns To which Payment well and truly to be made We oblige ourselves and *each* _____ of us by h*im*self _____ for the whole our and *each* _____ of our Heirs Executors and Administrators firmly by these Presents Sealed with our Seals Dated the *twenty fifth* _____ Day of *November* _____ in the *twenty second* Year of the Reign of our Sovereign Lord *George the second* by the Grace of God of *Great-Britain France* and *Ireland King* _____ Defender of the Faith and so forth And in the Year of Our Lord One Thousand Seven Hundred and *forty eight*

𝕿𝖍𝖊 Condition of this Obligation is such, **That** if *Joseph Tuck of Thornford aforesaid* _____ Administrator of all and singular the Goods Chattels and Credits of *his Brother Wm Tuck on board ye Grantham Indiaman* _____ Deceased do make or cause to be made a true and perfect Inventory of all and singular the Goods Chattels and Credits of the said Deceased which have or shall come to the Hands Possession or Knowledge of *him* _____ the said *Joseph Tuck* or into the Hands and Possession of any Person or Persons for *him* and the same so made do exhibit or cause to be exhibited into the Registry of *the Dean of Sarum* _____ at or before the *twenty eighth* Day of *February* next ensuing and the same Goods Chattels and Credits and all other the Goods Chattels and Credits of the said Deceased at the time of *his* Death which at any time after shall come to the Hands or Possession of the said *Joseph Tuck* _____ or into the Hands and Possession of any other Person or Persons for *him* do well and truly administer according to Law And further do make or cause to be made a true and just Accompt of *his* said Administration at or before the *the twentieth* Day of *November next* and all the Rest and Residue of the said Goods Chattels and Credits which shall be found remaining upon the said Administrators Accompt the same being first examined and allowed of by the Judge or Judges for the time being of the said Court shall deliver and pay unto such Person or Persons respectively as the said Judge or Judges by his or their Decree or Sentence pursuant to the true Intent and Meaning of a late Act of Parliament made in the two and twentieth and three and twentieth Years of the Reign of our late Sovereign Lord King *Charles* the Second, Intituled An Act for the better settling of Intestates Estates shall limit and appoint And if it shall hereafter appear that any last Will and Testament was made by the said Deceased and the Executor or Executors therein named do exhibit the same into the said Court making Request to have it allowed and approved accordingly if the said *Joseph Tuck* above-bounden being thereunto required do render and deliver the said Letters of Administration (Approbation of such Testament being first had and made) in the said Court then this Obligation to be Void or else to remain in full For~ and Vertue.

Sealed and Delivered (*being first duly Stamped.*) in the Presence of

John Richardson
John Loop

Joseph Tuck

John Tuck

Administration Bond, 1748. *Joseph and John Tuck of Thornford, Dorset, are bound in the sum of £38 duly to administer the goods, chattels and credits of William Tuck, seaman on the East Indiaman* Grantham, *and to make a true and perfect inventory of the same. Court of the Dean of Sarum, 25 Nov 1748.* (Wiltshire Record Office)

as appropriate. The first (shorter) section will name the individuals to be bound and state the amount of forfeit if the conditions are broken. This may well be in Latin, beginning 'Noverint universi per presentes...' but the wording is standard, and you can always compare it to a later English version or to the text given below in order to establish the meaning. The second part of the bond states in a rather long-winded fashion that should the conditions not be adhered to, then a financial penalty will result. Even if the first section of the bond is in Latin, the second part will usually be in English. The bond is then signed and sealed in the presence of witnesses - even more names for you to note down and think about.

Here is a translation of the first section of an eighteenth century Administration Bond, taken from page 64 of the second volume of *Genealogical research in England and Wales* by David E.Gardner and Frank Smith (1959) - still one of the most comprehensive guides to probate matters available anywhere:

> *Know all men by these presents, that we* William John and Morrice Jenkin of Kidwelly in the county of Carmarthen, yeomen, *are held and firmly bound to* the Reverend Father in Christ and Lord George by divine permission Bishop of St.Davids *in sixty pounds of good and lawful money of Great Britain to be paid to the said* Lord Bishop *or his certain attorney, his executors or administrators, To which payment well and truly to be made we bind ourselves and each of us by himself for the whole and in gross, our heirs, executors, and administrators and (those) of each of us, firmly by these presents. Sealed with our seals, dated the* 25 *day of the month of* February *in the* seventh *year of the reign of our sovereign Lord* George, *by the grace of God, of Great Britain, France and Ireland,* King, *defender of the faith, &c., and in the year of our Lord* 1720.

The second part of the bond mentions the name of the deceased, George Lawrence of Pembrey, Carmarthenshire. An Administration Bond is usually nothing like as informative as a will, of course, but it might contain enough clues to help you on your way.

Inventories

Whether a person left a will or died intestate, it was common practice in the late sixteenth and seventeenth centuries - and sometimes much later - for probate courts to insist that an inventory be made of the personal and household goods left by the deceased, with appraised values added. An inventory can give a most vivid picture of both the layout and the contents of an ancestor's home, listing furniture, fittings and movable goods room-by-room, each item priced by two or three independent assessors. Hay, corn and malt may be kept on the top floor, a cheese press might stand in the dairy, a wondrous array of kitchen equipment may fill the chimney area, an old abandoned cross-bow may be lying in the attic, and a variety of animals may be accounted for in the farmyard.

It is possible to build up quite a graphic picture of a home and grounds from the appraisal of Oliver Nickliss' goods and chattels made in September 1796. The inventory states that he had been a yeoman - and a relatively prosperous one, it would seem, though by today's standards the furniture would seem to be somewhat sparse. No doubt it was economical and sufficient for the needs of

Probate inventory for yeoman Oliver Nickliss *of Keyston, Huntingdon, 1769.* (Huntingdon Record Office)

Oliver and his family. The house comprised a parlour, kitchen, dairy, a hall (which was obviously large and extensively furnished), four bedrooms including one situated over the parlour, a cheese room and a brewhouse. The barn and yard contained hay and firewood, one haycock and two ladders. There was one pig and one cow in the grounds, with another cow in the close. The total value came to the grand sum of £46. 5s. 0d.

Do look at *Village Records* by John West (3rd. Ed., 1997) for a fascinating demonstration of the way in which it is possible to make a three-dimensional reconstruction of a house from a careful reading of probate inventories.

It is archival practice in some record offices to separate a will from its related inventory and from other relevant documents such as an estate distribution record. If you have found a will that interests you, do make active enquiries as to whether other associated probate papers exist.

Present location of probate and associated documents

Generally, wills, administrations, inventories and other related probate documents for the various courts such as those of an Archdeacon, Bishop or Dean, together with any existing records of a Peculiar, are to be found in Diocesan Record Offices which are often incorporated into County Record Offices. Check with the books by Anthony Camp and Jeremy Gibson, mentioned above, to determine which repository you will need to visit or to contact.

Locating pre-1858 probate and associated documents: a summary

We can now summarise the process you need to go through in order to discover relevant probate documents for your ancestors in the years before 1858:

- Determine the exact or approximate date of death of the person concerned, using burial registers or other evidence.
- Try to establish the place(s) in which your ancestor lived or held property.
- Use IHGS county maps or Lewis's *Topographical Dictionary* (1833 edition) to establish which ecclesiastical jurisdiction is involved.
- Use the Camp or Gibson books to find out which repository holds the records of the jurisdiction involved.
- Refer to any relevant will or admon calendars, usually with indexes, which have been published by the Index Library (The British Record Society) or by local antiquarian and Family History Societies and others, as books or on microform. Calendars covering some of the records of the Prerogative Court of Canterbury and the Prerogative Court of York (see below for details of these courts) are widely available; these should be held by large reference libraries, or may be consulted at the Society of Genealogists, on the open shelves of the British Library or in major university libraries. The latest edition of Gibson's *Probate jurisdictions: where to look for wills* should keep you abreast of what printed probate calendars have been published, and will mention the existence of typescript or manuscript indexes where these exist. Typescript or manuscript indexes will usually only be available for consultation in the appropriate record offices (though some will also be at the Society of Genealogists). If you are extremely lucky, you may even find that the full text or an abstract of an ancestor's will already exists in print.
- If you can find a reference to probate material which interests you in a published work, you could write to the relevant record office to see whether photocopies may be obtained and at what price. Alternatively, use a paid local researcher (see advertisements in *Family Tree Magazine*, the *Genealogists' Magazine* and elsewhere), or visit the record office in person.
- If you visit a record office in person you can do your own searching. Use indexes whenever you can, look for admons as well as wills, and remember that you will want to see all associated probate documents for your ancestor (a will, a bond, an inventory and so on). Do refer to a Probate Act Book if you can, as it should contain unregistered as well as registered wills and may contain details not given in the comparable calendar. Transcribe all these documents accurately and in full if you have time, or abstract the essential details if not. Request photocopies if possible, so that you can work on them at home at your own pace. You will need some practice in palaeography if

you are to produce an accurate transcript or extract.

Whether you are looking for wills, admons or related documents in calendars or in Probate Act Books, it is essential to remember that these record the date of probate (that is, when the will was 'proved' or the Letters of Administration granted), *not* the date of death as such. Just as wills could have been made some time before death, so the granting of probate may have taken several years to complete. Sometimes there would be various disputes and litigations to resolve, or near relatives would delay matters to see whether a testator's widow would die fairly soon afterwards or choose to remarry, so that affairs could be sorted out all at one time rather than proving a will before it was absolutely essential to do so. As a result, it does pay to search several years after a testator's known date of death for a relevant entry in a calendar or probate act book.

Roger Molford of Burrington, Devon, dictated his will on 25 February 1640 at which time he was 'sick and weak in body'. Within three weeks he had died, being buried on 20 March 1640. Because of various court actions and disputes, and maybe as a result of turmoil caused by the early years of the civil war, his will was not proved until thirty-two years later. His only surviving daughter, now Amy Rosier alias Molford, acted as executrix, his wife Zenobia and other daughter, Grace, having died during the intervening years. In the event, Roger Molford had no male heirs to inherit. The following example comes from the series of abstracts now in the Devon Record Office, made by Miss Moger before the disastrous bombing of the Exeter Registry during the Second World War destroyed practically all the Devon wills.

MOLFORD, Roger, of Brudge in Burrington, Gent. Sick and weak in body. Will dated 25th February 1640.
To the poor of Burrington 30s. To wife Zenobia all my furniture (except that standing in the Broad Chamber at Northam in such sort as it was given by my father to my daughter Grace and one other bedstead given to my daughter Amy) and after her death to my daughters Grace and Amy equally. To Christopher Baitson of Chumleigh, Clerk, and John Challacombe of Westleigh, John Davy als Richards of Yeaberley and George Risdon of Parkham, gents, and their heirs, all my lands etc. in Northam, Burrington, Abbotsham, Winckleigh, Tawton Episcopi and elsewhere, also my Rectory of Burrington and the Vicarage of the said parish to go also with the sheaf, garb and tithes and the nomination, donation etc., of the said Vicarage, upon trust to satisfy my debts and legacies and subject thereto to my daughters Grace and Amy and their heirs. The remainder to Edward Reed the younger, son of Edward Reed the elder, of Trayne, gent; Thomas Challacombe, son of John Challacombe of Westleigh, gent, and George Risdon the younger son of George Risdon the elder of Parkham, gent, and their heirs. Residue to my two daughters whom I make my executors.
Signed: Roger Molford. Witnesses: Anne Wood, John Bright.
Proved Exeter, Barum [Barnstaple] Archdeaconry, 7th June 1672, by Amy Rosier alias Molford, surviving executrix. On oath taken 9th May 1672 before Christopher Baitson.

The Prerogative Court of Canterbury

The records of the Prerogative Court of Canterbury include a magnificent series of wills (1383 to 1858), admons (1559 to 1858) and related probate documents, though the court itself was probably not formed until as late as 1443. Slowly but steadily the documents are being sorted, calendared and indexed by volunteers and professionals alike. The totality of PCC archives is at the Public Record Office in Kew. If it is the main series of wills and administrations which interests you, these may be consulted on microfilm both there and at the Family Records Centre in Myddelton Street. Photocopies can readily be made.

The Index Library (the British Record Society) has produced printed and indexed calendars of PCC wills and admons, while enterprising individuals such as J.& G.F. Matthews, J.H. Morrison and R.M. Glencross have filled various gaps with printed volumes of their own. There are printed PCC will calendars from 1383 to 1700; the Friends of the Public Record Office have produced a set of microfiche indexes covering the years 1701 to 1749, while for the period 1750 to 1800 you should refer to a set of printed volumes (also available on microfiche) published by the Society of Genealogists and edited by its former director, A. J. Camp. Admon calendars are in print, 1559 to 1660, and various other publications of the List and Index Society feature lists of inventories and other related probate documents. For a few selected annual PCC registers only, there are printed detailed abstracts of all or some of the wills proved in that year. These are: Register Soame (1620); Register Scroope (1630); Register Wootton (1657/8); Register Greenly (1750). Note that each annual PCC calendar would be known by the name of one of the testators featured within it; hence 'Soame', 'Scroope' and so on.

There were two courts of appeal from the PCC: the Court of Delegates (records are in the Public Record Office) and the Court of Arches (records are in Lambeth Palace Library, with cases 1660-1913 being published as volume 85 of *The Index Library* in 1972).

Many PCC records, then, are comparatively easy to access by way of printed indexes and calendars. Do make use of these, and benefit from the tireless efforts of earlier enthusiasts and scholars.

Essential further reading for all matters relating to the PCC is *Wills, inventories and death duties* by Jane Cox, published by the Public Record Office in 1988.

The Prerogative Court of York

The Prerogative Court of York was not established until 1577; before that time (and afterwards) probate was usually granted in the Exchequer Court, which was the responsibility of the Archbishop but was presided over by his representative, a Receiver-General, who acted originally as chief financial officer for the province. The Exchequer Court included as one of its functions that of acting as a Consistory Court in granting probate (from 1374) of those having *bona notabilia* solely within the diocese of York, the Archbishop himself being also the Bishop of York diocese.

For a significant period of time the Exchequer Court was also held in conjunction with the Prerogative Court; the two worked together and their wills were registered together, though separate act books were maintained, especially after 1624. The printed indexes published by the Yorkshire Archaeological

Society covering the years 1389 to 1688 under the title *Wills in the York Registry* contain references to a mixture of Prerogative and Exchequer Court wills and admons. At the Borthwick Institute of Historical Research, University of York, St Anthony's Hall, Peasholme Green, York YO1 2PW, this series is continued by way of typescript indexes, 1688 to 1731, but this is the only period for which separate indexes exist for probates within the Prerogative Court. Manuscript calendars of both courts combined complete the run to 1857.

Volume one of the Yorkshire Archaeological Society's Record series includes an index to Yorkshire wills proved in London during the time of the Interregnum, 1649 to 1660, and volume nine of the same series, entitled 'Abstracts of Yorkshire wills in the time of the Commonwealth at Somerset House, London...', is particularly useful for its detailed abstracts and index.

The general appeal court for the Province of York was known as the Chancery Court of York; its records are at the Borthwick Institute.

Death or Estate Duty will registers

The Legacy Duty Act of 1796 imposed a duty on legacies and residues of the personal estate of a deceased person. These duties were payable on certain types of bequests by groups defined by their degree of kinship to the deceased. This duty was extended by the Legacy Duty Act of 1805 and the Stamp Act of 1815 to money legacies and residues bequeathed in wills which were to be raised by the sale of real estate.

Registers of Death Duty abstracts for England and Wales (Inland Revenue, class IR26) extend from 1796 to 1903. From 1858 the wills and admons in question also feature in the records of the Principal Probate Registry at Avenue House (see below). Microfilm copies of the Death Duty Registers to 1858 may be consulted at the Family Records Centre and at the Public Record Office in Kew, which also holds original books from 1858 to 1903, though these will need to be ordered in advance of a visit. The relevant indexes (IR 27) may be seen at Myddelton Street, and the Society of Genealogists has copies of these to 1858.

The Death Duty Registers are an excellent finding aid to the court in which many (but not all) wills or admons were granted. The indexes give the name of the deceased and of the executors or administrators, together with the probate court concerned. From here, if you wish, you can then search for the relevant documents in the appropriate County Record Office, or at the PRO or the Family Records Centre if the Prerogative Court of Canterbury was involved.

Wills from 1858

From 11 January 1858, all wills and administrations for England and Wales have been proved in the Principal Probate Registry or in the District Probate Registries.

Bound alphabetical indexes to all these wills and admons are available for free public scrutiny at the Principal Registry of the Family Division, 1st Avenue House, 42–49 High Holborn, London WC1V 6NP (formerly located at Somerset House in the Strand). Up to the year 1870 wills and admons appear in the same index volumes but are kept separate, wills in the first part and admons in the second. Make sure, therefore, that you have covered every index. After 1870 wills and admons are combined into one alphabetical sequence, and indexes for very recent years are on microfiche. These indexes are not only extremely simple and straightforward to use, they are also very informative in their own right, as an example will illustrate:

> *1873. Titford, Sydney. Effects under £1,500.*
> *19 March. The will of Sydney Titford, formerly of 104 Rotherfield Street, Islington, but late of 52, Canonbury Park North, both in the county of Middlesex, gentleman, who died 17th December 1872 at 52 Canonbury Park North, was proved at the Principal Registry by Andrew Goring Pritchard of 41, Bedford Row in the said county, gentleman, the sole executor.*

Although the indexes are free to view, a fee has to be paid to see a copy of a will or admon, which you order at 1st Avenue House but which will need to be retrieved from an off-site repository. Family historians can avoid paying a fee to inspect documents which are at least one hundred years old by applying for a Literary Search Pass from the Probate Department Manager at 1st Avenue House in advance of a visit. Such a pass is valid for one year and allows the searcher to inspect up to forty documents in one day.

During a visit to 1st Avenue House, you will want to read and note down relevant details from the will or admon, though if time is precious you may order a photocopy of the document for your files, in which case a fee is paid on the spot and the copy will be sent through the post, usually within a few days.

Be aware that it may have taken some time for a will to be proved or Letters of Administration to be granted after a person died, so don't expect to find an entry immediately after the date of death. From 1858 onwards, probate should have been granted and the will proved within a year. In some cases, a further probate may have been taken out for various reasons, such as a will being contested by relatives who thought they were entitled to something from the deceased's estate, or someone discovering a bank or savings account which had not been included in the original probate. So, a number of years may have elapsed between death and a final grant of probate.

Opening hours at the Principal Registry are 10 am to 4.30 pm, Monday to Friday, except public holidays, and the last order time for documents is 3 pm.

What to do if you cannot visit Avenue House in person
If you cannot pay a personal visit to Avenue House, a number of options present themselves:

- The Hampshire County Record Office will sell microfiche sets of will indexes from 1858 to other record offices or institutions. You may refer to these at the Society of Genealogists or elsewhere. Having found your reference, you could order photocopies of the documents you need by post (see below).
- Some local probate registries hold sets of the national printed will and admon indexes, though over the years these have often been handed over to County Record Offices to make them more readily available. Check with your nearest probate registry and County Record Office to see whether they hold these indexes. If so, conduct a search and apply for a photocopy by post (see below).
- You can order photocopies of wills or admons by post. Obtain a copy of form RK1 from Avenue House; when it has been completed, send it to York Probate Sub-Registry, Duncombe Place, York YO1 2EA. A three-year search will be carried out for a nominal sum.

- You could use one of a number of record agents who advertise in *Family Tree Magazine* or other journals to search for a will for you and provide the necessary photocopy. Fees are usually very reasonable.

Here is an example of a will from the Principal Probate Registry:

The Last Will and Testament of Samuel Elstone, yeoman, of Higher Way, Tiverton, Devon, dated 4 July 1862.

In the name of God, Amen. The Last Will of Samuel Elstone, Yeoman, of Higher Way Farm in the parish of Tiverton in the county of Devon in perfect body and mind and knowing it is appointed unto men once to die. And as touching such worldly Estate and Goods wherewith it hath pleased God to bless me with in this life I give and despose of the same in the following manner and form. First I give and bequeath unto my daughter Emma the wife of Daniel Trude One Shilling, I give and bequeath unto my wife Elizabeth and nine of my children namely William, Samuel, Henry, Edwin, John, Mary Ann, Selina, Caroline Jane, Frederic all my Goods and Chattels money and securities for money credits and effects of what nature or kind whatsoever. But in case my wife should marry again and after the second marriage takes place, in that event, to leave the business and property to my nine children. But if either of the children should get married or wish to leave after they arrive at the age of twenty one years of age then for my two Trustees namely William Blake, Yeoman, Templeton, and William Elstone, Yeoman, Witheridge, both in the County of Devon, to decide what share of the property they shall have after all debts and expenses is paid. And lastly I charge my Goods and Chattles to the payments of all my just debts funeral and testamentary expenses to my wife Elizabeth and nine of my children as before mentioned joint Executrix and Executors of this my last will and Testament made by me.

In Witness whereof I have hereunto subscribed my name this fourth of July in the year of our Lord, One thousand, eight hundred and sixty two.

Samuel Elston...Signed, published and declared by me Samuel Elstone the Testator as and for my last will and testament in the presence of us who have subscribed our names as witness thereunto in the presence and at the request of the Testator and in the presence of each other... William Blake...Nutcombe Cornwall...

Probate: On the 13th day of February 1863 the will of Samuel Elston late of Tiverton in the County of Devon Farmer deceased was proved by the Oath of Elizabeth Elston, widow, the Relict of the deceased, one of the Executors she having been first sworne duly to administer, power being reserved to Mary Ann Elston, spinster, William Elston, Samuel Elston, Henry Elston, children of the deceased and to Edwin Elston, Selina Elston, spinster, John Elston, Caroline Jane Elston, spinster and Frederick in the will written Frederic Elston, minors, children of the deceased the other Executors when they shall attain the sum of twenty one years.

Effects under £600.

Wales

The counties of North Wales (Anglesey, Caernarvonshire, Denbighshire, Flintshire, Merionethshire and Montgomeryshire) were in the diocese of Bangor and/or St Asaph, a few parishes lying within the dioceses of Chester, Hereford and St David's. The records, except for Hereford, are in the National Library of Wales in Aberystwyth. Various indexes exist, those for the Consistory Court of Bangor, 1635-1700, having been published. The South Wales counties of Brecknock, Cardigan, Carmarthen, Glamorgan, Monmouth, Pembroke and Radnor came almost entirely within the diocese of St David's and Llandaff, except for eight parishes which came under Hereford. The Archdeaconry of Brecon had its own Consistory Court. Records of these courts (except those within the jurisdiction of Hereford) are at the National Library of Wales.

Nearly all of Wales came within the province of Canterbury (though parishes in the Diocese of Chester came under York), and the National Library of Wales holds a microfilm index of Welsh wills in the Prerogative Court of Canterbury covering most of the eighteenth century.

Scotland

The main collection of probate records for Scotland are at the National Archives of Scotland, General Register House, Edinburgh EH1 3YY.

Scottish 'testaments' deal only with movable property, not real estate. A 'testament-testamentar' is involved if there is a will, a 'testament-dative' if there is none. These were processed by the church through its commissary courts until the 1820s and by a sheriff court thereafter.

If you know where a person died or held property, you need to determine the appropriate commissariot or sheriff court. For lists of commissaries and of sheriff courts (1820s to 1875) by county, see *Tracing your Scottish ancestors*, published by the Scottish Record Office in 1990 (pages 31-33 and 37-38), a book which is also very useful in explaining many of the complications attendant upon the use of Scottish probate records. Maps published by the Institute of Heraldic and Genealogical Studies will give you the commissariot boundaries and the parishes within them. Name indexes to all commissariot records prior to 1800 have been published by the Scottish Record Society. If an ancestor died after 1875, you can refer to a series of annual volumes called *Calendar of Confirmations and Inventories*.

Most Scotsmen did not own their own dwelling house or land, but when they did, whether it was acquired by inheritance or in some other way, the transference of ownership should be recorded in the appropriate Register of Sasines, which date from 1617. Sasines are an excellent record of land ownership, and for further details you are referred to pages 52-63 of *Tracing your Scottish ancestors*, mentioned above.

Those who became 'heirs in heritage' of real estate had to prove their title, and details should appear in the so-called 'Retours', which formed part of the records of Chancery. An indexed summary of retours to 1700 was published in three volumes (1811-1816) under the title *Inquisitionum ad Capellam Regis Retornatarum Abbreviatio*, while the period 1700 to 1859 is covered by: *Decennial Indexes to the Services of Heirs in Scotland*, published 1863-1889. The early retours are in Latin, the later in English; many entries in the *Services of Heirs* volumes are a sheer delight, as the heir ('the person served') might recount several generations of descent in order to prove his or her title.

Ireland
Irish wills and administrations came under the jurisdiction of the church until 1858, when a Principal Registry was established and matters of probate were handled by the state. Tragically for all concerned, the collection of wills dating from 1536 deposited in the Four Courts in Dublin was practically destroyed during the troubles of 1922. Many indexes survived, however, together with important abstracts such as those made by Sir William Betham of most of the Prerogative Court of Armagh wills to 1800. Irish genealogists have made the unearthing of probate material of every kind one of their key priorities since the disastrous losses. The large collection of will transcripts and other relevant material held at the Society of Genealogists in London is listed in *Will indexes and other probate material in the Library of the Society of Genealogists* by N. Newington-Irving (1996), and the abstracts of Irish wills made by Lorna Rossbottom have been published on fiche by the Society. Several indexes are in print, and a significant amount of probate material has been published in *Registry of Deeds, Dublin: abstracts of wills 1708-1832* (3 vols., Ed. P.B. Eustace and E. Ellis [vol.3], 1956-1984). Detailed calendars from 1858, with the will books from the district probate registries, may be seen at the National Archives, Bishop Street, Dublin 8, while the Public Record Office of Northern Ireland is at 66 Balmoral Avenue, Belfast BT9 6NY.

For more detailed information on matters of Irish probate, see Rosemary ffolliot and Eileen O'Byrne's chapter on wills in D. Begley's *Irish Genealogy: A Record Finder* (1987).

The Channel Islands and the Isle of Man
The Channel Islands were nominally in the Diocese of Winchester, but have always handled probate matters separately.

In **Jersey**, probate was subject to the ecclesiastical court of the Dean of Jersey until 1949. Records are at the Judicial Greffe, Royal Court, Jersey, and include wills 1660-1694 and admons 1848-1964. Wills are indexed, admons are calendared.

In **Guernsey**, grants of representation are still issued by the ecclesiastical court of the Bailiwick of Guernsey, Bureau des Connetables, St Peter Port. Wills and admons date from 1660, and include Alderney, Sark, Herm and Jethou. Wills from 1841 which involved the inheritance of real estate are at The Greffe, Royal Court House, St Peter Port, Guernsey.

The Isle of Man came within the Province of York, and some Manx wills may be found with the records of the Prerogative Court of York. The Consistory Court of Sodor and Man (wills from 1600, indexed from 1659) and the Archdeaconry Court of the Isle of Man (wills from 1631, indexed) had jurisdiction throughout the island at different times of the year. The jurisdiction of these two courts continued to 1874; from 1874 to 1885 the Consistory Court alone handled probate matters, and after 1885 such business has been with the High Court of Justice. Probate records from 1847 to 1910 are at the Manx Museum; after 1910 they are at the Deeds and Probate Registry.

Wills and administrations: hints and reminders

- Every area of England and Wales is covered by a bishop's diocese, but do not assume that a diocese is the same thing as a county. Some dioceses encompass only part of a county, others include territory in more than one county.
- A deceased person may have had debts in more than one jurisdiction, in which case the process outlined above for those holding scattered property would apply.
- Much probate material has not survived the ravages of time; in some cases a reference to a will may be found in a calendar, but the original documents may nevertheless be missing.
- Children were often provided for in a marriage settlement, and therefore may not be mentioned in a will.
- 'Cut off with a shilling'. Unless this is definitely stated in these terms in a will, don't assume the worst. A token shilling may be left to a married daughter who had already received her portion or dowry at the time of her marriage, or to a son who had already been given land or financial help during the testator's life.
- Take note of the names of witnesses and of executors mentioned in a will; they may be officials, they may be friends, but they may be family.
- Transcribe a will or administration exactly as written. If you make a pedigree from the information given and attach it to your copy, this can give you 'at-a-glance' information which may tie in with your research into other records.
- Not everyone left a will, but it is essential to search for one, not just for that of a direct ancestor but also for those of relatives and in-laws - and even friends and neighbours.
- There may have been a dispute within a family about a will or administration. 'Testamentary causes' will be found in diocesan archives or in the records of the Court of Arches for the Prerogative Court of Canterbury. Disputes related to probate matters could also find their way into chancery or other equity courts.

Further reading

Begley, D. *Irish genealogy: a record finder.* 1987.

Bevan, A. *Tracing your ancestors in the Public Record Office.* (5th.Ed.) 1999.

Camp, A. *Wills and their whereabouts.* 1974.

Collins, A. *Basic facts about using wills after 1858 at First Avenue House.* 1998.

Cox, J. *Affection defying the power of death: wills, probate and death duty records.* 1993.

Cox, J. *Wills, inventories and death duties: a provisional guide.* 1988.

Gibson, J. *Probate jurisdictions: where to look for wills.* (4th.Ed.) 1997.

Gibson, J. *Wills and where to find them.* 1974.

McLaughlin, E. *Wills before 1858.* (5th.Ed.) 1995.

Milward, R. *A glossary of household, farming and trade terms from probate inventories.* (3rd.Ed.) 1991.

Moore, J.S. *Goods and chattels of our forefathers.* 1976.

Overton, M. *A bibliography of British probate inventories.* 1985.

PRO Pocket Guide. *Using wills*. 2000.

Scott, M. *Prerogative Court of Canterbury wills and other probate records*. 1997.

Sinclair, C. *Tracing your Scottish ancestors in the Scottish Record Office*. (Revised Ed.) 1997.

Society of Genealogists. *Index to the Bank of England will extracts 1807-1845*. 1991.

Society of Genealogists. *Will indexes and other probate material in the library of the Society of Genealogists*. 1996.

Steer, F.W. *Farm and cottage inventories of mid-Essex*. 1969.

West. J. *Town records*. 1983.

West, J. *Village records*. (3rd.Ed.) 1997.

CHAPTER 8

Parish Chest Records and the Old and New Poor Laws

We must now return once more to the parish. Having traced your ancestors by using the step-by-step approach outlined in previous chapters, you should have drawn up a family tree which includes known names, dates and places. The time has now come to seek further information from the records, not only to confirm that your research is correct, but to find out just what happened to your ancestors during their lifetimes. In this way you will travel back in time through the fortunes, or misfortunes, of the family, discovering more about individuals and their way of life. Some will be ordinary, some not so ordinary as you might have supposed.

You will find that most families had their ups and downs throughout the generations and that an apparently rigid class system allowed significant movement between the classes. You may discover teachers, lawyers, clergymen, yeomen, landowners and magistrates, tradesmen, craftsmen, miners, factory workers, servants and agricultural labourers.

Some members of the family may well have been incapable of working through ill-health exacerbated by a poor diet, overwork and poor living conditions. They may have suffered from illnesses or handicaps which in today's world would be treatable and curable but which were debilitating in the 'good old days'.

Many of our ancestors fell foul of the law and were dealt with harshly by the justices and courts for what we would now consider to be relatively minor misdemeanours. These offences were very often committed as a result of straitened circumstances, when the imperative was to feed and clothe a family, though no doubt some broke the law for the sheer joy of it.

Parish chest records

As we attempt to put some flesh on the bare bones of a pedigree, it makes sense to look first at what are referred to as 'parish chest' records, most of which are not now kept in a chest at all, but are in the safe keeping of a County Record Office or other local repository.

Henry VIII had made the parish the basic unit in what we would nowadays think of as local government; in other words, parishes had a civil as well as an ecclesiastical jurisdiction, though in parts of Yorkshire, Lancashire and

Cheshire, local government was centred more on the 'township' than the parish as such - so Halifax, for example, contained twenty-six townships, each with its own record-generating jurisdiction. Complementary to parochial and township records are those of the Clerk of the Peace and the county-wide records of the Quarter Sessions and Petty Sessions.

In 1538 a stipulation by Thomas Cromwell, Henry VIII's chief minister, insisted that a 'sure coffer' made of sturdy oak be kept in each church to store all the parish books, records, registers and documents relating to parish business. This coffer, known as the 'parish chest', also contained the parish silver and communion plate.

Vestry minutes
The minister of the parish would be instituted to the living, often by the lord of the manor or some other person who held the 'gift of the living'; a rector might be a layman, in which case he would appoint a substitute, a 'vicar', to look after the moral and spiritual welfare of the parishioners.

The rector or vicar had some help from various local worthies in the execution of his duties. Each year, a parish council comprised of responsible citizens and some rate-paying householders, known as the vestry, administered affairs and elected parish officers to carry out their various duties. All except the parish clerk were unpaid. The vestry meeting was chaired, traditionally, by the parish minister. Such parochial parliaments first developed around the fifteenth century; the vestry would discuss and vote upon relevant business, and later acquired other powers of decision and supervision in the parish. There were two types of vestry meetings, the 'closed' or 'select' and the 'open'; the latter could be attended by all rate-payers and was favoured by parishes which operated under more democratic principles.

Vestry minutes can be most revealing, bearing in mind the power that this august body of men held within their grasp as they levied fines, audited parish accounts, set the poor rates, and, if necessary, made arrangements and payments for the emigration of parish paupers to the colonies.

It was not uncommon for the vestry members to open their meetings in the church vestry, after which they would promptly adjourn, only to re-open in the warmth and comfort of the local hostelry. The vestry accounts for such parishes would always include a substantial sum for bread, cheese and ale - all on the parish rates!

Glebe terriers and tithes
Certain records which may be found in a parish chest directly concern the affairs of the incumbent, be he a rector or a vicar.

A glebe terrier consists of a survey of the land held by a beneficed clergyman; the boundaries are described, and adjoining owners or tenants may be mentioned. These terriers generally commence in about the sixteenth and seventeenth centuries; some will be found amongst parish chest papers, but a large number are with diocesan records.

A rector or vicar of a parish was entitled to a tenth part of the main produce of the land, such as grain crops and wood, and this was known as a praedial tithe (arising from the produce of the land). He could also claim the tenth part of the produce of stock and labour such as milk, wool or pigs, known as a mixed tithe (coming from stock on the land) and a personal tithe (from the labour of the

The Disbursements of M^r
John Walker & Peter Lamb
Churchwardens from Easter
1791 to Easter 1792

	Peter Lambs Disbursements	£	S	D
	Paid for Sparrows at various Times	1	1	5½
	Paid Baxter for Mend^g Church Wall	0	2	0
July 21th	Paid Ric Corthorn for Matts for the Church	0	2	6
	Paid for Hedge Hogs various Times	0	2	4
Sep^t 22	Paid the Ringers at Wm Hills	0	5	0
	Paid at the Visitation	0	7	0
Oct 7th	Paid the Presentment Bill	0	7	0
D^o 12th	Paid Geo Chambers Qu^tr Bill	1	3	3
D^o 31th	Paid for Hedghogs	0	1	2
Novr 5th	Paid the Ringers at Wm Lowthers	0	5	0
D^o 12th	Paid for a Hedghog	0	0	4
	Paid for a Bill Rope	0	4	0
	Paid Presentment Bill & Exp^s	0	9	6
	Paid Glos Clarks Bill	0	5	6
Novr 20th	Paid Wollarson for Mend^g Church Wall	0	2	0
	Paid for two Hedghogs	0	0	8
	Paid for two Broomes for Street	0	0	6
Decr 19th	Paid Mr Head for Visitation Expen^s	0	15	0
Jany 10th	Paid for Broomes for the Street	0	2	0
1792	Paid for a Hedghog Feb 27th	0	0	4
Mar^h 29th	Paid Wm Chamberss Paving Bill	5	5	4
	£	11	2	6½

Churchwardens' accounts, Yaxley, Huntingdon, 1791–2. *Payments include those for destruction of vermin: hedgehogs and sparrows.* (Huntingdon Record Office)

occupiers of the land). All these tithes were handed over by parishioners to the church. Tithes were then divided into great or rectorial tithes (for a rector, consisting of corn, hay and wood) and small or vicarial tithes (made up of other produce, for a vicar). Produce might be stored in a tithe barn, of which several examples still exist today in country areas.

Gradually this system became outdated and very unwieldy, and by the Tithe Commutation Act of 1836 all tithes were to be converted into cash payments by the commissioners, though commutation had happened in many parishes long before and would continue for many years afterwards. The 1836 Act resulted in a series of Tithe Awards, arranged alphabetically by landowners, which specify occupiers, acreage and the annual tithe payment. Also given on the award is a number which refers to the parish tithe map which shows houses, field names, lands and boundaries. The map and the award can be easily cross-referenced to discover exactly where an ancestor lived within a parish. Tithes were eventually abolished in 1936. Three copies were made of each Tithe Award: the one made for the commissioners will now be at the Public Record Office, class IR18; the copy made for the bishop will be in the appropriate Diocesan or County Record Office, and the incumbent's copy should form part of a parish chest collection.

Churchwardens' accounts
Two churchwardens (more in a large parish) would be appointed and duly sworn on Easter Tuesday each year. One was the Vicar's Warden and the other the People's Warden. This office was an ancient one dating back to the twelfth century. The churchwardens' duties were many and varied, and at times could be interchangeable with those of the overseers of the poor and the parish constable. They reported regularly to the ecclesiastical court which held jurisdiction over their parish, such as that of the Archdeacon or Bishop, on any decay in the church fabric and on the morals and welfare of the parishioners and the minister, 'presenting' whether anything was amiss or irregular in the parish. Churchwardens' presentments can be exceptionally informative, and will be found among diocesan, not parochial, records.

Churchwardens' account books and papers can be very comprehensive. A record was kept of income - principally derived from ratepayers (usually named) - and of disbursements such as payments made to local tradesmen and suppliers, to paupers and to those who brought in dead vermin. Then there was the cost of maintaining and cleaning the church and grounds, the purchase of sacramental wine and bread and a fee to the parish clerk for the keeping of the registers. There might be charities to administer and pews to be allocated at an appropriate rent.

Overseers of the poor accounts
This particular office was created by an Act of 1572 followed by another in 1597/8 which ordered the appointment of overseers by the justices. In 1601 came the Poor Law Act, made permanent in 1640, which was to be the basis of poor law administration in England and Wales for nearly two hundred years until 1834.

Overseers of the poor, responsible rate-paying householders and pillars of the community as they were, had an onerous task. They maintained the able-bodied poor and set them to work; relieved the sick and aged, known as the 'impotent poor'; apprenticed pauper children; assisted the parish constable in his duties and set a rate to tax every inhabitant and occupier of land to pay for the upkeep of the poor. They also had to provide a House of Correction for law-breakers, vagrants and women who had given birth to illegitimate children, and also a poorhouse for parish paupers.

Overseers' account books and vouchers list the names of ratepayers in the parish, and itemise payments of every kind to named paupers by way of clothing, food and other support. Some poor people were maintained by the poor rate from the cradle to the grave. These accounts can be very detailed, providing information about a parish which is as useful to local historians as to family historians. We will have more to say about the poor later in this chapter.

The parish or petty constable's accounts
The post of parish constable was an ancient one and was important in that he had to maintain law and order in the parish community. He was supervised in his duties by the churchwardens and the justices of the peace. This was not a popular job and there was a widespread practice of paying someone else to do the work. This post was eventually superseded by the Parish Constables' Act of 1842; from this time on, parish constables were appointed at special sessions of the justices until 1862, and lists of appointments will be found in the records of the Clerk of the Peace. Parish constables survived until around 1862 when county, city and other police forces were established throughout the country.

The constable had powers of arrest and could charge anyone who had committed a crime or a breach of the peace; he was empowered to hold such a person in custody in the stocks, the local lock-up, blind house or cage - or even in his own home - until such time as the prisoner was brought before the magistrates. If sentence was passed, a warrant would be issued and the constable would deliver the prisoner to gaol. Another of his duties was to escort vagrants to the next parish on their way to their parishes of settlement. From 1757 parish men were chosen by ballot to serve for three years in a county militia but, if they or the parish could afford it, a substitute could be provided. Part of a constable's function was to ensure that this procedure ran smoothly.

Constables' accounts and vouchers may be found in a parish chest collection and their expenses may also be given in the overseers of the poor and churchwardens' accounts.

Surveyors of the highways' records
The 1555 Highways Act gave responsibility for the upkeep of the highway to parishes, and provided for one or two surveyors to be appointed to ensure that all roads and bridges within the parish were maintained. The appointed men might be known as surveyors of the highways, overseers of the highways, waywardens or stonewardens. This was another unpaid and unpopular appointment. All able-bodied parishioners were required to give a certain number of days' labour on the roads. Able-bodied paupers were also set to work picking stones from the fields for the roads, and often their names will be listed, along with details of the small payment each received. By 1691 power of appointment of the surveyors was transferred from the parish to the justices.

Surveyors of the highways' documents usually consist of highways accounts and vouchers.

Local censuses and inhabitants' lists
Lists of local inhabitants were only made for a few parishes, at various times and

for a variety of reasons. Where they survive, most will be with parish chest records. Family historians will associate the word 'census' with the decennial national census returns from 1841 onwards, but various lists of inhabitants have been compiled in certain localities over many centuries, and can be thought of as censuses or inhabitants' lists in their own right.

Various parishes compiled such name lists in the process of preparing returns for the national censuses of 1801 to 1831. Other local censuses took place through the years, and range in date from the sixteenth to the twentieth centuries. One excellent example from Hampshire was published as *Comyn's New Forest: 1817 directory of life in the parishes of Boldre and Brockenhurst*, edited by Jude James in 1982 and based upon Rev Henry Comyn's detailed house-by-house, village-by-village survey of every parishioner's family and lifestyle during the last six months of his curacy there. Another representative census available in print appears as volume 52 of the publications of the Bedfordshire Historical Record Society, *The inhabitants of Cardington in 1782* (1973); this contains exceptionally useful personal and family details, though the exact reason for its compilation is unknown. In 1988 the Dorset Record Society published *Puddletown, house, street and family: an account of the inhabitants of Puddletown parish, Dorsetshire, 1724* by C.L. Sinclair Williams.

Other records which can be considered as a type of census are lists of communicants, pew lists and incumbents' visiting books, some of which have been transcribed and published by Family History and other societies. Wiltshire Family History Society has published all available early censuses for the county, including pew rents and incumbents' visiting books. Here is an example from Chiseldon:

Chiseldon, Wiltshire. List of inhabitants of the parish taken on 15 February 1787.
Richard Arman, sen. sister, 1 child. Chiseldon
Richard Arman, jun. wife, 7 children. Chiseldon
Caroline Berry, brother, sister, house shared with John Cook & Isaac Heath. Chiseldon
Mr & Mrs Calley, 5 children, 12 servants. Burderop & Hodson
John Edwards, wife or housekeeper. Badbury
William Jerom, widower, 4 children, 3 grandchildren. Chiseldon
John May, son, house shared with William Hat. Coate
Hannah Werrel [husband left her], 2 children. Burderop & Hodson
[From Wiltshire Record Office, Calley Papers]

The Old Poor Law

Much of the work of the principal officers appointed by each parish concerned the upkeep of the poor. This was in the days before national poverty relief, and each parish had to balance the needs of its poor with the burden placed upon its ratepayers. Meticulous records were kept in all matters pertaining to poor relief - hardly surprisingly, in view of the great sums of money involved. As a result, you may learn far more about your pauper ancestor than about those who were law-abiding and conscientious ratepayers.

The dissolution of the monasteries under Henry VIII left a vacuum to be filled: monasteries had been great providers of alms, and once this service was denied to the population, there was every risk that the country might be swamped by paupers and 'sturdy beggars'. Eventually the Poor Law Acts of 1601 and 1640, which made poor relief the responsibility of the parish, became the foundation of poor law administration for nearly 200 years.

Many paupers were supported in their own homes by relief of various kinds. Other parishes, however, had their own poor houses, and following an act of 1722/3 parishes were encouraged to build or rent a workhouse, which may have been only a poor hut on the common or waste land. If the parish did not provide the means for a poorhouse, then paupers may have been compelled to take other paupers into their homes. If a parish was very small, or could not afford to build its own poorhouse, it was urged to unite with another parish to make such a scheme a viable proposition. Some parishes were much more generous than others in dealing with their poor, and would provide rent and food allowances, pay for a doctor when necessary and cover funeral expenses.

If a poorhouse or workhouse was provided, it would often accommodate not only adult paupers, but also young children. Babies might be kept in the poorhouse, but many were sent out to be nursed by someone who was paid a few pence a week. As a result of this practice, a Parliamentary Committee reported in 1715 that 'many poor infants are inhumanely suffered to die by the barbarity of the nurses who are a sort of people void of commiseration or religion hired by churchwardens to take off a burden from the parish at the easiest rates they can and these know the manner of doing it efficiently.' Children who survived this terrible practice would then often be apprenticed to 'husbandry' or 'house-wifery' (sometimes just to be used as unpaid skivvies) at the early age of seven years or so. If a vagrant couple with children happened to trespass into a parish, then their children could be apprenticed by the parish authorities against the will of the parents, once more relieving the parish of a financial burden. A person harbouring a vagrant could be heavily fined from ten shillings up to forty shillings.

Gilbert's Act of 1782 endeavoured to remedy the inhumane conditions obtaining in many workhouses, and to this end inspectors were appointed to conduct matters. Thanks to Gilbert's Act, children under seven years of age were allowed to stay with their parents, and paupers were not to be sent to workhouses more than ten miles from their homes. Able-bodied paupers could no longer be sent to the workhouse and, at long last, the humiliating practice of making paupers wear distinguishing badges was abolished, providing that individuals could prove that they were of 'very decent and orderly behaviour'.

About 1795 the Speenhamland system of outdoor relief, which had begun in Speenhamland, Berkshire, was adopted, and wages were made up to equal the cost of subsistence. This was based on a scale of relief for a family related to the poor rate and the current price of bread. This system was eventually adopted throughout the country, encouraging employers to pay low wages and persuading some people that they now had enough to exist on, and therefore did not need to work in order to maintain themselves. Finally, after various unworkable and outmoded systems had been tried and abandoned, we arrive at the year of 1834 and the Poor Law Amendment Act.

The New Poor Law
With the advent of the Poor Law Unions as a result of the 1834 Poor Law Amendment Act, the whole poor law system changed radically - and not for the better, so far as paupers were concerned. The old poor laws were abolished in

England and Wales, and parishes were formed into 'Unions' which encompassed a number of local parishes and which would build a Union workhouse or poorhouse. In fact, some 15,000 parishes were amalgamated into around 600 Unions. In a number of large cities, including London, some of the old workhouses were retained as Union workhouses. Large workhouses were built to house paupers from their Union parishes which were to contain those impotent poor who were unable to support themselves. The responsibility of the parish for its own poor was now transferred to new Poor Law Unions and their Boards of Guardians. Absolute poverty, not just mere poverty, was the criterion adopted, and life was made deliberately harsh in the new Union workhouse, for it now seemed to be the view that it was a crime to be poor and without means of subsistence. Conditions were made as unpleasant as possible in an effort to encourage the poor to seek work, and to this end employers were exhorted (not always with success) to provide a living wage. Guardians had to supply a special and adequate diet from a list of supplied dietaries which contained specific amounts of solid food - enough, as it was stated, to 'maintain the reasonable health of the inmates'.

The authorities had hoped to do away with 'outdoor relief' but the increasing number of paupers made this impossible, and the practice continued. If a pauper died in the workhouse in the earlier days of the Union, the body would often be taken back to the parish of settlement for burial, a fact reflected in some Union minute books.

Special arrangements were made for 'tramps' on the move, and there was provision of workhouse schools for children, and of infirmaries for the sick.

Any man or woman who abandoned his or her family with a resultant burden on the Union poor rates would be eagerly sought by the authorities, and a *Poor Law Unions' Gazette*, price 2d, was established 'for giving information of all persons who desert their families'. Here is an example from such a Gazette:

> *Saturday, February 20 1858: Wellington [Shropshire] Union: James Burness alias Black Jemmy, labourer, aged about 40, 5 ft 8 ins high, dark complexion, dark hair and whiskers, stoops a little in the shoulders; deserted his wife and family at Wellington, about 9 months ago, whereby they have become chargeable to this Union; is supposed to be in the neighbourhood of Bilston, his wife has since deserted the family, and is believed to be with him; she is a short stout woman, very much marked in the face with small-pox. £1 reward.*

The work of the Guardians was closely and strictly supervised by the Poor Law Commissioners in London. Records were kept of all those in receipt of relief, outdoor and indoor, and lists were printed and published. Minute books recorded the day-to-day Union business of the 'house' and supplied detailed information about paupers, including settlements and removals. In the early days of the Unions, the local registrar was obliged to appear before the Guardians to read out marriage notices for couples who wished to marry in the Register Office, and these notices often appear in the first minute books. Other Union records which may be found in local record offices include: birth and death registers of those in the workhouse, admissions and discharges, creed registers, workhouse school registers, registers of boarding out of workhouse children and punishment books. Census returns from 1841 to 1891 for Union workhouses also need to be searched if it is suspected that family members were residing in the 'house', though sometimes only the initials of inmates are given.

Extensive correspondence between Union Guardians and the Commissioners survives in the records of the Ministry of Health (Class MH) in the Public Record Office, and can be a valuable source of family information, supplementing that found in Union minute books.

Poor Law Unions were established in Ireland and Scotland a few years after 1834. Their records are similar in content to those for England and Wales, and you may expect to find minute books, admission and discharge registers, birth and death registers and accounts of those receiving outdoor relief.

Life was physically and psychologically harsh for inmates of the Union workhouse. They were forced to wear standard pauper uniforms, and the rules were that adults rose at 5 am in summer and 7 am in winter. Work would take place from 7 am or 8 am to midday, and then from 1 pm to 6 pm, bedtime being at 8 pm. Women worked in the laundry or at other hard domestic tasks and men worked at whatever was available. The workhouse master and matron enforced the rules of 'industry, order, punctuality and cleanliness' at all times. Husbands were separated from their wives and children, and the only communication allowed between them came by way of very occasional meetings - and then only if the Guardians' permission was obtained. Inmates were divided into various categories - 'aged or infirm' men and women; 'able-bodied' men and women over 16 years of age; boys or girls aged from seven to fifteen years; and children under seven years of age. Each group had its own separate living accommodation and exercise yard. Young children were usually allowed to stay with their mothers during any leisure time and to sleep with them at night. Children of pauper parents were to be apprenticed by the workhouse authorities, although from 1844 education was provided for workhouse children.

All in all, the workhouse system was always open to abuse by the masters, matrons and staff in charge, and the use of cruelty in Unions was the subject of Parliamentary Commission enquiries. Although many poor lived in the workhouse with its austere and forbidding conditions, many others were not resident but were 'relieved' by the poor rate and were known as the 'outdoor poor'. Lists should be found of such people.

The Poor Law Amendment Act of 1834 and subsequent acts were eventually abolished under the Local Government Act of 1929, which established Area Guardians Committees. The Poor Law finally came to an end with the National Assistance Act of 1948, which brought about the closure of these miserable and unhappy places where many of our ancestors had existed until the end of their lives.

The Poor Laws: records
Records regarding the poor were usually kept in great detail, though survival of these can be patchy. The complexities of the settlement laws gave rise to a vast amount of litigation, and you will find printed records of relevant legal cases extracted from Quarter Sessions and elsewhere in libraries with specialised collections of law books.

Settlement certificates
In 1662 the Act of Settlement insisted that every individual was to have an official parish of settlement. The Act stated that a stranger staying in a parish

Settlement certificate, 1745, for William Titford and his wife Joan. *Even though they had been in Hawkhurst, Kent, for 34 years and were moving only a few miles away to Cranbrook, they still needed a certificate from their parish of original settlement – Frome, Somerset, which they had left in 1711.* (Centre for Kentish Studies, Maidstone)

could be removed by the overseers within 40 days if he had no means of being able to work, or did not rent property worth £10 per annum. After 40 days such a stranger could claim settlement in his new parish and therefore, if the need arose, he could claim poor relief if he fell on hard times, thus becoming a charge on the parish poor rate. This Act also authorised justices to punish persistent vagrants.

Two more Settlement Acts followed in 1691 and 1697. The 1697 Act stated that strangers would henceforth be allowed to enter a parish, provided they possessed a settlement certificate from their parish of settlement which stated that if they became in need of poor relief, they would be taken back by that parish. For example, if a stranger entered a parish for temporary work he was obliged to bring a certificate from his home parish which guaranteed that he would be returned there if he became in need of poor relief. In some parishes, a stranger would be obliged to enter into a settlement bond for a certain sum of money, giving names and addresses of two sureties, thus ensuring that he would not be a drain on the parish if he became in need of poor relief. Some of these are known as 'bonds to save the parish harmless'.

The administration of these laws was a complex matter, and often caused confusion amongst the parish officials and magistrates, but in essence the law was quite clear: that parish officials would not relieve a pauper, that is, give him poor relief, unless he was in his own parish of settlement - and that parish was not necessarily that of his birth.

A person was able to gain a settlement in a parish in several ways:

- By being born there of legally-settled parishioners, and by never moving out and away.
- By being born there, if illegitimate, providing that it was the mother's settlement parish.
- By working there at least one full year (365 days) as a yearly servant and receiving a full year's wages.
- By serving a full apprenticeship by indenture to a 'settled' parishioner.
- By holding a parish office.
- By paying parish rates or by completing 40 days' residence, after giving due notice in writing.
- By owning or renting property worth at least £10 per annum.

A woman took the settlement parish of her husband when she married, as can be made clear from the following example. William Pollett (or Pollard) was settled in the Somerset parish of Podimore Milton. On 16 April 1723 he married Martha Titford in her parish of settlement, Frome, also in Somerset. From that point onwards the couple would both be officially settled in Podimore Milton, since Martha would take her husband's parish of settlement as her own. Now in the event they both wanted to live and work in Frome, so a settlement certificate was necessary. This was duly issued, and a transcript of the essential information appears below. This certificate was handwritten; in later years many were printed, with the blanks filled in as appropriate:

Somerset:
We Edward Smith Churchwarden & William Hunt Overseer of the poor of the Parish of Puddemore Milton in ye County aforesaid do

hereby own & acknowledge William Pollett & Martha his wife to be Inhabitants legally settled in ye Parish of Puddemore Milton aforesd. Witness our hands & seales the tenth of March in the tenth yeare of ye Raign of or Soveraigne Lord George King of Great Brittain et.
... To the Churchwardens & Overseers of ye Poor of ye Parish of ffrome Selwood in ye County of Somerset or to any or either of them. Signed April 1st, 1724.
[From an original document in Somerset Record Office]

The appropriate signatures, including those of Justices of the Peace, then follow. William Hunt, the Podimore Milton overseer, makes his mark only, a great blob. Imagine what problems an illiterate overseer would create for a parish!

Removal orders and examinations

If a person without a certificate entered a parish in which he or she did not have an official settlement, and seemed likely to become chargeable, then an examination would be made by the justices. From this examination on oath, the justices would determine which was that person's parish of settlement; as a result the intruder would then either be allowed to stay, or would be removed by means of what was known as a removal order, sometimes accompanied by a pass showing the route to be taken back to the parish of settlement. This would apply even within a city or town which consisted of more than one parish; no one was allowed to move across town to live without the appropriate documentation, as in the case of Richard Dangerfield and his family, who were removed from the parish of St Peter's, Marlborough, Wiltshire, to St Mary's, Marlborough on 18 September 1758.

Removal orders would often take a person or a family back to their place of settlement miles away across the country, sometimes to a parish they had never known, or only known briefly as a small child. It was not uncommon for a husband and wife to have their children taken from them, each being removed to separate scattered parishes.

Settlement examinations can be extremely detailed and may provide evidence of a place of birth, parents' names, movement around the country, trade, service in the army or navy, marriage, children and so on, and can supply vital family information which may be found nowhere else - as the following example of an examination made by the Borough Justices of Marlborough will illustrate:

Borough of Marlbrough in Wilts. *To wit. The examination of Wm. Johnson, taken on Oath the 12th Day of June 1737 before Thomas Beaven, Gentl., Mayor & Wm.Gough, Gentl.,two of his Maj'ties Justices of the peace of the said Burrough, as followeth:*
Saith, That he was born in the City of Limerick in the Kingdom of Ireland, That he is a Weaver and Woolcomber by Trade and that he work'd at his said trade a Year and a halfe wth one Moses Vine of Kenta Street in the parish of St. George's in the B...ugh of Southwark - Then maried with one Mary Bowles of Swansey in Wales, but a Servt. at that time at the Bell and Bare in the Burrough of Southwark aforesd. and went with his said wife to Bristoll to work and work'd there wth one Charles Crawley without Castle Gate abt three months,

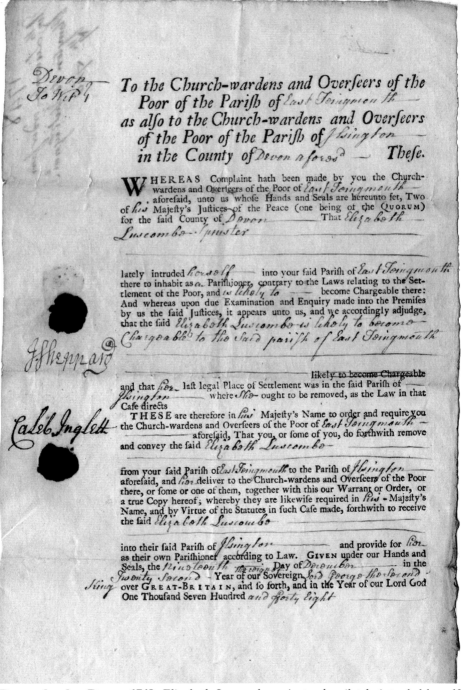

To the Church-wardens and Overſeers of the Poor of the Pariſh of *East Teignmouth* as alſo to the Church-wardens and Overſeers of the Poor of the Pariſh of *Ilsington* in the County of *Devon aforeſaid* — Theſe.

WHEREAS Complaint hath been made by you the Church-wardens and Overſeers of the Poor of *East Teignmouth* aforeſaid, unto us whoſe Hands and Seals are hereunto ſet, Two of *his* Majeſty's Juſtices of the Peace (one being of the QUORUM) for the ſaid County of *Devon* That *Elizabeth Luscombe Spinster*

lately intruded *herself* into your ſaid Pariſh of *East Teignmouth* there to inhabit as *a* Pariſhioner, contrary to the Laws relating to the Settlement of the Poor, and *is likely to* become Chargeable there: And whereas upon due Examination and Enquiry made into the Premiſes by us the ſaid Juſtices, it appears unto us, and we accordingly adjudge, that the ſaid *Elizabeth Luscombe is likely to become Chargeable to the said parish of East Teignmouth*

~~likely to become Chargeable~~ and that *her* laſt legal Place of Settlement was in the ſaid Pariſh of *Ilsington* where *she* ought to be removed, as the Law in that Caſe directs

THESE are therefore in *his* Majeſty's Name to order and require you the Church-wardens and Overſeers of the Poor of *East Teignmouth* aforeſaid, That you, or ſome of you, do forthwith remove and convey the ſaid *Elizabeth Luscombe*

from your ſaid Pariſh of *East Teignmouth* to the Pariſh of *Ilsington* aforeſaid, and *her* deliver to the Church-wardens and Overſeers of the Poor there, or ſome or one of them, together with this our Warrant or Order, or a true Copy hereof; whereby they are likewiſe required in *his* Majeſty's Name, and by Virtue of the Statutes in ſuch Caſe made, forthwith to receive the ſaid *Elizabeth Luscombe*

into their ſaid Pariſh of *Ilsington* and provide for *her* as their own Pariſhioner according to Law. GIVEN under our Hands and Seals, the *Nineteenth* Day of *November* in the *Twenty Second* Year of our Sovereign *Lord George the Second* King over GREAT-BRITAIN, and ſo forth, and in the Year of our Lord God One Thouſand Seven Hundred *and forty Eight*

Removal order, Devon, 1748. *Elizabeth Luscombe, spinster, has 'lately intruded herself' into the parish of East Teignmouth and is 'likely to become chargeable there'. She is to be removed to her last place of settlement, Ilsington.*

& his said wife with him - Then left his said wife & went back to London again & work'd for himselfe, till about Five or Six Weekes agoe [During wch time, he left his said wife behind him at Bristoll aforsaid] Then went to the Devizes & work'd there abt three Weekes with one Mrs Pile - Then went to Bristoll to seek for his said wife; But when he came there, understood she was gone up to London after him. Five Weekes before - Then was making his way up towards London again, and Tuesday last met her with two Men, abt four or five miles beyond Bath - Ask'd her wt she had done wth the Child, & she told him she had left it at the Six Bells in Marlbrough, to wch place he Saith he is now come for his said child.

Saith, That he was maried to his said wife, abt Michas last, at the hand and penn in the Fleet, within the said City of London; and when he went away from her as aforesaid to London, he left her big wth Child & therefore Suppos'd She had been brt to bed, when he so met her, & ask'd her for the sd Child as before is Set Forth...

Sworn before us the Day and Year aforesaid. Wm. Johnson; Thos. Bevan; Will. Gough.

Rec'd of the Churchwardens and Overseers of St.Peter's Marlborough A Male Child which was found att the Ring of Bells in ye sd. Parish last Sunday Morning. I own my Self to be the true father of the Child and do promise the Parish to take due Care of the same as Witness my hand this 12th day of June 1737.

Witness: Tho. Hodges; Wm. Johnson; Anne Hodges.

Wm. Johnson from ye Citty of Lymerick and Mary Bowls from Swansey being ye Fathr & Mothr of Thos. Johnson.

The settlement laws were not substantially altered until the passing of the 1876 Poor Law Amendment Act and were still being applied, in some cases, into the twentieth century.

Vagrancy

The vagrancy laws were much harsher than the settlement laws, in that the parish authorities would remove a vagrant from their parish after examination, as a 'rogue and vagabond, wandering and begging'. He or she would be punished according to law and escorted and passed from one parish to another, usually by the constable, from House of Correction to House of Correction, until the parish of settlement was reached and the vagrant could be cared for 'as the law provides'. Children who were found wandering were no exception to this law and were subjected to the same treatment - an examination, followed by the appropriate punishment and removal by a signed pass.

If a single woman or a widow of child-bearing age, on her own, with a child or pregnant, appeared without warning in a parish, the authorities would be anxious to rid themselves of this burden and she would be examined and removed with all speed. By 1743, children born illegitimately within a parish which was not their mother's parish of settlement would be deemed to be legally settled in their mother's parish. If the father of an illegitimate child could be 'persuaded' to marry the mother, especially if he was from another parish and single, then the woman and her child would become settled in his parish.

An Act of 1743/4 placed vagrants into three categories: 'idle and disorderly

Middlefex } THESE are to defire you, to permit and fuffer
to wit. } the Bearer hereof

Robert Little with his Wife Rachael and one child named Ann

Rd. J. George Hand Sq.

Kensington 9/
Hammersmith ... 6d 2 May
Colnbrook 9 May 3
Maidenhead — 1/0
wargrave 1/0 May
S. Giles Reading 1/ 5
Theale — 1/

peaceably and quietly to pafs unto *Broad Hinton in the County of Wilts*

without any of your Lett, Hindrance, or Mo-
leftation, whatfoever, *they* ———demeaning
themselves orderly and not exceeding the
Space of *Eleven days* ——— from the Date
hereof, to accomplifh the faid Journey.

Given under my Hand and Seal, being one of
His Majefty's Juftices of the Peace for the faid
County of Middlefex, the *fecond* Day of
May ———— in the Year of our Lord One
Thoufand Eight Hundred *and one at the
Public Office Great Shirebro' Street*

John Scott

To all Juftices of the Peace, Mayors,
Sheriffs, Bailiffs, Conftables, *and
all other His Majefty's Officers, whom
it may concern.*

Pass for Robert Little and his family *to travel from London to Broad Hinton in Wiltshire, 1801. The family has eleven days to make the journey; the places reached are listed on the left.* (Wiltshire Record Office)

Bastardy Examination, Dover, Kent, 1819. *Elizabeth Crapan names Charles Town, servant, as the father.*

persons', 'rogues and vagabonds', and 'incorrigible rogues'. As can be seen, there were many devious ways of a parish ridding itself of undesirable persons.

There had always been persistent vagrants who for one reason or another tramped the countryside causing a nuisance, possibly because they had 'itchy feet', or because they were homeless, out of work, or trying to evade the law. Women who had been abandoned by their husbands and those who were married to soldiers who had embarked for foreign shores were often apprehended whilst making their way back to their place of settlement. These were the ones who were dealt with severely by the magistrates for consistently breaking the vagrancy laws. Vagrants could be sentenced to a public whipping or to a spell of hard labour, they could be branded or, as a last resort, transported to the colonies.

In the early days of the poor laws Salisbury city was plagued with vagrants from all over the kingdom:

> *On 13 September 1624, Francis Symons, wandering, confessed that she lived incontinently with William Goodman, a joiner and lewd fellow, who impudently affirmed they were married. She was punished by a public whipping and sent to Blandford in Dorset, where she said she had been born. Goodman was committed to prison and examined on the 15 September 1624, when he confessed that he and Frances Symons lived lewdly, not being married. He was also punished and sent back to Bristol where he said he had been born.*

[From Salisbury City Vagrancy Records, Wiltshire Record Office]

Bastardy

It is fairly rare for family historians to discover no evidence of illegitimacy in their ancestry. An Act of 1575/6 decreed that mothers and fathers of a bastard child were to be punished and sent to prison by the magistrates. An Act of 1609 did not really improve matters concerning illegitimacy, as this stated that any 'lewd' woman having a bastard who was chargeable could be sent to the House of Correction for a year unless she gave security for good behaviour.

From the seventeenth century until the middle of the eighteenth century illegitimacy increased, and another Act in 1732/3 stated that a pregnant woman had to declare to the overseers of the poor that she was pregnant and to give the name of the father. Entries in parish registers at this time will often include entries such as: 'reputed father...as she saith' or, as shown in a baptism at Milton Lilbourne on 5 August 1787:

> *John, bastard son of Ruth Tarrant, husband gone, and Guy Warwick.*

The next Act of 1743/4 laid down that a bastard born in a place where the mother was not settled was to have its mother's place of settlement and the mother was to be punished by a public whipping.

The task of the overseers and churchwardens was to examine a woman on oath and to extract from her the name of the putative father of her bastard child, already born or about to be born, and to make the man in question enter into a bastardy bond or indemnity bond, agreeing to pay a sum of money for the woman's 'lying in' and maintenance until the child was of an age to be apprenticed or put out to work.

On 1 February 1826, George Titford, a labourer of Ringwood in Hampshire, entered into a bond concerning a female bastard child of Hannah Nippard's which was likely to become chargeable to the parish. George Titford 'did beget the said bastard child in the body of her the said Hannah Nippard', and having no reason not be adjudged the father, entered into a bond agreeing to pay the churchwardens and overseers one pound towards the lying-in costs of the said Hannah, and thereafter one shilling and sixpence per week 'towards the keeping, sustenation and maintenance of the child for as long as it shall be chargeable to the parish of Ringwood'. Not only that, but Hannah Nippard was obliged to pay sixpence per week so long as the child remained chargeable, 'in case she shall not nurse and take care of the child herself'.

There follows an example taken from a book of Bastardy Examinations relating to the parish of Dover in Kent. The book covers the period 1813 to 1823; at the front, 'Examinations in bastardy before birth' are listed, while the back section features 'Examinations in bastardy after birth'.

The reputed fathers in this book are of all social classes, some living in Dover, some further afield, not a few being absent in the navy, the army or the militia. So Mary Briggs, wife of John Briggs, formerly of the West Kent Militia, accuses James Durban of the Derby Regiment of Militia, now in Ireland, of being the father of the child she is carrying; Elizabeth Cole, spinster, accuses Joseph Stalkart, mariner belonging to His Majesty's Revenue Cutter *Rattlesnake*; Mary Ann Smithett, spinster, accuses William Davis late of Dover but now of London, journeyman to H.Bowman, linen draper. Ann Welch, spinster, had already given birth to her bastard child 'in the Kingdom of France' and christened it Charles William Stewart. She accuses Archibald Stewart, Captain in the Rifle Brigade, First Battalion, now in Limerick in the County of Limerick, Ireland, of being the father. A full entry reads as follows:

> *The Examination of Deanna Morgan (singlewoman) taken upon oath this fourth day of December 1818 before me, Jonathan Osborn Esq. one of His Majesty's Justices of the Peace in and for the town and port of Dovor* [sic] *in the County of Kent concerning the Father of the Bastard of which she was lately delivered as follows:*
> *The said Examinant saith that on the eighteenth day of February 1815 she was delivered of a female Bastard child at Bruges in the Kingdom of the Netherlands and that Kenneth Mac Kensie General in His Majesty's Service did beget her with child of the said Bastard and is the Father thereof and the said Bastard is likely to become chargeable in the Parish of Saint Mary the Virgin* [Dover]. [Signed by J.Osborn and by the mother, as 'Deanea Morgan']

Over the years, some men adjudged to be fathers would default in their maintenance payments, and their names and the reason for their consequent imprisonment may appear in the calendars of prisoners in the local gaol. Local newspapers, too, often reported names of men who defaulted on maintenance payments.

Of course, another solution open to a parish faced with cases of bastardy was to use bribery or threats to 'persuade' the father of the child to marry the mother with a licence obtained and paid for by the parish. For all that, in some cases it is obvious that 'reputed' fathers must have been accused unjustly.

The papers to look for in bastardy cases are examinations, bastardy bonds and bastardy affiliation orders; in certain cases a warrant was issued once a reputed father had decided to abscond.

From 1844, a mother of an illegitimate child could apply to the justices for a maintenance order against the father, but the onus was now on the woman to prove her case and it is from this period onwards, to the latter part of the nineteenth century, that orders for bastardy maintenance and 'cases in bastardy' may be discovered in Petty Sessions records.

Apprenticeship indenture, 1721, *for Henry Durdall, son of Richard Durdall of New Sarum, to be apprenticed to Charles Thomas of Bristol, chimney sweeper, by the terms of the Duke of Somerset's Charity.* (Wiltshire Record Office)

Pauper apprentices

Pauper children could be forcibly apprenticed, often against the will of their parents. A small amount of money would be paid by the proposed master to the parish, and the term to be served was often much longer than the usual seven years, thus relieving the parish of a costly burden. Girl paupers could be apprenticed from the age of seven years to the age of twenty-one, while the upper age for boys was twenty-four. In 1768 this age for boys was reduced to twenty-one.

Parish apprenticeships commended themselves to the authorities for two good reasons. Firstly, the child was learning a useful trade (although very often such apprentices were used as a household menial who belonged to their master or mistress until their term of service was up). Secondly, the churchwardens and overseers were ridding themselves of a charge on the poor rate during the period of the apprenticeship. The employer gained cheap labour, so everyone - except the hapless apprentice - was well satisfied. In the nineteenth century a very large number of pauper children from the south of England were apprenticed to work in northern mills where labour was much in demand.

If a boy apprentice should be impressed into the navy by some unfortunate chance, his master was entitled to all his pay and his prize money!

Another type of apprenticeship was the charity apprenticeship, usually bestowed by some benevolent member of a parish in his or her will for the good of the poor children of the parish. This type of apprenticeship had terms set down by which the parish officials, the master or mistress, and the apprentice had rights and conditions which usually ensured reasonably fair treatment. Indentures relating to pauper and charity apprenticeships will often be found in parish records and may well be referred to in churchwardens' or overseers' accounts. Of course, there were always apprentices who absconded from their masters, and warrants for their apprehension may be found in surviving Petty Sessions records. If apprehended, they may have been sent to the General Quarter Sessions for trial and sentence.

Parish chest records and the Poor Laws: hints and reminders

- Overseers of the poor accounts often show items such as 'badges' at one penny or one halfpenny each. These were the badges which paupers were forced to wear on their clothing - a large 'P' followed by the initial letter of the name of the parish. So a pauper from Faringdon in Berkshire would have a badge bearing the letters 'PF'. Penalties for not wearing these badges could result in loss of relief and even imprisonment in the local gaol.
- Tradesmen would be employed to work on the parish roads by the surveyor of the highways, so accounts may indicate what trade your ancestor followed.
- Sometimes the records of a workhouse will contain lists of births and baptisms which took place within its walls. Many births were of illegitimate children, and some private workhouse baptisms may not have been recorded in the parish registers. Some workhouse births may even not be registered after the advent of general registration in 1837.
- Some Poor Law Union Boards of Guardians had a system of vaccination for smallpox. Records may have been kept, giving names and ages.

Further reading

Bier, A.L. *The problem of the poor in Tudor and early Stuart England.* 1983.
Camp, A. *My ancestors moved in England and Wales.* 1994.
Chapman, C. *Pre-1841 censuses & population listings.* (4th.Ed.) 1994.
Cole, A. *An introduction to Poor Law documents before 1834.* (2nd.Ed.) 2000.
Cox, C. *Churchwardens' accounts.* 1913.
Crowther, M.A. *The workhouse system 1834-1929: the history of an English social institution.* 1981.
Digby, A. *The poor law in nineteenth century England and Wales.* 1982.
Evans, E.J. *Tithes, maps and apportionments and the 1836 Act.* 1993.
Gibson, J. and Medlycott, M. *Local census listings 1522-1930: holdings in the British Isles.* (3rd.Ed.) 1994.
Gibson, J. and Rogers, C. *Poor Law Union records in England and Wales.* 4 vols. (2nd.Ed.) 1997.
Hammond, J.L. and B. *The town labourer.* Reprint, 1995.
Hammond, J.L. and B. *The village labourer.* Reprint, 1995.
Kain R.J.P, and Prince, H.C. *Tithe surveys for historians.* 2000.
Longmate, N. *The workhouse.* 1974.
McLaughlin, E. *Annals of the poor.* (5th.Ed) 1994.
McLaughlin, E. *Illegitimacy.* (5th.Ed.) 1992.
McLaughlin, E. *The poor are always with us.* 1994.

Marshall, J.D. *The Old Poor Law 1795-1834*. 1985.

Munckton, T. *Somerset Paupers: Unremembered Lives*. 1994.

Price, F.D. *The Wigginton Constable's book 1691-1836*. Banbury Historical Society, Vol.11. 1971. With a substantial introduction on the office of constable.

Reid, A. *The Union Workhouse*. 1994.

Richardson, J. *The local historians' encyclopedia*. (2nd.Ed.) 1986.

Rose, M.E. *The English poor law 1780-1930*. 1971.

Rose, M.E. *The relief of poverty 1834-1914*. (2nd.Ed.) 1986.

Slack, P. *The English poor law 1531-1782*. 1995.

Tate, W.E. *The parish chest*. 1946. Several times reprinted.

Turner, M.E. *Enclosures in Britain 1750-1830*. 1984.

Wiltshire FHS. *The compleat parish officer*. 1996 reprint of a 1753 original.

Wiltshire FHS. *The handy book of parish law*. 1995 reprint of an 1872 original.

Wiltshire Record Society. (Vol 46) *Bradford Settlement Examinations 1725-98*. 1990.

Wood, P. *Poverty and the workhouse in Victorian Britain*. 1991.

CHAPTER 9

Diocesan Records

Above and beyond the parish lay two broader jurisdictions, the county and the diocese. We will deal with the county and its records in the next chapter, but will look first at the diocese - that is, the area that came under the overall control of a Bishop but which would be further sub-divided into archdeaconries and various other units of ecclesiastical jurisdiction. Beyond the diocese, of course, came the provinces of Canterbury and York, but their voluminous records are beyond the scope of the present book.

Turn the pages of *The Phillimore atlas and index of parish registers* and look at the county maps. Here the various jurisdictions are outlined with distinguishing colour lines, and you'll see how counties differ in terms of the complexity of ecclesiastical control within which they operated. In truth, nothing is simple; London reveals a complicated network of ecclesiastical areas of influence, the ridings of Yorkshire are riddled with peculiars, and a county like Derbyshire, which looks simple enough, was within the diocese of Lichfield, which lies across the county border into Staffordshire. The point here is a simple one: know your ecclesiastical areas, and never confuse a county with a diocese.

Our ancestors who lived out in the country, far from the nearest cathedral town, would nevertheless have been aware of the importance of the diocese in which they lived as they decided to apply for a marriage licence or needed to sort out matters of probate. The niceties of exactly which archdeaconry they lived in, within which diocese, would have been of more than passing academic interest to them. Not only that, but in preparation for the next visitation by the Archdeacon, the Bishop, or some other dignitary, the churchwardens and the 'apparitor' or 'summoner' (a kind of legalised sneak) would have been keeping their eyes open, rooting out examples of bad conduct to report in the required presentments.

Churchwardens' presentments can yield fascinating information about what our ancestors were allegedly doing or not doing in centuries past. In 1615 the churchwardens of the parish of Bratton in Wiltshire made their presentment to Henry Cotton, Precentor of Salisbury, for Bratton lay within his peculiar. They charged various parishioners with misconduct: William Pavvier and his wife Maude were 'with child before they were married'; Edith Bollin 'useth not the company of her husband'; Thomas Walter and Valentine Perry were 'at a Tiplinge House in the time of Divine Prayer' and Thomas Titford, shoemaker, was not attending his parish church. These rogues were cited to appear before the Precentor at his court in Salisbury to answer the charges made against them

Churchwardens' presentment, Uffculme, Devon, 1664, *in the Peculiar of the Prebend of Uffculme in the Diocese of Sarum. They list those who have died since the last visitation and, amongst other items, state that a child has been left unbaptised, that another was base born, and that the arrival of the child of Willyam and Rebecka Bartlett, born in June, followed too close on their marriage in April.* (Wiltshire Record Office)

in the presentments. William Pavvier failed to attend the court, and so did Thomas Walter. Both were duly excommunicated. Thomas Titford did make an appearance, arguing his case that 'Edington parish church is nearer than his own parish church, and that he doth rather frequent thither to hear Divine service than to his own parish church'. Thomas was fined the usual twelve pence and went back home.

Churchwardens would clearly have been collectors of gossip, and were no doubt keen to report any form of moral misconduct brought to their attention. Ecclesiastical dignitaries such as the Precentor of Salisbury had their own church courts, to which malefactors could be summoned to appear. Such courts took themselves very seriously, with attornies known as 'proctors' and a scribe to summarise the proceedings. Unfortunately, those summoned to appear at such courts seem generally to have held them in low regard; absentees would be deemed to be 'contumacious' and might eventually be excommunicated - one of the few punishments available to the frustrated court officials, and one which could eventually be lifted, after a period of time, by confession, prayer and/or the payment of a fine.

When a full-blown court case did take place, either one brought by the court itself or by an aggrieved party, a great deal of interesting matter could be recorded, including the depositions of witnesses who have a good deal to say about themselves as they start off their evidence.

From the family historian's point of view, the records of the presentment of Thomas Titford of Bratton, modest enough as his crime was, provide us with two snippets of information which are available nowhere else. To begin with, his occupation of 'shoemaker' is given, and then his explanation as to his absence from church, if true, helps us define where he was living at the time - namely, the one small portion of the parish of Bratton which was nearer to the neighbouring church of Edington than to Bratton church itself.

Diocesan Record Offices are now very often incorporated into County Record Offices, the County Archivist doubling up as Diocesan Archivist, or else into large reference libraries. This makes life easier for the family historian, in that bishops' transcripts, marriage licence allegations and bonds and probate material can be consulted under one roof.

Any diocese would have a great deal of other business to transact day by day; some of the resulting written records are of direct relevance to family historians, others are less so. Here is just a flavour of the documentation you could expect to find. Note that in many cases there will be separate records for each jurisdiction.

- Church court records: act books, caveats, court papers, deposition books. Details of punishments (penances, excommunications, fines).
- Visitation records, including churchwardens' presentments.
- Bishops' registers. Many are of very ancient date, and several have been published.
- Records concerned with benefices, tithes, parish terriers.
- Consecrations, faculties, institutions of incumbents.
- Ordination papers.
- Details of licences granted to parish clerks, schoolmasters, surgeons, physicians and midwives. Here is a nomination for a licence for a parish clerk:
  ... that I Ferdo Warner, Vicar of Rowde [Wilts.] have elected and publickly declared in the parish church of Rowde on Sunday, April 16th 1732, Francis Drake to be Clark of the Parish aforesaid, being a Person of a Sober life and conversation and fitly qualify'd both in Singing and Ringing for That office. 9 May 1732.
- Lists and details of dissenters, including Roman Catholics.
- Charters.

The general run of diocesan records, it must be said, has been largely overlooked by family historians. Some are in Latin, and abbreviated Latin at that, which can be daunting; C.T. Martin's *The record interpreter* (2nd.Ed. 1982) should be a great help in this regard. Nevertheless, if you are interested in a diocese which has an orderly manuscript or printed catalogue of its records, you could unearth great treasures.

Further reading

Chapman, C. *Ecclesiastical courts, their officials and records*. (2nd.Ed) 1997.
Christie, P. *Of chirche-reves and of testaments: the church, sex and slander in Elizabethan North Devon*. 1994.
Cox, J. *Hatred pursued beyond the grave: tales of our ancestors from the London church courts*. 1993.
Emmison, F.G. *Elizabethan life: morals and the church courts*. 1973.
Hair, P. *Before the Bawdy Court*. 1972.
Howard-Drake, J. *Oxford church courts: depositions 1542-1550*. 1991. This is one volume in a continuing series.
Ingram, M. *Church courts, sex and marriage in England, 1570-1640*. 1987.
Le Neve, J. *Fasti Ecclesiae Anglicanae*, or a calendar of the principal ecclesiastical dignitaries in England and Wales. 1854. Excellent for biographies of senior Anglican clergy. A three-volume reworking by T.D.Hardy of the original 1716 edition. The University of London Institute of Historical Research is currently publishing a new edition in several volumes.
Smith, D.M. *Guide to the Bishops' Registers of England and Wales*. 1981.
Tarver, A. *Church court records: an introduction for family and local historians*. 1995.

Printed catalogues of diocesan records include those for the dioceses of Chichester, Gloucester, Lincoln, Salisbury and Winchester.

CHAPTER 10

County Records: Crime, Charities and the Coroner

We have seen how the parish in England and Wales was not just concerned with ecclesiastical affairs, but was the basic unit of local government. Beyond the parish lay the old-established jurisdiction exercised by counties.

It was partly as a result of the need to store and preserve county-wide archives such as those of Quarter Sessions that County Record Offices were established, in the days before the huge growth of interest in family history. So you can expect surviving county records to be well cared for and catalogued; a significant number of transcripts of these also appear in print, and if you're interested in Quarter Sessions records for various periods covering Hertfordshire, Buckinghamshire, Warwickshire or a number of other counties, you need look no further than printed books.

Much of the county authorities' day-to-day business had to do with crime, its perpetrators, its victims and those who had witnessed it, though the justices also had administrative duties and were a key element in the day-to-day government of counties until the 1888 Local Government Act set up County Councils to administer their affairs.

In the past there were a great many crimes, major and minor, which attracted harsh punishments. A convicted criminal could be sentenced to imprisonment, often with hard labour, and at one time over two hundred crimes, many of them apparently minor in today's terms, could be punished by hanging - a sentence frequently commuted to transportation to the American or Australian colonies.

Petty or minor crimes would be dealt with by Petty Sessions or Borough Sessions; more significant matters would go to the Quarter Sessions courts of a county, leaving the Assizes to handle a range of business, including the more heinous crimes. Records of Petty Sessions, Borough Sessions and Quarter Sessions will be found in County Record Offices. Assize records are in the Public Record Office, but have been dealt with in this chapter because of the close working relationship that existed between the Quarter Sessions and Assize courts.

Petty Sessions

Petty Sessions courts operated at the first level of justice; here two Justices of the Peace (magistrates) would deal with the more trivial offences ('summary' matters) such as minor theft, poaching, assault, drunkenness, furious driving (in the days before and after the advent of motor cars), cruelty to animals, settlements and vagrancy. Petty Sessions would also be concerned with absconding husbands, wives and apprentices; deserters from HM's forces and the militia; bastardy cases; maintenance defaults; non-payment of rates; the registration of aliens and the licensing of alehouses and inns.

Nineteenth century justices' minute books containing details of bastardy cases, together with Petty Sessions papers, may well prove to be of value, as from the late eighteenth to the late nineteenth century several contain details of maintenance applications by mothers of bastard children, often naming putative fathers. From 1926 some adoption records dealt with by the courts appear in Petty Sessions Divisional records, but these are subject to the one-hundred-year closure rule, access being denied to all but adoptees themselves.

The survival of Petty Sessions records, it must be said, is patchy, but they are always worth seeking out.

Quarter Sessions

Quarter Sessions courts had jurisdiction over a county, and operated from the fourteenth century to 1971. They dealt with matters somewhat less serious than those handled by the Assize courts, but these could still be crimes punishable by death or transportation.

As the name implies, the Quarter Sessions met four times a year. They would be held in different major towns and cities within the county at Easter, Trinity (Midsummer), Michaelmas (September) and Epiphany (January). In 1835 the Municipal Corporations Act removed the administrative control of cities, boroughs and towns from the justices.

Quarter Sessions records can be classified as follows:

● Great Rolls. These often date back to the sixteenth century and were used as a type of general file of business transacted at each sessions. Here you will find jury lists, justices' qualifications and oaths, sacrament certificates, returns of bailiffs, coroners' inquisitions, indictments, depositions, recognizances, presentments, writs, calendars of prisoners, removal orders and bastardy cases subject to appeal, matters concerning insolvent debtors, the highways, footways and bridges, and so on.

● Indictment Books. These will contain written accusations by one or more persons concerning an alleged crime.

● Order Books. These contain the formal records of court proceedings, but also include much useful information arising from the justices' non-criminal jurisdiction.

Here is a typical record of the judicial function of the Quarter Sessions:

Sessions held at Bedford, 11th April 1659:
Indictment of Anthony Bray, of Bedford, yeoman, and Magdalen his wife, "for counterfeiting false orders, supposing the robbing by Turkish pirates off the Isle of Akon in Ireland, and thereby deceiving the people by false collections". Both plead not guilty. He acquitted by verdict. She found guilty. To stand on the pillory at Bedford, Ampthill, and Woborne, on the market days two hours, with a paper on her hat expressing her offence and to be branded with the letter "C" on the

forehead with a hot iron at Bedford.
[From *Bedfordshire County Records Vol.II: the Sessions Minute Books 1651-1680*. No date. pp.50,51]

Here is a court dealing with a matter of bastardy maintenance:

Somerset General Sessions. Wells. January 1614/5.
Whereas in the third year of His Majesty's reign an order was made at Wells for John Churley of Stawley husbandman to give security for the discharge of that parish (from the maintenance) of the base child of Johane Brewer; and afterwards Nicholas Brewer grandfather of the child gave ten pounds for its use and benefit to John Govyer, Richard Potter, and Andrew Barby: it is now referred to Sir Francis Popham Knt., Thomas Warre and Thomas Brereton, Esquires to call before them the parties named and to take order to secure the money to the parish.
[From E.H. Bates (Ed.). *Quarter Sessions Records for the County of Somerset, Vol.I. 1607-1625*. Somerset Record Society. 1907. p.127]

Records of prisoners at Quarter Sessions may be found in more than one repository, and consist of annual criminal registers which have been gathered together under the counties of England and Wales. Many appear in the Home Office deposited documents at the Public Record Office. The Public Record Office also has calendars of prisoners in gaol after trial by Quarter Sessions. Other prisoners' records can be discovered in County Record Offices, while some still remain with prison or police authorities.

Calendar of the Prisoners in the Gaol of the City of Gloucester and County of the same city. For trial &c. at the Epiphany Sessions on Monday 11 January 1841:
John Bidmead aged 22. Committed November 10th 1840 on suspicion of having, within six weeks last past, feloniously stolen a wheelbarrow, of the value of twelve shillings, the property of Joseph Page, within the said City.
William Washington aged 42. Committed November 13th 1840 on the oath of William Henry Hughes and others, with having, on the 12th day of November last, within the Parish of St.John the Baptist, feloniously stolen about twenty-five yards of merino, of the value of twenty shillings, the property of the said William Henry Hughes.
Prisoners under Sentence in the City Gaol:
William Lea aged 23. Assault with intent. Spring Assizes 1839. Three years at hard labour.
Elizabeth Clewer aged 18. Larceny. The Sessions 1840. Two years at hard labour.
Summary Convictions:
George Smith aged 21. Rogue and vagabond. Convicted Nov.1840. Two cal. months.
William Etheridge aged 24. For leaving his master's service. Convicted Dec. 1840. 1 cal. month.
John Emery aged 25 and William Jones aged 23. For cutting the throat

and killing a dog. 2 cal. months each or pay a fine of £2. 17s. each.
[From calendars of prisoners, Gloucester Record Office]

Borough Sessions

Boroughs had their own jurisdiction by way of Borough Sessions. A typical borough would have a mayor and council, a gaol or bridewell and a workhouse. Borough Sessions documents will be similar to those of Petty and Quarter Sessions, and with luck should include details of apprentices, charities and coroners' inquests, together with burgess rolls, inhabitants' lists, rentals, vagrants' examinations, council minutes and so on.

The Clerk of the Peace

The county Clerk of the Peace was the officer appointed to assist the justices in Quarter Sessions and to keep county records. Such records were generated as a result of stipulations laid down by various Acts of Parliament and contain a wealth of documentation of great value to the family historian. The post of Clerk of the Peace was abolished in 1971/2.

You should find a great deal of useful information in the records of the Clerk of the Peace:

- Oaths of allegiance, declarations and sacrament certificates. A series of acts, commencing with the Test Act of 1672, insisted that all persons seeking significant public office should take oaths of allegiance and supremacy and provide evidence that they had received the Sacrament according to the custom of the Church of England.
- Lists of persons qualified to serve on juries.
- Lists of licensed victuallers, together with enrolled recognizances for the maintenance of order and good government of alehouses.
- Licences issued to butchers to allow them to kill, dress and sell meat in Lent and on fast days.
- Details of 'badgers', so called because they wore a badge to show that they had been licensed by the justices to sell corn and other victuals. Such people were also known as 'laders' or 'kidders'. Cattle drovers also had to apply for licences to trade. Dated licences and registers dating from 1551/2 to 1772 show names, occupations, abode and names of sureties.
- Registers and deputations of gamekeepers and certificates under various acts, commencing with the Game Laws of 1710.
- Copies of vagrants' passes and examinations, bastardy returns and removal orders.
- Turnpike Trusts; maintenance and repair of highways and bridges; registers of barges under the Defence Acts of 1798 and 1803.
- Inspection of woollen mills and other factories.
- Licensing of private asylums with certificates of admission, removals, discharges, deaths and the names of those who had absconded. Returns of pauper and criminal lunatics. Some asylum records may be subject to a closure rule.
- Poll books and registers of electors from 1832. See chapter 11.
- Licensing of sedan chairs, hackney carriages, cars and motor cycles.
- Returns of parish constables under the Parish Constables Act of 1842 until

around 1862. In the event, many county police forces had been set up under the County Police Act of 1839.

- Monthly returns of county police forces, giving disposition and numbers, with admissions registers stating the names of constables, their description, details of where they were born, whether married, and if so, the wife's birth place.
- Accounts of payments to the overseers by the County Treasurer for relief of militia men and their families, with lists of militia men and rolls of militia substitutes (who could come from anywhere in the country).
- Recruitment of men under the Navy Acts of 1794/5, with names of those enrolled.
- Maimed soldiers' petitions.
- Enrolled Deeds. Following the Statute of Inrolment of 1535, details of some transfers of land by bargain and sale were lodged with Clerks of the Peace.
- Bonds and contracts for transportation of felons to the American colonies and elsewhere.
- A number of registers of summary convictions and depositions was kept separately from the Quarter Sessions Great Rolls and Petty Sessions documents. These could include details of juvenile offenders under 14 years of age and of convictions for poaching and other offences against the game laws, the selling of beer without a licence and the swearing of profane oaths.
- Numerous societies and organisations were obliged to register with the clerk, especially friendly societies, savings banks and masonic lodges. Under the Unlawful Societies Act of 1799, all those who operated printing presses had to be registered, as did freemasons, who had to submit certificates and lodge registers giving members' names, addresses and occupations. The origins of freemasonry in England date back to the late seventeenth and early eighteenth centuries. If an ancestor is thought to have been a freemason, the name of his lodge and details of his date of entry may be obtained, on payment of a fee, from: The Secretary, The United Grand Lodge of England, Freemasons' Hall, 60 Great Queen Street, London WC2B 5AZ. The Society of Genealogists published *My ancestors were Freemasons* by Pat Lewis in 1999.

Charities

For many centuries past, bequests in wills have been left for charitable purposes, often according to the whims and eccentricities of the donor. A sum of money would usually be invested in stocks and consols, or in property which would generate an annual revenue, and the proceeds would be used for charitable or educational purposes.

Unfortunately, in some parishes, charity affairs were mismanaged to such an extent that bequests were frittered away. Other parish officials managed so well that after centuries some of these charities are still in existence today.

An Act of 1812 required trustees of charities (with some exceptions) to register a memorial with the Clerk of the Peace. This had to include a statement of real and personal estate, gross annual income, the object of the charity, the names of founders, trustees and persons in possession of the deeds of the foundation. Charity Commissioners were permanently established in 1853 to safeguard and oversee the control of existing charities. The usual types of charities provided endowments for charity schools, hospitals or apprenticeships. Many offered clothing and house repairs for poor men, women and children, together with some much-needed food - often in the form of a loaf of bread to be given to all who attended morning service on a certain Sunday in the year, with an enlightening sermon preached in memory of the benefactor.

In Thorverton, Devon, in 1694, Mary West left a yearly rent charge of 35s 2d out of a house in Exeter to provide petticoats for poor women of the parish. In 1628 Robert Drake of Littleham left land in trust for charitable and public uses for the relief of his poor relations!

A letter was found in the archives concerning a great-grandmother who in 1859 had been given ten shillings from a charity bequeathed by a Miss Elizabeth Benet of Wroughton, Wiltshire. An investment of two hundred pounds was to bring in about seven pounds annually to purchase new frocks for a number of poor girls in domestic service who had given satisfactory service. The letter reads as follows:

> *Mr Watts, Sir,*
> *I beg to inform you that we have a girl liveing with us name Mary*
> *Collier Daughter of John Collier She have no Mother She have been*
> *liveing with us Severel years She is a very good girl and I think She is*
> *Deserveing the Chariety money if you would be kind enough to give it*
> *to her it will be Thankfilly received by her.*
>
> > *from your most hu'ble Se'nt.*
> > *D. Cowley*

'D. Cowley' turned out to be Mary Collier's uncle, David, a baker in the village of Wroughton, with whom she had gone to live when she was seven years old on the death of her mother. You may feel that this makes a charming little cameo to include in a family history? You will find a reference to Elizabeth Benet's bequest in a huge two-volume folio publication of the House of Commons, dated 1816 and entitled *Abstracts of the returns of charitable donations for the benefit of poor persons made by the ministers and churchwardens of the several parishes and townships in England and Wales, 1786-1788:* 'Wroughton: Eliz. Benet. 1750. By will. For poor girls going out to service. Bequest in money. Now vested in Benit Gerrard. Gross amount given: £200.0.0; annual produce of the money: £7.0.0.' Such details make these abstracts of returns well worth consulting if you can find a set. Later in the nineteenth century comprehensive lists of charities were published in several volumes, and copies of *The annual charities register and digest* will bring you further up to date.

Charity documents preserved in the keeping of the Charity Commissioners are open for inspection at St Alban's House, 57-60 Haymarket, London SW1Y 4QX.

If you are interested in a specific charity then you need to make enquiries at the appropriate County Record Office to see whether its records have been deposited. Some Family History Societies have published transcripts of county and parish charity records, and trade directories can be useful if you wish to establish the existence of charities within particular localities.

Coroners' inquests

Coroners' inquests were held whenever a sudden death occurred. Relevant documentation will appear in Quarter Sessions records, and from the middle of the eighteenth century brief details of inquisitions, giving names, dates, places and cause of death, together with coroners' bills for fees and travelling expenses, should be found in separate collections in the Clerk of the Peace records. Records of Coroners' Inquisitions are closed to the public for 75 years. Certain cities and boroughs also had the right to hold inquests in the case of sudden and unexpected deaths. Here is an example from the City of Bath Coroners' records:

> *17 May 1792. James Hoskins and Edward Vallis were lying dead in the parish of Bathwick within the liberties of the City of Bath. Henry Phelps of Walcot, co.Somerset and Thomas Pridewood, also of Walcot, masons, said that on the 15th of May they saw the two labouring men at work in the crown of a stone arch under the area of a house situated in Henrietta Street belonging to Laurence Freed, builder. The stonework of the arch sank and fell in and the two men were suffocated and killed. Verdict: Accidental death with the materials of the said men coming to the value of 10s.*

Where a death certificate indicates that a coroner's inquest had been held, it is worthwhile seeking the actual inquest report and/or a newspaper account. Although parish register burial entries should indicate that a coroner's inquest took place, unfortunately many do not. Until recently, if an inquest jury recorded a verdict of death by murder or manslaughter, it was the coroner's task to send the offender to gaol to await trial. Until 1961 suicide was deemed to be a felony, and an inquest would be held; suicides were usually denied burial in consecrated ground.

The extensive records of Petty Sessions, Quarter Sessions and the Clerk of the Peace can be a fascinating area of research for the genealogist. Many County Record Offices publish guides to these records and you should attempt to familiarise yourself with the holdings of any particular record office before paying a visit.

The Assizes

The Assize courts, which dispensed justice over a wider area than simply one county, dealt with the most serious crimes such as murder, bigamy, treason and counterfeiting, but you will also find records of those accused of more trivial offences such as a failure to scour a ditch or repair a bridge. Assizes were held four times a year in various locations when the justices were sent on what were known as 'circuits'. English and Welsh counties were grouped into circuits; so, for example, the Oxford Circuit encompassed the counties of Berkshire, Gloucestershire, Herefordshire, Monmouthshire, Oxfordshire, Shropshire, Staffordshire and Worcestershire, with records dating from 1558 to 1971. The Western Circuit became particularly notorious in the years following the unsuccessful Monmouth Rebellion of 1685, when Judge Jeffreys meted out retribution to all those found guilty, sentencing many men to death or to transportation for life. The Assizes came to an end in 1971 and Crown Courts were established in their stead.

Records of the Assizes include indictments and depositions, gaol calendars, order books, minute books and other miscellaneous papers. All Assize records

Sentences of prisoners at Salisbury Assizes, 1800. *Sheep-stealing could bring the sentence of death, and the theft of stockings seven years' transportation.* (Wiltshire Record Office)

except those for London and Middlesex are held in the Public Record Office, classes JUST and ASSI 1-76, and a useful class list of the Clerks of Assize records was published by the List and Index Society in 1965. Matters were rather more complex in London, and you are referred to the London, Middlesex and Westminster and Surrey sections of *Quarter Sessions records for family historians* by Jeremy Gibson (4th. Ed. 1995) for an explanation of the way in which jurisdictions worked in the London area. Do bear in mind the caveat which appears in *Guide to the Middlesex Sessions records* (1965), that the voluminous sessions records for London 'are not a series to be tackled without careful preparation'. Manuscript and/or printed records are at the Corporation of London Record Office, the Guildhall Library, the London Metropolitan Archives (formerly the Greater London Record Office) and the Surrey Record Office.

Sometimes, where there were suspicious circumstances, a case would be referred to the Assizes from a Coroners' Court:

Forest of Dean Coroner's Division. Maurice Frederick Carter, elected Coroner. 23 March 1868.
Isaac Edmonds, 19 June 1868, at East Dean, died on the 17 June. Witnesses: James Williams, collier, Enoch Simmonds, foreman, James Woodhouse, collier, all of Ruspridge. Run over by a train of iron ore. A portion of his head was cut off. The trams were under the charge of William Drew. Verdict: manslaughter against William Drew. To take trial at the ensuing Assizes. Drew bailed under £50.
[From: Coroners' papers held at Shire Hall, Gloucester]

Assize indictments for the counties of Essex, Hertfordshire, Sussex, Surrey and Kent have been published by HMSO for various dates in the sixteenth and seventeenth centuries. For Kent these extend to the year 1675, and an example follows:

Maidstone Assizes, July 1662.
Indictment of Gregory Lylly of Lynsted, labourer, for burglary. On 1 May 1662 he burgled the house of Thomas Cranmer and stole a brass kettle (15s), a blanket (9s), 6 pewter dishes (£1), an iron scale beam (2s) and a bridle (6d).
On 1 May 1662 he burgled the house of Ann Newland, widow, and stole a copper kettle (10s) belonging to Simon Greenstreete.
Found guilty of larceny but not of burglary; claimed clergy but unable to read; to hang.

Another indictment should give food for thought to the dedicated family historian:

Maidstone Assizes. July 1675.
Indictment of Thomas Browne, yeoman, and Thomas Knowler, victualler, of Herne, for forging a record. On 5 May 1675, while pretending to search the parish register of Birchington for the baptism of Mary, daughter of Robert Oxbridge, they inserted the entry '18 Februarii baptizatus fuit Maria filia Roberti Oxenbridge' among the baptisms recorded for the year 1659.
The outcome of this indictment is not recorded.
[From J.S. Cockburn (Ed.) *Calendar of Assize Records: Kent indictments 1660-1675*. 1995. pp.55,377]

Haydn's *Dictionary of Dates*, a popular book published in many editions throughout the years, records much information about major crimes and summarises some of the sentences involved:

> *William Corder, for the murder of Maria Marten, Bury St. Edmunds, 8 August 1828. Hanged.*
> *Catherine Walsh, for the murder of her child. Old Bailey 14 April 1828. Hanged.*
> *The Rev'd. Dr. O'Halloran for forging a frank. 9 September 1818. Transportation.*
> *Mr Henry Fauntleroy, banker of London, for forgery. Hanged 30 October 1824.*
> *Bird, a boy of 14 yrs, for the murder of a child. Hanged 1 August 1831.*
> [From Haydn's *Dictionary of Dates*, 1866 edition]

Local and national newspapers are another useful source for reports of petty misdemeanours and the results of trials from Quarter Sessions, Assizes and coroners' courts:

> *Coroner's jury at Weymouth [Dorset] returned a verdict of wilful murder against Capt.Wolse, and the officer and men employed by him in the Impress Service, in the fatal affair occasioned by an attempt to rescue a seaman who had been impressed.*
> [From *Gloucester Journal*. 20 April 1803]

Courts of the Great Sessions for Wales from the sixteenth century to 1830 are held at the National Library of Wales, Aberystwyth. Wales only became part of the Assize system in the nineteenth century. Other related records may be found in the appropriate Welsh record offices.

The Palatinates of Chester, Lancaster and Durham had their own system of law courts (records are in the Public Record Office) but joined the Assize system during the nineteenth and twentieth centuries.

County records: hints and reminders

- If an apprentice was ill-treated by a master or mistress, the employer could be taken in front of the magistrates. In some cases the apprentice would be discharged and re-apprenticed elsewhere, and the master or mistress punished, but courts generally seem to have favoured masters in such disputes. Certificates of discharge may be found in Quarter Sessions records. If an apprentice absconded from his master, warrants would be issued for his or her arrest; these may be found in the records of the Petty Sessions or those of the Clerk of the Peace.
- If a husband deserted his wife and family, a warrant could be issued for his apprehension. Warrants may be found in parish, Petty or Quarter Sessions records.
- If a workhouse inmate absconded wearing institutional uniform, a warrant would be issued by the magistrates for his apprehension.
- By the 1844 Poor Law Amendment Act, a woman who had given birth to an illegitimate child was allowed to sue for maintenance in Petty Sessions courts.

Further reading

(County records)

Bateson, C. *The convict ships 1787-1868*. 1988.

Beddoe, D. *Welsh convict women: a study of women transported from Wales to Australia*. 1979.

Cale, M. *Law and society: an introduction to sources for criminal and legal history from 1800*. 1996.

Cockburn, J.C. *A history of English Assizes 1558-1714*. 1972.

Chambers, J. *The Swing Riots 1830*. A series of county-by-county volumes on machine breakers. Various dates.

Emmison, F.G. and Gray, I. *County records: Quarter Sessions, Petty Sessions, Clerk of the Peace and Lieutenancy*. 1987.

Emsley, C. *Crime and society in England 1750-1900*. 1991.

Gibson, J. *Local newspapers 1750-1920: a select location list*. 1987.

Gibson, J. *Quarter Sessions records for family historians: a select list*. (4th.Ed.) 1995.

Gibson, J. and Hunter, J. *Victuallers' licences: records for family and local historians*. (2nd.Ed.) 2000.

Griffiths, A. *Chronicles of Newgate*. 1987 reprint of an 1883 original.

Hawkings, D. *Bound for Australia*. 1987.

Hawkings, D. *Criminal ancestors: a guide to historical records in England and Wales*. 1992.

McLaughlin, E. *Quarter Sessions: your ancestor and the law*. 1995.

Norvall, M. and Rothman, D.J. *The Oxford history of prisons: the practice of punishment in western society*. 1995.

Oldham, W. *British convicts to the colonies*. 1990.

Richardson, J. *The local historians' encyclopedia*. (2nd.Ed.) 1986.

Saul, P. *The family historian's enquire within*. (5th.Ed.) 1995.

Sharpe, J.A. *Crime in early modern England 1550-1750*. 1986.

Wigfield, W. McDonald. *The Monmouth Rebels*. 1985.

(Charities)

Alvey, N. *From chantry to Oxfam: a short history of charities and charity legislation*. 1995.

Jordan, W.K. *The charities of rural England*. 1961.

(Coroners)

Cole, J.A. *Coroners' records of a Borough: Marlborough, Wiltshire, 1773-1835*. 1994.

Cole, J.A. *Coroners' inquisitions for the Borough of Malmesbury, Wiltshire, 1830 to 1854*. 1994.

Cole, J.A. *Wiltshire county coroners' bills 1815 to 1858*. 1997.

Gibson, J. *Quarter Sessions records for the family historian*. (4th.Ed.) 1995.

Gibson, J. and Rogers, C. *Coroners' records in England and Wales*. (2nd.Ed.) 2000.

Hunnisett, R. *Sussex Coroners' Inquests 1558-1603*. 1996.

Hunnisett, R. *Wiltshire Coroners' Bills 1752-1796*. 1981.

CHAPTER 11

Some Contemporary Printed Sources

Not everything of value to the family historian comes in the form of handwritten documents. Do take a close look at contemporary printed records whenever you get the chance.

Newspapers and magazines

Newspapers can be one of the most valuable aids to family historians. Most contain a wealth of names, and in effect are historic time capsules as they give news of events as they actually happened.

Newspapers began in the seventeenth century, but until the middle of the eighteenth century you will find little in them by way of personal items. From this time on they should always be searched for local, social and family events in an ancestral area; look for birth, marriage, death and burial notices, obituaries, divorce notices, lists of bankrupts, accounts of coroners' inquests, details of criminal activities, sales of property and business partnerships dissolved. Advertisements can also be great fun and very informative. Reports of deeds of valour or great service to the community may be found alongside those of sordid scandals. Try to look at more than one newspaper - perhaps one national and one local - to get a balanced view. Local, national and international news, political and social history - all will be found within the pages of a newspaper. You may even, for example, find nineteenth and early twentieth century lists of those visiting spa towns to take the waters!

Newspaper editors were always on the look-out for unusual or bizarre items to liven up their pages. Here's a typical example, quoted by Tom Wood in his 'Genealogical Miscellany' feature in *Family Tree Magazine* (April 1997):

> *The Lincolnshire, Rutland & Stamford Mercury*, 30 October 1812:
> *Marriage: On Thursday last at Tadcaster, Mr.Wilson of Bramham to Miss Bearcliff of Hutton, both near Tadcaster: the united ages of the Bride, Bride-groom and Bride-groom's Man, are 220 years, and what is very singular, those three persons have only one eye each.*

In 1666 the *London Gazette* reported the Great Fire of London as it actually happened, but the main value of this publication lies in its reports of official appointments within the state, the church and the military. Here you will also find details of medal awards, bankruptcy proceedings and much else. The Guildhall Library in London has a complete set of the *Gazette*.

Other important publications include the *Gentleman's Magazine* (1731 to 1868) and various similar publications, some short-lived but arranged along the same lines. The *Gentleman's Magazine* has both separate and cumulative indexes, which should help you locate lists of births, marriages and deaths, together with obituaries and details of bankrupts and promotions. A complete run of this publication may be found in the British Library, the Public Record Office and the Society of Genealogists. Several major reference libraries have full or partial sets and indexes. Expect to find the unexpected in the pages of this magazine:

> Obituary, 1811. Vol.81. Part 2. Page 197:
> *Suddenly, on his arrival at Derby, to be exhibited at the races (on the day he attained his 31st year), John Cummins, a dwarf, only 31 inches high.*

Never be surprised to find that an ancestor of yours was declared bankrupt. It happened even in the best of families. You are most likely to come across a reference to bankruptcy in the pages of a newspaper, in an eighteenth or nineteenth century publication such as the *Gentleman's Magazine* or one of its many imitators, or in *Stubbs' Commercial Year Book and Gazette Index* (first published in 1870). Legal records regarding bankruptcy may be found in the Public Record Office, and adjudications have appeared in print in the *London Gazette* since 1684, and continue to do so. Entrepreneurial printers were not slow to benefit from the afflictions of others, so you will find various published lists of bankrupts; these not only provided information to creditors and others, but no doubt served to titillate the curiosity of neighbours. The Society of Genealogists has published an alphabetical list of bankrupts, 1774-1786, and a bankrupt directory, 1820-1843, on microfiche. Other ephemeral publications of a similar type include those which feature unclaimed dividends and money, next-of-kin being sought, and so on. If you can find a copy of *Missing heirs and next of kin: chance is the salt of life - you may be one of the lucky ones*, published by the *News of the World* earlier this century, you should be well entertained.

The Times newspaper (from 1785) is a storehouse of useful information. There are printed and CD-ROM indexes to its contents, and many libraries have microfilm copies of the newspaper itself from its early days.

The Illustrated London News, founded in 1842, cast its net wider than London itself, reporting happenings at home and abroad. Here you will find reports of Paris fashions alongside the names of bankrupts, accounts of disasters next to weather reports. Look out, too, for advertisements and for announcements such as the following:

> *21 August 1847. Bristol Consistory Court sentenced a brewer named Evans to stand in church in a white sheet for having defamed the character of a young woman.*
> *8 March 1862. Two witnesses and one attorney who were engaged at the Liverpool Police Court yesterday week respectively rejoiced in the names Debt, Death and Daggers.*

2 July 1864. More than 10,000 emigrants arrived at the port of New York in the week ending June 4.
12 January 1865. Gales all over the country.

The largest collection of newspapers in the United Kingdom is at the British Library Newspaper Library, Colindale Avenue, London NW9 5HE. The library is open from 10 am to 4.45 pm, Monday to Saturday, with closure on public holidays and for one week in late October for stocktaking. Briefly, the collection includes national and local daily and weekly newspapers from around 1800, periodicals, magazines, trade papers and yearbooks from the mid nineteenth century onwards and large holdings of Commonwealth and foreign newspapers. Of particular interest for family historians are the various nonconformist periodicals and magazines and the *Poor Law Unions' Gazette*.

The catalogue system provides two sets of entries, one arranged geographically by countries, counties and towns and the other by titles of newspapers. Many of the newspapers are now on microfilm to prevent wear and tear on the originals. A reader's ticket is needed, but this is usually provided on the spot on production of identification such as a driving licence.

Some bibliographies of newspapers for certain counties have been published, and these are worth checking. It is also advisable to take a general map of the areas you intend to search to help when deciding just where to look for newspaper coverage of a particular area. Photocopying facilities are available at the Newspaper Library.

The Burney Collection of Newspapers from 1603 to 1800 is housed in the British Library, as is the fascinating Thomason Collection of printed ephemera for the Civil War and Commonwealth period.

The Bodleian Library at Oxford has a collection of newspapers dating from 1622 to 1800. In the case of the British Library and the Bodleian, any request to use their collections must be made in writing, giving your reasons for wanting to consult these newspapers.

Many County Record Offices, local studies libraries and reference libraries hold microfilm or original copies of their local newspapers, often from the commencement of publication.

The India Office Library has a collection of Indian newspapers in English dating from 1780, which is one of the finest in existence. The late nineteenth and early twentieth centuries are particularly well covered. This is an on-going collection which includes comprehensive collections of serials and official gazettes published in and relating to South Asia. There is a catalogue system with full entries under both title and place of publication. Photocopying facilities are available. The address is: Oriental and India Office Collections, British Library, 96 Euston Road, London NW1 2DB.

Directories, poll books and electoral registers

The first printed directory appeared in London in 1677, listing merchants and bankers. From these modest beginnings directories grew in size and scope to include private residents, officials, craftsmen, farmers, carriers and others, with thousands of names and addresses. Often a short but invaluable history of the village, town or city will be included; here you will find the names of local landowners and dignitaries past and present, details of local buildings of importance, charities, chapels, churches, schools, canals and railways, together

52 KILMARNOCK AND KINGUSSIE ADVERTISEMENTS. [1907.

M. MUIR & CO., Kilmarnock,

Builders, Contractors and Monumental Sculptors.

ESTIMATES GIVEN FOR ALL KINDS OF MASON, BRICK AND DIGGER WORK.

M. MUIR & CO.'S

Monumental Works,

BANK PLACE, Kilmarnock (opposite Post Office).
'PHONE 104.

MONUMENTS, TOMBSTONES, CROSSES, and every style of Cemetery Memorial, in Granite, Marble and Freestone.

The Largest, Finest, and Cheapest Stock in the West of Scotland.

Particulars and Prices on application.

THOMAS THOMSON & SONS,

General Contractors and Coal Agents.

Works supplied with Best Steam Coal and Dross.

ESTIMATES ON APPLICATION
FURNITURE REMOVAL
THOMAS THOMSON & SONS.
BY ROAD

Truck Loads to any Station.

FURNITURE REMOVALS A SPECIALITY.

46, High Street, and 41, Dean Street, Kilmarnock.

TELEPHONE 10Y.

Telegrams, "GRANT, KINGUSSIE."

W. GRANT & SON,

Tweed Manufacturers,

—KINGUSSIE.—

Carriage Rugs.   **Home Spuns.**

——SPECIALITIES IN——

CRÊME TWEEDS, RUGS & PLAIDS ; also The " FLORA MACDONALD " TWEED.

Advertisement page from Slater's Directory for Scotland, 1907.

with a precise location of the place in question and the number of inhabitants. The main listings will give the names of public houses and posting inns, with a list of carriers, stating their names and times of their arrivals and departures. Many large towns had their own directories from the late eighteenth century onwards, and you may find inhabitants listed by street as well as alphabetically, but smaller places were only catered for at intervals, often being included with the nearest town. Publishers who produced directories for most of Britain include Pigot, Slater, Kelly and White.

Trade and street directories can be of great help if you are trying to locate an address in order to consult one of the census returns from 1841 to 1891. Be aware that many tradesmen and others of modest means living in towns would move address frequently, often from one rented dwelling to another.

Several early county directories such as those published by Pigot in the 1820s and 1830s are now appearing as reprints, and a number can be purchased on microfiche.

The first telephone directory appeared in April 1880. As the telephone became a popular means of fast personal contact for business and personal reasons, so directories giving names, addresses and numbers were issued and even those who ran quite a modest business may have had a telephone during the early years of the twentieth century.

Even modern telephone directories, in print or on CD-ROM, can be useful in helping you locate the present-day occurrence of an unusual surname which interests you. Why not plot such distribution on a map and try contacting some individuals to see if they fit in with the family tree?

Directories may be found in larger reference libraries, local studies libraries or County Record Offices. One of the largest collections of provincial and London directories is held by the Guildhall Library, Aldermanbury, London, while BT Archives, 3rd Floor, Holborn Telephone Exchange, London WC1V 7EE, has a collection of telephone directories which can be viewed by prior appointment.

Poll books, not to be confused with poll taxes, first appeared in the late seventeenth century and can be thought of as directories of the more prosperous inhabitants of any particular place. Entrepreneurial local printers were usually responsible for these publications; the information they provide and the way in which that information is classified and arranged is not uniform, but all constitute significant name lists of county and borough voters in parliamentary and certain other elections. Some give trades and addresses, all specify the candidate(s) voted for in the days when such information was public knowledge, and there are often lists of voters living out-of-county.

Not everyone approved of the idea that voters' names and voting preferences should be published for all to see, and J. Stockdale of Pall Mall's printed Westminster Poll Book for 1818 includes the text of a handful of abusive letters he had previously received. He is called a 'blackguard', a 'vile wretch', a 'footman's fag', a 'despicable parasite' and 'the basest reptile that ever crawled upon the face of the earth'. One enraged inhabitant of Westminster threatened to pursue him 'with unrelenting vengeance...as a warning to all traitors', more than one elector offered to put him to death, and a correspondent rather lacking in the refinements of spelling upbraided him in the following terms:

Mr Stokdale: Hiff you poublishis hour names has woted for Burditt,
dam my blud hiff i wont nok yoor branes hout the fust time has i

*ketchis yoo hand i vont never rest til i finds yoo - i ham has
hindependint a gemmen has any man thof i does karry hon the traid
hof an naker. i ham sur a Pouple Hof Kalib Baldvin.*

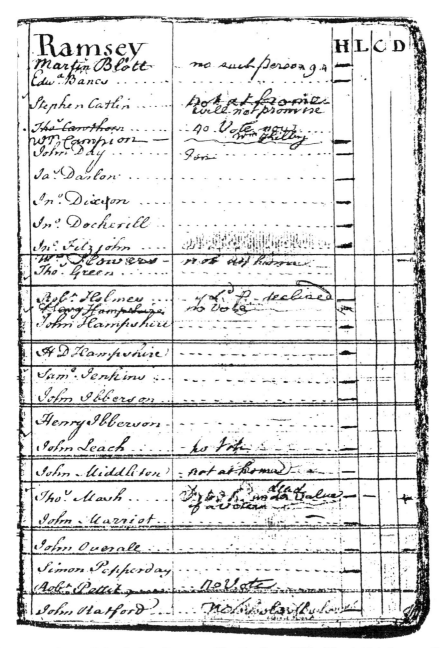

A manuscript poll book for Ramsey, Huntingdon, 1790. *The initial letters of the
candidates' surnames head the right-hand columns.* (Huntingdon Record Office)

Poll books continued to be published up to the General Election of 1868; their final demise was occasioned by the introduction of the secret ballot. These were essentially ephemeral publications printed in limited quantities, so originals are very scarce. Copies should have found their way into County Record Offices and local studies libraries, and there are significant collections at the Society of Genealogists, the University of London Institute of Historical Research, the Guildhall Library, the British Library and elsewhere. Stuart Raymond (author of the FFHS Genealogical Bibliographies of Counties) has begun publishing facsimile reprints of certain poll books at an affordable price.

Following the Reform Act of 1832, registers of electors with details of their qualifying property began to be printed. Unlike poll books, these list all eligible electors, not just those who voted in a particular poll. You should find electoral registers in County Record Offices or local studies libraries.

Parliamentary Papers

The same nineteenth-century thoroughness which inaugurated national registration of births, marriages and deaths and decennial censuses is also much in evidence when it comes to Parliamentary Papers. Very few aspects of life, public and private, escaped the scrutiny of various Select Committees and Royal Commissions: here you will find investigations into the work of men, women and children in agriculture, coal, tin and copper mining, lacemaking and brickmaking; you can read about climbing boys, dame schools, crime and punishment, apprenticeship of children from the south to mills in the north, child prostitution and the boarding out of workhouse children. Most reports contain names, and many contain thousands of names. The evidence given to the investigating commissioners can be read in full, and maybe your own ancestors were amongst those who gave their testimony, helping in some small way to change the law and to make life better for working people? Here is an example from the 1832 Parliamentary Commission into Factories:

> **Evidence given by Samuel Coulston, tailor, living near Leeds with three daughters, the youngest aged 7 yrs.**
> *Commissioner: At what time did the girls go to the mills?*
> *Samuel: For about six weeks they have gone at three o'clock in the morning and finished at ten or nearly half past at night.*
> *Commissioner: What intervals were allowed for rest or refreshment?*
> *Samuel: Breakfast a quarter of an hour, dinner half an hour and drinking a quarter of an hour.*
> *Commissioner: Did this excessive term of labour occasion much cruelty?*
> *Samuel: Yes, with being so very much fatigued the strap was frequently used.*
> *Commissioner: Have any of your children been strapped?*
> *Samuel: Yes, every one.*
> *Commissioner: Had your children any opportunity of sitting during those long days of labour?*
> *Samuel: No.*

Parliamentary Papers are a largely untapped source for family history. Many may now be seen on microform in the larger reference libraries, and can usually be ordered through the inter-library loan system.

Maps

We've included maps amongst 'contemporary printed sources', though many of the most interesting ones are hand-drawn in manuscript rather than printed.

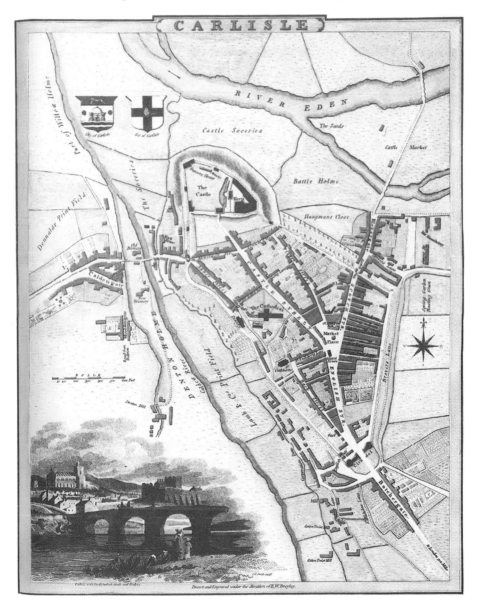

Carlisle in the early 1800s, *from* The British Atlas: Comprising a Complete Set of County Maps of England and Wales; with a General Map of Navigable Rivers and Canals; and Plans of Cities and Principal Towns.

Family historians can make good use of maps of all types, from general maps of Britain as a whole to detailed estate or town maps if these can be found.

Maps date back to very early times, some of the earliest being rudimentary if not inaccurate. Nevertheless, you could find early maps by Camden, Speed or Ogilby not only quaint, but also useful as your research takes you back in time.

The Public Record Office houses a great quantity and variety of maps, and County Record Offices, local studies libraries and reference libraries between them usually hold extensive collections for their own area, ranging from railway, canal, estate and manorial survey maps to town and city plans of varying dates. Many deposited family and estate records contain privately-commissioned maps of the owners' land and property holdings, and you will also need to look for enclosure and tithe maps, with their accompanying documentation giving names, acreage and rent.

When researching in a record office or library, it's a good idea to take with you maps which cover a county or region, together with a parish map if you can obtain one. That way you can get a feel for the geography of the area in which your ancestors lived; you can see which parishes lie next to each other, you can gain an idea of communication routes between them by road, track, river, canal or railway, and if you discover a reference to a parish which is new to you, you can soon establish where it is. At some point you'll need to refer to, or to buy, a good gazetteer, preferably one produced in Victorian times, which will be full of detail. If you come across a place name that even a good gazetteer won't identify, either refer to the extensive place name lists published to accompany census reports, or use a volume in the English Place Name Society series of books, if one exists for your county. History and geography are not separate subjects, as they taught us at school - they are all part of one seamless robe.

Further reading

(Newspapers and magazines)

British Newspaper Catalogue of the British Newspaper Library. 8 Vols.
Chapman, C.R. *An introduction to using newspapers and periodicals.* 1993.
Cranfield, G.A. *Handlist of English provincial newspapers and periodicals 1700-1760.* 1961.
Gibson, J. *Local newspapers 1750-1920: a select list.* 1987.
Handover, P.M. *A history of the London Gazette 1665-1965.* 1965.
McLaughlin, E. *Family history from newspapers.* (2nd.Ed.) 1994.
Murphy, M. *Newspapers and local history.* 1991.
The Newspaper Press Directory.
Tercentenary handlist of English and Welsh newspapers, magazines and reviews 1620-1920. 1920. Reprint, 1966.
Westmancoat, J. *Newspapers.* 1985.
Williams, K. *The English newspapers: an illustrated history to 1900.* 1977.
Willings' *Annual Press Guide.*

(Directories, poll books, electoral registers)

Atkins, P.J. *The directories of London, 1677-1977.* 1990.
Gibson, J. and Rogers, C. *Electoral registers since 1832; and burgess rolls.* (2nd.Ed.) 1990.

Gibson, J. and Rogers, C. *Poll books c1696 - 1872*. (3rd.Ed.) 1994.

Goss, C.W.F. *The London directories 1677-1855*. 1950.

Humphery-Smith, C.R. *A catalogue of directories and poll books in the possession of the Institute of Heraldic and Genealogical Studies*. 1978. A new edition is in active preparation.

Norton, J.E. *Guide to the national and provincial directories of England and Wales, excluding London, published before 1856*. 1984.

Shaw, G. and Tipper, A. *British directories: a bibliography and guide to directories published in England and Wales (1850-1950) and Scotland (1773-1950)*. (2nd.Ed.) 1997.

Sims, J. *A handlist of British parliamentary poll books*. 1984.

Society of Genealogists: *Catalogue of directories and poll books in the possession of the Society of Genealogists*. 1994.

Tupling, G.H. *Lancashire directories 1684-1957*. 1968.

(Parliamentary Papers)

Bennett, A.A. *Working life: child labour through the nineteenth century*. 1991.

Ford P.& G. *Hansard's breviate of British Parliamentary Papers 1696-1834*. 1953.

Ford P.& G. *A select list of British Parliamentary Papers 1833-1899*. 1969.

(Maps)

Bartholomew's Gazetteer of Great Britain. Various dates, but refer to an edition before 1974 for information regarding historic counties.

Baynton-Williams, A. *Town and city maps of the British Isles 1800-1855*. 1992.

Booth, J. *Looking at old maps*. 1979.

David & Charles (publishers). Reprints of the first editions of *1" Ordnance Survey maps for England and Wales*.

English Place Name Society. Series of place name publications for English counties.

Foot, W. *Maps for family history*. 1994.

Gardner, D.E. et al. *A genealogical atlas of England and Wales*. 1965.

Gardner, D.E. et al. *A genealogical atlas of Ireland*. 1964.

Gardner, D.E. et al. *A genealogical atlas of Scotland*. 1963.

Gilbert, M. *British history atlas*. 1968.

Harley, J.B. *Maps for the local historian: a guide to British sources*. 1972.

Hartop, B.B. and Rodger, M. *Johnston's Gazetteer of Scotland*. 1958.

Humphery-Smith, C.R. *The Phillimore atlas and index of parish registers: England, Wales and Scotland*. 1995.

Oliver, R. *Ordnance survey maps: a concise guide for historians*. 1995.

Pigot & Co.'s British atlas: counties of England, comprising the counties of England with additional maps of England and Wales, and London 1840. 1990.

Smith, F. *A genealogical gazetteer of Scotland* 1979.

Smith, F. *A genealogical gazetteer of England*. 1977.

CHAPTER 12

Manorial and
Other Landholding Records

Did your ancestor own land, and if so, on what terms? If he didn't own it, under what conditions did he occupy it? The concept of land ownership is deeply imbedded in the collective psyche of most developed nations, and has been so for centuries.

Most land in England and Wales today is registered; its ownership is a matter of official record, and details about it are readily discovered. How different, then, from the way things were for centuries past, when bundles of dusty documents recording a succession of transfers of land from one person to another were carefully stored away to prove that the present owner's title to land was a legitimate one! For safety's sake, details from such documents were often copied onto rolls which formed the records of various courts of law, a process known as 'enrolment', but very often no public record was made at all. Following Land Registration Acts passed in the nineteenth century and those of 1925 to 1971, it was no longer necessary to keep deeds once a title was registered, and many were sold for scrap, used to help the war effort or acquired by bookbinders.

We will start with a look at the manorial system, one which had power over people's behaviour as well as over the ownership or occupancy of land.

Manorial records

Our ancestors must sometimes have found it irksome that they were caught within a web of legal and administrative jurisdictions which could affect their everyday lives. They were answerable to the parish and to the Archdeacon or the Bishop; wrongdoers could find themselves hauled before the ecclesiastical courts, Petty Sessions, Borough Sessions, Quarter Sessions or Assizes according to the severity of an alleged crime.

This was not the end of the story, however. There were other long-established jurisdictions which made regulations and set parameters within which individuals could operate, complete with punishments and sanctions to punish those who did not conform. Forest Courts had significant powers over those royal domains which monarchs originally used for hunting purposes, and if you visit the Speech House deep in the Forest of Dean in Gloucestershire to this day, you'll find a Forest Court House which is still operational. Counties were divided into Hundreds (sometimes known as 'Wapentakes' or some other term), and many people found themselves answerable to Hundred Courts, having to attend meetings as often as once a month.

The one system of courts which impinged most often upon people's lives, however, be they country or town dwellers, was that of the manor courts. The beauty of manorial records for the family historian is that they can take you, with luck, back in time before the advent of parish registers in 1538.

Following the victory of William the Conqueror and his followers in 1066, very few of the ruling classes in Britain were other than Norman sympathisers. The feudal system came into operation, whereby even wealthy landowners held their land from the King as tenants in chief; below them on the social scale came other tenants who held land of their lord and had certain duties imposed upon them as a result.

The manorial system formalised these relationships, concerning itself with the organisation of the affairs of the manor, including the cultivation of the soil and the land tenure of the tenants. In effect it was its own system of local government in which everyone knew his or her place. It did not altogether operate as a local dictatorship, however, for there was a relatively effective system of law and order which even the Lord of the Manor was expected to observe, and feudal relationships of interdependence operated, in theory at least, by way of custom and common consent.

The villein, an unfree tenant, was very much under the will of the Lord. He held land at the Lord's will, but was given very few privileges. He was allowed to graze his cattle on the common, and also to collect hay and firewood. He was not usually able to possess freehold land, nor even let his daughter marry without the Lord's permission. The villein paid the Lord a rent for his land, usually in kind or by working part of the time for him, and when a villein died, a fine known as a 'heriot' was levied before the next person in line could take over the land holding. Gradually, especially after the Black Death which reduced the supply of labour, the villein was able to improve his position on the social scale.

Another class of tenants at the poorer end of the feudal hierarchy included serfs or cottars. The exact meaning of these terms and the conditions under which such people lived often varied from manor to manor. Some were bought and sold like slaves.

The essence of the manorial system lay in the various forms of land tenure:

A **freeholder** was a landowner, who, although paying rent to the Lord, was not obliged to carry out any of the feudal tasks associated with the agricultural life of the manor.

A **leaseholder** held his land by virtue of a lease that would expire after a specified term of years or upon the deaths of each of a number of named individuals.

A **copyholder** held his land of the Lord by custom of the manor, his title consisting of a copy of the court roll in which his admittance is referred to. Even wealthy landowners who might hold many acres of freehold land could also be copyhold tenants and thereby owe allegiance to the appropriate Lord of a Manor. Copyhold tenure was only abolished in 1926, though isolated examples of its use may be found at a later date. You may find that your house deeds include examples of its use. The end of copyhold meant that there was no longer a need for court rolls or copies from such rolls to be retained for legal purposes. Fortunately certain legal restraints were applied at that time. So manorial documents, which are still bought and sold for their antiquarian interest and may well be in private hands, are not allowed to be exported abroad without specific permission being sought. Not only that, but a Manorial Documents Register has been established; this is a compilation of manors, arranged in county order, which details the location of all known existing records, but only where an owner has registered the fact of their existence. Possibly as many unregistered documents exist as registered ones; a close study of the descent of an individual manor might still lead you to a collection of manorial records held by a solicitor or in a private muniment box. By the time the register was established the manorial system was already in decline, and many documents had already been lost, destroyed or used for lampshades. The register will be found at The Royal Commission on Historical Manuscripts, Quality House, Quality Court, Chancery Lane, London WC2A 1HP. A personal visit is recommended, though you could always make a written enquiry concerning the whereabouts of documents for one or two specified manors. Note that this is a register only; Quality House can let you know where records may be found, but does not hold such documents itself. If you know precisely where your ancestors came from, you might find it useful to contact the local County Record Office in the first instance.

Records of proceedings in manorial courts
At the heart of the manorial system lay the regular meetings of the Court Baron and the Court Leet which, at times, functioned as one. Not every Lord had the privilege of holding a Court Leet, which would deal with many minor offences (including hedges or ditches being in disrepair, unruly dogs and so on) and was in effect a law court of first instance. Attendance at the Court Baron was compulsory for tenants, and the manor court rolls or books which record the proceedings can yield information of great genealogical value. At first sight, a handwritten record of manor court proceedings can be intimidating, especially if the language used is Latin, as it often was until the year 1733 except for the period of the Interregnum. Fortunately, the arrangement of manor court records follows a fairly consistent pattern. The name of the manor should appear first, followed by a statement outlining the kind of court it was, the name of the Lord of the Manor and that of his Steward (who would often preside in the Lord's stead), then the date. Sometimes the heading at the top of a court record will refer to a 'Customary Court'; you will also often see reference to the 'View of Frankpledge', a hangover from an earlier system whereby each person within a tithing of the manor was responsible for the good behaviour of every other person in that tithing. The jury or 'homage' would then be listed, with the names of those who were 'essoined' (that is, excused their attendance) and those defaulters who had failed to attend without excuse and were thus at the Lord's 'mercy'. Then come details of such matters as squabbles between neighbours, transfers and surrenders of land, the management of common land, and sometimes a recitation of the rights of the Lord of the Manor and his tenants and of the customs of the manor. As land or property changed hands at death or for some other reason, you might find several generations of your ancestors named, with relationships specified.

Luckily, help is at hand to enable you to make some sense out of manorial documents. Denis Stuart's *Manorial Records* (1992) should be a great help, especially when read in conjunction with the same author's *Latin for local and*

Jurors to Enquire for our Sovereign Lord the King and the Lord of the Manor aforesaid.

John Say ——— Sworn	William Humphris Mons. Coller
Theophilus Johnson	William Neath
Charles Barrett	Stephen King
Thomas Maysey } Sworn	John Morris } Sworn
George Hunter	John Bristow
Thomas Coventry	William Ewen
William Bonny	William Humphris Shep:keeper

First The Jurors *afore said* upon their Oaths Present ~~and afore said~~ John Hobbs Constable for the Borough, William Kemble Tythingman for the Borough, Thomas Maysey Tythingman of Lower Town, George Hunter Tythingman for West Swindon, Thomas Mills and John Humphris Carnalls, Anthony Farmer & W.m Parker Leather Sealers, Matthew Harwell Ale Taster, William Ewen and Henry Pinnick Affeerors, and Richard Heath Beadle and Cryer who were all Sworn to Serve their respective Offices for the year ensueing accordingly.

Also — They Present John Godding Ephraim Hollogg and John Walker forthwith to repair their several Chimneys being very ruinous and greatly out of repair and not only a publick Nusance to the Inhabitants but very dangerous and if the said Chimneys are not Sufficiently repaired *within the month* ~~by past~~ ~~Subjecting for the forfeit~~ ~~ to pay~~ ~~and for which they do amerce the~~ Ten Shillings for each Chimney.

Also — They Humbly request and desire the Lord of the Mannor to repair the Market Cross, and provide Weight and Scales for the Carnalls, and also to Erect a Blind House within the Borough the same being greatly wanted.

Also — They present all the persons under written who Owe suit and Service to this Court and have not appeared here this Day and Amerce them four pence each. To Witt Joshua Lewis, Richard Mills, Peter Woofford, W.m Tinson Sen.r W.m Tinson Jun.r Anthony Martin, Ambrose Barrett, William Catwell, Tho.s Ross, being all duly Summoned.

Goddard Manor Court Book, Swindon, 1750. *The men constituting the sworn homage or jury are listed first, then their presentments.* (Wiltshire Record Office & Capt J.W.H. Goddard)

family historians (1995). In the event, those who were charged with recording the proceedings of a manor court needed a manual of some sort to help them on their way. Many such guides were published, and you should find a copy in a specialist law library. Sir William Scroggs's *The practice of Courts Leet and Courts Baron*, published in the eighteenth century, includes 'Full and exact Directions for holding the said Courts, and making up the Rolls or Records thereof'. One of the most popular manuals for court officials was Giles Jacob's *The Complete Court Keeper*, which contains, inter alia, 'The Manner of holding Courts Leet, Courts Baron, and Courts of Survey...and the Forms of Entring those Courts in the Minute-Books and in the Court-Rolls...'. Because Jacob's book went through many editions, it is possible to use an early example (the Second Edition of 1715, for instance), which contains much text in Latin, and compare it with a later edition, after the 1733 watershed (such as the Sixth Edition of 1764), in order to see a translation of the wording from one to the other. We are not talking here about Classical Latin, but the more mundane use of that language for the events of everyday life - so with patience you should soon become more confident in reading apparently illegible documents.

If you're lucky, the manor which interests you may have surviving accounts, rentals or a survey of its lands and tenants; if so, you'll have plenty of names to trawl through until you find the ones that interest you. If you're even luckier, there may be printed transcripts of manorial proceedings which feature your own family and include the names of friends and neighbours. Printed volumes exist for manor courts held at Wakefield, Manchester, Wimbledon and many other places.

Your ancestor may have committed one of a number of crimes that warranted his or her appearance before a court. Anita Travers, in an article published in *The Genealogists' Magazine* [Vol. 21, No. 1. March 1983] points out that there were more than sixty offences liable to be dealt with by the Court Leet and more than forty by the Court Baron. These included such offences as murder, treason, rape, arson, counterfeiting and burglary, all of which were referred to the Assizes. Less heinous offences such as assault, bloodshed, forestalling and regrating, using false weights and measures, breaking the assizes of bread and ale, selling corrupt victuals, bawdiness, eavesdropping, gossiping, diverting or fouling highways or watercourses or failing to maintain the watch or 'hue and cry' (that is, rallying all available help to pursue an offender), were punishable by a fine or a period in the stocks or pillory.

Be careful: a manor and a parish did not necessarily cover the same area. Often there were a number of parishes in one manor or a number of manors in one parish, the latter being more likely, as there were always many more manors than parishes in the country as a whole. Sometimes you will find various manors grouped together into what was known as a 'Liberty'.

There was a delegation of responsibilities by the Lord of the Manor to various people to enable the system to run as smoothly as possible:

- A **Steward** (or 'Seneschal') was appointed and would often run the manor on the lord's behalf. He would preside over the court meetings, ensure that everything was conducted in a proper fashion, and keep a written record of proceedings. Note that sometimes a 'Lord' of a Manor might be a corporate body or an ecclesiastical dignitary such as a bishop.
- The **Bailiff** was an overseer of the estate who was appointed by the Steward

and was often referred to as the Steward's Manager. He was usually responsible for the announcement of the court meetings and could act as the record keeper.

- The **Reeve** was responsible for arranging those duties which the tenants were obliged to fulfil for the Lord. He was elected and paid for by the villeins and was usually a member of that class.

Manorial Rental, Aldermaston, Berks, *taken at the death of Sir Humphrey Forster, Bart, 1711. Freehold and copyhold quit rents are kept separate.*

- A **Hayward** was responsible for the general repair of hedges and fences around the manor. It was he who rounded up stray cattle and impounded them in the pinfold, and acted as agent for the Lord concerning the sale of corn and other similar commodities.
- The **Constable**'s duty, then as now, was to keep the peace. He also summoned jurors to serve in the courts.

Manorial terms

Some of the unfamiliar words used in manorial records have been referred to in passing. Others include: **affeerors** (officers appointed by the court to assess penalties for proven offences); **amercement** (a fine paid in the manorial court by a tenant who was said to be 'in mercy' of the court); **custumal** (details of the customs of a manor); **demesne** (land retained by a Lord of the Manor for his own use); **fealty** (an oath of allegiance to the Crown made by an incoming tenant); **messuage** (a dwelling house with outbuildings and surrounding land); **moiety** (usually a half portion of an estate); **seizin/seisin** (possession of land rather than ownership of it); **entail** (an estate which passed to lineal descendants only, said to be held by 'fee tail'); **waste** (uncultivated land within a manor).

Other records of landholding

Deeds

The Statute of Inrolment of 1535 encouraged individuals to enrol details of transfers of land by bargain or sale. Many such enrolled deeds are to be found in the Public Record Office, but some were lodged with the Clerk of the Peace and will be among county archives. These enrolled deeds, where they exist, can give an indication of an ancestor's place of residence, together with family names.

During the early eighteenth century an attempt was made to establish local deeds registries, but such a scheme only came to fruition in the counties of Middlesex (from 1708) and Yorkshire (West Riding from 1704, East Riding from 1708 and North Riding from 1736). Registration was not compulsory, but was generally observed, resulting in an exceptionally useful series of records. These registries are now closed, but their archives are held at:

Middlesex Registry of Deeds, London Metropolitan Archives, 40 North-ampton Road, London EC1R OHB

Registry of Deeds, West Yorkshire Archive Service Headquarters, Newstead Road, Wakefield, W. Yorks WF1 2DE

East Riding Registry of Deeds, County Hall, Champney Road, Beverley HU17 9BA

North Riding Registry of Deeds, North Yorkshire County Record Office, County Hall, Northallerton, N. Yorks DL7 8AF

There are Registries of Deeds for Scotland and Ireland:

National Archives of Scotland, HM Register House, Princes Street, Edinburgh EH1 3YY

Registry of Deeds, Henrietta Street, Dublin.

Enclosures

Until the eighteenth century most land in England was cultivated on the 'open field' system which was generally on the principle of three arable fields, one of which was laid down with crops for the winter, the second sown in the spring and the third left to lie fallow. A farmer or tenant would hold a number of strips in each field. There could be no choice or variety, as every strip in the field had to be sown with the same crop and cultivated and harvested at the same time. In addition, each strip had to be separated by a small earthen bank, giving a network of footpaths to enable men to have access to their strips without encroaching on neighbours' plots.

Obviously this system was not economical; men would quarrel, one would weed and cultivate and another would not. Eventually the system of enclosing the land by hedges and ditches gained momentum, and holdings were consolidated and enlarged. Not only that, but there was division and take-over of the common land, where the poorest men and women had been able, from time immemorial, to sow a few crops and graze their animals. Even the ancient right to wood and wasteland disappeared under this system of enclosure, which brought about untold misery and privation to many labourers and their families, almost to the point of starvation. Some counties such as Essex, Surrey, Devon and parts of the Midlands had experienced enclosure during Tudor times, but over a large part of central and northern England the method of open-field farming continued until well into the eighteenth century.

The introduction of new crops and farming procedures by such men as Jethro Tull, Thomas Coke and Viscount Townshend revolutionised farming methods; this, together with the fact that enclosure of the fields and commons benefited the wealthy landowners, served to accelerate the rush to enclose every possible piece of land. From 1760 to 1797 some 15,000 private Enclosure Acts were passed through Parliament. In 1801 a General Enclosure Act was passed which did away with the need for private Acts, and in 1836 another Enclosure Act was passed which authorised enclosure of the fields if two-thirds of the interested parties were in agreement. In 1854 yet another Enclosure Act gave commissioners the right to consider any applications they received, and they were also authorised to allocate some land for exercise and recreation. At long last the enclosures were complete and were eventually brought to an end by the Curtailment of Enclosures Act in 1876. A certain number of open fields with their strips have been preserved for posterity, such as those at Braunton in North Devon and at Laxton in Nottinghamshire.

A good deal of documentation accompanied the practice of enclosure, and can have great value in helping you place your ancestor in his or her surroundings. For private and general Acts of the late eighteenth century onwards, the original award document with map was given to the parish concerned, with a copy to the Clerk of the Peace. At least one of these versions should be in the appropriate County Record Office, though some have found their way into the Public Record Office.

Feet of fines

A 'fine' in this sense refers to the final agreement made in writing at the end of a law suit that a particular person had title to a specific piece of land. The suit itself proceeded by way of a fiction that there was some dispute between certain individuals as to who had title to the land in question. The agreement was written out three times on a piece of parchment; after cutting, one part was given to each of the two parties to the agreement, while the third part, at the 'foot' of the sheet, was filed among the rolls of the Court of Common Pleas, thus forming a lasting and registered proof of what had occurred. The cutting process would be carried out in a wavy pattern (just as it was with a two-part indenture), thus creating 'indented' edges which could be married together at a later date to guarantee the authenticity of the various parts. Latin was the language used for these documents until 1733.

Feet of fines from the twelfth century will be found in classes CP25 and CP27 at the Public Record Office, and several early examples have been printed. Records of so-called 'Common Recoveries', which also proceeded by way of a legal fiction, are in classes CP40 and CP43.

Further reading

Alcock, N.W. *Old title deeds: a guide for local and family historians*. 1994.

Bennett, H.S. *Life on the English manor*. 1987.

Cornwall, J. *An introduction to reading old title deeds*. 1993.

Dibben, A. *Title deeds*. (2nd.Ed.) 1990.

Ellis, M. *Using manorial records*. 1994.

Gonner, E.C.K. *Common land and inclosure*. 1966.

Harvey, P.D.A. *Manorial records*. 1984.

Hone, N.W. *The manor and manorial records*. 1925.

Knocker, H.W. 'Manorial records' in *The Genealogists' Magazine* (1932). Vol.6. pp.92-100.

Levett, A.E. *Studies in manorial history*. 1937.

McLaughlin, E. *Manorial records*. 1996.

Modus tenendi Cur Baron cum Visu Franci Plegii. The Manorial Society, publication no.9. 1915. Useful reprint of an original of 1510, in that it gives extensive examples of recorded court business in both English and Latin.

Molyneux-Child, J.W. *The evolution of the English manorial system*. 1987.

Palgrave-Moore, P. *How to locate and use manorial records*. 1985.

Park, P.B. *My ancestors were manorial tenants*. (2nd.Ed.) 1994.

Richardson, J. *The local historian's encyclopedia*. (2nd.Ed.) 1986.

Stuart, D. *Manorial records*. (2nd. Ed.) 1992.

Tate, W.E. and Turner, M.E. *A Domesday of English enclosure acts and awards*. 1978.

Thirsk, J. *Tudor enclosures*. 1958.

Victoria County Histories of English counties. Where a volume has been published for an area which interests you, it will be essential reading for details of manorial ownership.

Vinogradoff, P. *The growth of the manor*. 1905.

Yelling, J.A. *Common fields and enclosures in England 1450-1850*. 1977.

CHAPTER 13

Name Lists of Taxpayers and Others

Do you pay your taxes? Did your ancestor pay his, willingly or under duress? The payment of taxes may have been bad news for our ancestors, but tax records with names and details of payment are good news for the family historian. Fortunately a significant number of tax returns and inhabitants' lists have survived from various periods including the seventeenth century, thus compensating at least in part for the havoc caused to the keeping of vital records during the Interregnum.

Taxes and subsidies

Lay Subsidies were a series of taxes levied periodically on the movable assets of the lay population (clerics being assessed separately). The amount paid would vary according to the needs of the country, or the ruling monarch, at the time, though the very poor were exempt. The Great Subsidy of 1542-5 theoretically lists all people over sixteen years of age and is of particular value.

Original Lay Subsidy records are in the Public Record Office Exchequer series E179, and range in date from the fourteenth century to the end of the seventeenth. Various county subsidies have been published by county record societies and others.

A particularly useful list of various taxes imposed by Parliament from 1290 to 1700 appears in *Somerset Protestation Returns and Subsidy Rolls* by A.J. Howard and T.L. Stoate (1975), pp.xi-xvi, and the List and Index Society has published a detailed calendar of the subsidy returns in class E179.

Poll tax

Poll taxes were first levied in the fourteenth century, and then again between 1660 and 1697. Very few of the resultant lists of heads of households with families and servants have survived, some in city archives and a few in the Public Record Office (Class E179).

Hearth tax

Various hearth tax returns were compiled during the years 1662 to 1689 and provide one of the most valuable seventeenth century name-list sources for the

Part of a hearth tax return of 1662, *Faversham, Kent. It begins with the names of 'The Mayor and Juratts', followed by the 'Commoners', and gives the number of chargeable hearths in each case.* (Crown Copyright. HMSO)

family historian. Parishes in each county made a return of names, indicating the number of taxable hearths for each person. You will usually find separate lists of those exempt from payment on the grounds of poverty.

The hearth tax was an imaginative attempt by Parliament to charge people according to their ability to pay, but was as unpopular in its day as the Community Charge became in the 1980s, and was short-lived.

Hearth tax records, 1662-1666 and 1669-1674, may be found in the Public Record Office ('Exchequer duplicates', class E179) and in a number of County Record Offices. Several sets of county hearth tax returns have been published, and other similar volumes are in active preparation.

Window tax

Window tax was first imposed from 1696 to replace the hearth tax, and applied to occupiers, not owners. Many householders bricked up their windows in order to evade this unpopular tax - and you will still see evidence of this when looking at various older houses to this day. Window tax records are not plentiful, but those which survive will be found in County Record Offices or in PRO class E181.

Land tax

Land tax was first imposed on a regular basis in 1693, mainly on real estate. From 1772 the returns list all occupiers in each parish as well as owners, and from 1780 duplicates had to be lodged with the Clerks of the Peace in order to establish the qualification for those voting in parliamentary elections. These deposited returns may be seen in County Record Offices, though from 1832 they become less regular. Copies of the 1798 Land Tax for the whole of England and Wales (except Flintshire) can be seen in the Public Record Office (class IR23). A typical land tax return will specify names of occupiers and owners, acreage, type of land and the tax paid.

Various other taxes were imposed at different times, so you will find, for example, that a printed volume of 'Ship money returns' for the county of Suffolk, 1639-1640, was published in 1904. By an Act of 1794/5 all those using hair powder had to obtain an annual certificate by paying a duty of one guinea. Surviving certificates and registers, many of which include the names of those servants who were obliged to use hair powder by their employers, should be found with the records of the Clerk of the Peace in County Record Offices.

Sometimes individuals would make payments of various kinds on a voluntary, not a mandatory, basis. In 1641/2 monies were raised by an Act of Parliament from every parish in the country for 'Distressed Protestants in Ireland', who were then victims of a rebellion and had been murdered in their thousands. Surviving returns may be found in the Public Record Office, classes E179 and SP28. The so-called 'Free and Voluntary Present' to King Charles II gave rise to some useful lists of the better-off who agreed to pay in 1661 in order to help Parliament raise money for the King on his restoration. Occasionally, occupations are given alongside the names of subscribers. Returns survive for over thirty English and Welsh counties and are at the Public Record Office (Class E179).

Devon (two Witt) — Assessment made this 10th day of June
Witheridge Hundred — by Roger Cock & John Froxford Apprs. upon
Meshaw Parish — in Pursuance of an Act passed in the 36th year
of His Majesty's Reign for Granting to his
Majesty by a Land tax to be Raised thirty nine Pounds three
Shillings and Sixpence half penny Payable to His Majesty
King George the third for this present year 1807

Names of the proprietors	Names of the Occupiers	Eastates	£ s d
Mr Wm Marks &co	Roger Cock — —	Barton & Congabo	11..1..4
Mr C. Woolacott	Do — — —	Dryhill — —	1..1..1
Do — —	Do — — —	Cottamedons —	0..5..9
Mr Wm Tropcumb —	Do — — —	Moundlake —	0..14..1
Do — — —	Elizabth Adams	Moortenment	0..4..4
the Rest Wm Tanner	Do — — —	Parsonage —	4..4..3
Mr Jno Tolley —	Jno Froxford —	Whitstone — —	2..16..1
Mr Wm Adams	Himself — — —	Narracott — —	2..2..1..½
Mr Hugh Tolley	Himself — —	Blackland —	1..8..1
Mr Henery Torington	Himself — —	Littlemeshawmoor	2..2..1..½
Do —	Wm Torrington	Bornpark —	0..14..1
Rest Wm Tanner	Joanthan Nichols	Prescott — —	2..2..1..½
Mr Wm Loosemore	Himself — —	Northdown — —	1..7..8
Mrs Martha Eastmond	Herself — —	Meshammills —	1..13..2
Rest H. Morrison	Henery Torrington	Jeeks — — —	0..10..7..½
Do — — —	Do — —	Carringdown —	0..5..10
Do — — —	Do — —	Jeeksmoor —	0..3..6..½
Do — — —	Jams Loosemore	Southhall —	1..17..2
Sir John Davy Bart	Jacb Adams —	Dowrland — —	0..14..1
Mr Richd Cock —	Himself — —	Broadsmoor —	0..14..1
			£39 3..6..½

Roger Cock and } Assesors 22 June 1807
John Froxford }
We Return our Selves Collectors

Land tax assessment for Meshaw, Devon, 1807, *giving names of proprietors and occupiers, and of the 'Eastates' and the amount assessed.* (Crown copyright. Devon Record Office. LTA Meshaw 1807)

Further useful seventeenth century name lists

Protestation Oath Returns

Early in the year 1642, with King Charles I at loggerheads with Parliament, all men over eighteen years of age were required to take an oath '...to live and die for the true Protestant religion, the liberties and rights of subjects and the privilege of Parliaments'. The text of the oath was read out in churches, and the names of those who signed or refused to sign were duly recorded. Most surviving lists are in the House of Lords Record Office, and a number have been printed, including those for Cornwall, Devon, Nottinghamshire and Derbyshire, Oxfordshire and North Berkshire, Lincolnshire and Somerset.

Association Oath Rolls 1696

Following a Jacobite plot to assassinate King William III, the Act of Association in 1696 required anyone who held public office to take a Solemn Oath of Association for the better preservation of His Majesty's Royal Person and government. In the event most men of any social standing took the oath and had their names enrolled. Survival of these rolls is patchy, but they can be of enormous value; the roll for Frome in Somerset, for example, contains a comprehensive list of names which constitutes a census of practically every adult male living in the town at the time. Original rolls are in the Public Record Office, class C213. A very useful list of those which survive, compiled by Cliff Webb, can be seen in *The Genealogists' Magazine* for December 1983.

Further reading

Gibson, J. *The Hearth Tax, other later Stuart tax lists and the Association Oath Rolls.* (2nd.Ed.) 1996.

Gibson, J. and Dell, A. *The Protestation Returns 1641-42 and other contemporary listings.* 1995.

Gibson, J., Medlycott, M. and Mills, D. *Land and window tax assessments.* (2nd.Ed.) 1998.

Hoyle, R. *Tudor taxation records.* 1994.

CHAPTER 14

Education and Apprenticeship

Life for most of our ancestors was divided between time spent at work and time spent at home, these two being intermingled if a person worked at home or on land adjacent to it. As ways of earning a living grew more sophisticated and specialised for the self-employed and the employee alike, chances of success would be enhanced if education and/or training was available. In that sense, at least, little has changed over the years.

Education

Britain's two oldest universities of Oxford and Cambridge and many of its public schools originally offered an education to scholars who were far from wealthy, but as time went on education of the quality they provided became a perquisite of those who could afford it, while a number of charitable foundations helped the children of poorer families acquire at least the basics of reading and writing. The great majority of men who entered the Anglican church had been educated at Oxford or Cambridge.

Roman Catholics would look to the friendlier countries of mainland Europe when it came to higher education, and a significant number of British students chose to be students at universities such as Leyden in Holland where their religious beliefs would be no bar to admittance. Eventually denominational public schools flourished in Britain, and the so-called Dissenting Academies offered higher education to nonconformists. Those choosing to enter the legal profession as barristers were catered for by the Inns of Court in London, which they would attend in addition to, or instead of, a university. Admissions registers for all four Inns of Court have been published, though the volume for the Inner Temple covers only the sixteenth and seventeenth centuries. Solicitors would enter into articles, or would spend time at one of the Inns of Chancery, junior cousins to the Inns of Court.

If an ancestor of yours attended a public school or a university in England, Scotland, Wales or Ireland, you will probably be able to determine at least some biographical details about him by consulting printed registers of students. *Alumni Cantabrigienses* by J. and J.A.Venn, featuring students of the University of Cambridge, is a magnificent biographical compilation, second only in scope to the *Dictionary of National Biography*. *Alumni Oxonienses*, compiled earlier by the indefatigable Joseph Foster, is useful but not so comprehensive in its details. You will also find printed alumni registers starting at an early date for Trinity College, Dublin, and for Scottish universities. The Society of Genealogists in

London has a fine collection of printed registers for schools and universities.

As for the 'ordinary' people who made up the rest of the population, there was a variety of schools which provided education of some sort, but it must be realised that until the Education Act of 1880 made schooling compulsory for all children up to ten years of age, the majority of our labouring ancestors did not receive any kind of an education and were never able to read or even to sign their names.

A number of schools provided for the education of children: charity schools, dame schools, private schools, industrial schools, reformatory schools, poor law union workhouse schools, ragged schools, Sunday schools, Church of England and nonconformist schools. Records of these, where they survive, are generally to be found in County Record Offices. Records of schools under the control of a Local Education Authority will either still be at the school or in County Record Offices. School registers, log books, admission registers and the occasional punishment records can be of great value, providing information about our forebears which may not be found elsewhere.

Punishment books and medical log books are usually subject to a closure rule - of one hundred years, in some cases - and school log books are also subject to a closure rule of thirty years from the date of the last entry.

By the late nineteenth and early twentieth centuries, parents and guardians who habitually neglected to provide efficient and elementary instruction for their children without reasonable excuse could be summoned to attend the Petty Sessions; at the worst their children could then be sent to the Union workhouse school where there would be some guarantee of their receiving the required education. Where these records exist, names of parents and children can be found, together with addresses.

In cases where children were evacuated to so-called safe rural areas during the Second World War, there should be fairly detailed records of evacuees in the school admission registers of these places.

Apprenticeship

Apprenticeship was the system of training for all skilled trades. It was maintained by guilds from about 1350, and received definite statutory sanction by the passing of the Statute of Apprentices in 1563, at which time there was a growing social problem of how to occupy the time of young able-bodied men who had been impoverished by the dissolution of the monasteries. The Statute stated that a uniform term of seven years' apprenticeship should be served as a condition of the right to practise any manual trade, and this was quite rigidly enforced until well into the eighteenth century.

Parishes would bind poor boys and girls to husbandry, to housewifery or to other menial trades (see our earlier chapter on parish chest records), but private apprenticeships would be arranged by mutual agreement, and a two-part indenture would be drawn up, one half being kept by the master, the other being handed to the apprentice. The survival of any such indentures is purely a matter of chance, but where more formality or some corporate body was involved, then original documents or details may survive. There are many original indentures relating to men who became freemen of the City of London held by the Corporation of London Record Office; several London livery companies have published lists of apprentices or of relevant court minutes; Cliff Webb is producing a series of indexed apprenticeship records taken from the archives of London livery companies, and Rob Cottrell has published fiche indexes to bindings of the independent Company of Lightermen and Watermen of the River Thames, 1692-1949. For a detailed study of apprenticeship and other matters relating to the Freedom of the City, refer to *My ancestors were Freemen of the City of London* by Vivienne E. Aldous (Society of Genealogists, 1998). London livery companies are still very much alive, actively involved in the life of the City, and new ones are being formed to take account of changing trades, occupations, crafts and professions. The system of freedom by apprenticeship is still operated in many cases.

From 1710 stamp duty was liable on all apprenticeship bindings nationally at the rate of sixpence in the pound on all premiums of £50 and under, and one shilling in the pound on sums over £50. This tax remained in force until 1810. Much valuable information is given in these registers: the year, the apprentice's name, that of his or her master or mistress with place and trade, and the amount of premium paid. Up to the year 1760 the name and place of abode of the apprentice's father are also given. The original records of this apprenticeship tax are to be found in the Public Record Office (Inland Revenue, IR1 and index, IR17). A typescript index of the Inland Revenue records, 1710 to 1774 (together with some original indentures), can be consulted at the Society of Genealogists, and has been published on fiche by Primary Source Media of Reading (formerly Harvester Press), the final fiche index of masters (1762 to 1774) being added by the Society of Genealogists in 1994. Some lists of stamp duty apprenticeships have been printed - for Surrey, Warwickshire and Wiltshire, for example - as have registers of apprentices for the City of Oxford, 1697-1800 and South-ampton, 1609-1740. Many erstwhile apprentices became freemen of a city or a borough; published freemen lists include those for Canterbury, Chester, Exeter, Gloucester, Great Yarmouth, Grimsby, Guildford, King's Lynn, Kingston-Upon-Thames, Lancaster, Leicester, Newcastle Upon Tyne, Norwich and York.

Further reading

(Education)

Chapman, C.R. *The growth of British education and its records.* 1991.
Coulson, I. and Crawford, A. *Archives in education.* 1995.
Foster, J. *Alumni Oxonienses 1500 to 1886.* 1887-1892. Reprinted, 1980. Supplemented by *Oxford men and their colleges,* 1893.
Jacobs, P.M. *Registers of the universities, colleges and schools of Great Britain.* 1964.
Morton, A. *Education and the State 1833-1968.* 1997.
Parker, I. *Dissenting academies in England.* 1914. Reprinted 1969.
Peacock, E. *Index to English speaking students who have graduated at Leyden University.* Index Society. 1883.
Raven-Hart, H. and Johnston, M. 'Bibliography of the registers (printed) of the universities, inns of court, colleges and schools of Great Britain and Ireland' in the *Bulletin of the Institute of Historical Research* (ix.19-30, 65-83, 154-170; x.109-113) 1931-2.
School, university and college registers and histories in the library of the Society of Genealogists. 1996.
Sturt, M. *Education of the people.* 1967.
Sutherland, G. *Elementary education in the nineteenth century.* 1971.

Thomas, D.H. *Reformatory and industrial schools*. 1988.

Titford, J. A series of articles on the printed registers of schools, universities and other institutions of higher education is featured in *Family Tree Magazine* from September 1997 onwards under the overall title of 'Have you tried ... Guide to printed sources for family historians'.

Venn, J. and J.A. *Alumni Cantabrigienses* 1251 to 1900. 1922-1954. Reprinted 1974.

(Apprenticeship)

Camp, A.J. 'Was he apprenticed?' in *Family Tree Magazine*, Vol.1, No.3. March/April 1985.

Gibbens, L. 'Records of apprenticeship: a lesser-used source' in *Family history news and digest*, Vol.10, No.4. September 1996.

Raymond, S.A. *Londoners' occupations: a genealogical guide*. 1994.

[Worshipful Company of Glaziers]: *The outwith London guilds of Great Britain*. No date.

CHAPTER 15

Sailors, Soldiers, Airmen and Police Officers

Whether or not your ancestor was lucky enough to undergo some form of education or to follow an apprenticeship, the time would come when he would have to work for a living. There may be no surviving record of his working life, but if he joined a profession and became a lawyer, a doctor, a surgeon, a clergyman, an engineer, a surveyor, an architect - or even a civil servant or a politician - you may be lucky enough to find evidence of his career and accomplishments. *Occupational sources for genealogists* (2nd.Ed. 1996) by S.A.Raymond is a useful bibliography of printed books on this subject.

Where an individual was employed by the state in some capacity or other, very detailed records were often kept, and will have stood a good chance of survival over the years.

We will concentrate here on archives relating to those who joined the forces as volunteers or conscripted men, found themselves in the militia, went to sea with the Merchant Navy or were involved in the policing of the community in which they lived. Most family historians should have an ancestor who fits into at least one of these categories.

Naval ancestors: Royal Navy
Most records of the Senior Service are held at the Public Record Office.

Officers are featured in various manuscript classes, in the *Navy Lists* (beginning as Steel's *Navy List* in 1782) and in a number of naval biographical dictionaries, including D. Syrett and R.L. DiNardo's *The commissioned sea officers of the Royal Navy 1660-1815* (1994). For naval ratings, you can refer to the easily-accessible continuous service records which commence in 1853; before that date you can examine muster books and pay books, but only if you know the name of the ship on which a man served. If an ancestor received a Chatham or Greenwich pension, he will appear in the relevant indexed registers.

The Royal Marines can trace their origins back to 1664; Description Books (1750-1888) in the Public Record Office also provide an alphabetical summary of the information given on the Attestation Papers (1790-1883), with plenty of personal details of those who served. There are no published records of officers' service.

For details of other records, including Royal Navy apprentices, sea fencibles,

(6)

Bounty paid.	Nº.	Entry.	Year	Appearance.	Whence and whether Prest or not.	Place and County where born.	Age at time of Entry in this Ship.	Nº. and Letter of Tickets.	MENS NAMES.	Qualities	D. D.D. or R.	Time of Discharge.
£5.0.0	101	13 July	1796	July 31	from the List Nº 194	Newcastle	21		Willⁿ Dunbar	Ab	DD	25 July
£5.0.0	"	"	"	"	Dº Nº 195	New York	20		James Sealey	Ab		
£10.0	21	"	"	"	Dº Nº 212	Yewton Somersetshire	23		Benjⁿ Tilford	Sm	DD	1ˢᵗ January
£10.0	"	"	"	"	Dº Nº 213	Sigherolle Northamptonshire	26	BG (160)	Willⁿ Brown (1)	Sm	DD	1ˢᵗ July
	5	2ⁿᵈ	"	"	Dº Nº 149	County Downe Ireland —	30		Henry Chambers	Ab	D	6 August
		10 June	"	Augˢᵗ 6	from the Sandwich Lynn Col.	Lynn	20		John Beech	Sm	D	16 Decʳ
		15	"	"	"	Wittle	20		Thoˢ Hammond — To the 1ˢᵗ Novᵗ 1797 Then	Sm Ord	R	24 April
		16	"	"	Volᵗ Gravesend	Smyrick Staffordshire	20		John Brittle	Sm	D	13 Novʳ
		"	"	"	"	London	40		Richᵈ Baker	Sm	DD	8 Octᵗ
	110	"	"	"	"	Ardley Essex	21		Thoˢ Dymes — To the 1ˢᵗ Novᵗ 1797 Then — To the 1ˢᵗ March 1800 Then	Sm Ord Sm		
	"	"	"	"	"	Deagnum Dº	22		John Deeks	Sm	DD	29 Decʳ
	23	"	"	"	Late Sparkler	London	26	BG (69)	Richᵈ Fowler	Sm	DD	1ˢᵗ July
	21	"	"	"	Enterprize	London	20		Thomas Rogers — To the 1ˢᵗ Novᵗ 1797 Then	Sm Ord		
	27	"	"	"	Hannon & Mary, Davis	Battersea Surry at Waresham & Hyde taken 10 Feb 1800	24		Abraham Ben⸺ — To the 20 October 1796 Then — To the 9ᵗʰ Febʸ 1800 Then	Sm Carp crew Carpʸ		
	5	26	"	"	Volᵗ Feversham	Feversham	20		James Bennett	Sm	DD	1ˢᵗ Febʸ
£10.0	29	"	"	"	Glenmore Bry list sent to bounty board	County Downe Ireland	21		George Shortell — To Sept 1ˢᵗ March 1800 then	Sm Ord		
£1.0.0	"	"	"	"	"	Ballescrain Ireland	26		Daniel Ryan — To the 12 Novᵗ 1797 Then	Sm Ord	D	22 April
£1.0.0	"	"	"	"	"	Cork	25	BH 303	John Gullivan	Sm	DD	2ⁿᵈ June
£1.0.0	"	"	"	"	"	Basinstock Hampshire	21	BG (150)	Geoˢ Fuller — To the 1ˢᵗ Novᵗ 1797 Then	Sm Ab	DD	8ᵗʰ July
£1.0.0	120	"	"	"	"	London	20		Willⁿ Parlen — To the 1ˢᵗ Novᵗ 1797 Then — To the 1ˢᵗ May 1798 then	Sm Ord Ab	DD	22 April

Part of a muster roll for HMS York, 1800–1. *This is the left-hand page of a two-page entry and features sailors born in England, Ireland and America.* (Crown copyright. HMSO)

the Naval Medical Service, dockyard employees, etc, see *Naval records for genealogists* by N.A.M. Rodgers (1988).

A quantity of records, diaries and photographs of naval interest are held at the Royal Naval Museum, Portsmouth, the Maritime Museum, Greenwich, and the Royal Marines Museum, Eastney, Portsmouth.

Memorials for those lost at sea during the two World Wars with no known graves are situated at Southsea, Hampshire, bearing inscriptions of 9,666 names. There are similar memorials at Plymouth and at Chatham.

Naval ancestors: Merchant Navy

A significant number of our ancestors, particularly those living on or near the coast, would have enlisted into the Merchant Navy. Research into Merchant Navy ancestry may involve the use of records in more than one repository.

Registers of births and deaths at sea on any ship registered in Great Britain from 1 July 1837 (Marine Register Book) will be found in the Miscellaneous Indexes of the Registrar General at 1 Myddelton Street, Islington, London EC1R 1UW.

The Public Record Office holds surviving Merchant Navy crew lists and agreements and official logs from 1747 to 1860. After this date only a 10% sample of such records is held by the PRO, the remainder (1861 to 1938) being in the possession of the Maritime History Group, Memorial University of Newfoundland, St John's, Newfoundland, Canada A1C 5S7, which operates a research and photocopying service for a fee. The Public Record Office at Kew has a microfiche list of its own holdings and of those now in Newfoundland.

Lloyd's Captains' Registers are in the Manuscript Section of the Guildhall Library, Aldermanbury, London, and contain details of the careers of captains and mates of merchant ships who held masters' certificates and were active between 1869 and 1947. Records of the Corporation of Trinity House are also held at this Library, while original petitions for pensions from Trinity House, giving particulars of the family of the petitioner, are held by the Society of Genealogists. An indexed catalogue of these records was published in 1987.

Lloyd's Register of Shipping, 71 Fenchurch Street, London EC3M 4BS, holds a number of relevant records and has information leaflets available.

The Registry of Shipping and Seamen, PO Box 165, Cardiff CF4 5FU, only holds records relating to the last thirty years, and has deposited other documentation with the Public Record Office and with the National Maritime Museum, Romney Road, Greenwich, London SE10 9NF.

Miscellaneous papers of local interest are held by some record offices, and locations of these are given in the class lists at the PRO.

Merchant Navy passenger lists before 1890 have not survived, with the exception of those for a few ships arriving in the UK between 1878 and 1888. These, together with surviving passenger lists from 1890 to 1960, are held at the PRO, classes BT27 and BT32.

You are strongly advised to read around this subject (and to have sight of PRO and Guildhall Library leaflets on the Merchant Navy) before embarking on this area of research.

Army ancestors

The great majority of records relating to the army will be found at the Public Record Office. Officers are featured in various manuscript classes and in the printed *Army Lists* (published regularly from 1754). The most detailed records for other ranks who were discharged to pension are the attestation and discharge documents which constitute the class known as Soldiers' Documents (Class WO97). These are arranged by regiment up to 1872, but are steadily being indexed by name from 1760 onwards. Other relevant classes include the Description Books, Muster Rolls and Medals Rolls. There are also various records of the militia and volunteers.

Public Record Office Class WO364 (First World War Soldiers' Papers) has recently been made available to searchers. The majority (60%) of records of service of soldiers who served in the British army during the First World War were destroyed by enemy action in 1940, but the records in Class WO364 were obtained as a substitute from other government departments, and as such contain different types of records not normally seen in soldiers' documents. WO364 consists of over 4,500 reels of microfilm and is arranged alphabetically by surname. Additionally, the Imperial War Museum, the National Army Museum in London and various regimental museums have archives, books and photographs relating to the army in general or to certain regiments in particular.

The Commonwealth War Graves Commission, 2 Marlow Road, Maidenhead, Berks SL6 7DX, has a great many records on database relating to those who were killed in the First and Second World Wars, including the whereabouts of graves and memorials. Printed registers may be purchased and photographs of memorials obtained. Also on database are records of civilian casualties killed during the Second World War. Graves for other wars since, for example those of the Falklands or the Gulf, are recorded by the Ministry of Defence, PS4(CAS)(A), Room 1012, Empress State Building, Lillie Road, London SW6 1TR. 1.7 million names of Commonwealth servicemen who died in the two World Wars, plus 60,000 civilian casualties commemorated in 20,000 cemeteries around the world, are featured in the Commonwealth War Graves Commission's 'Debt of Honour Register' which may be searched on the Internet at www.cwgc.org/.

A relational database CD-ROM published by the Naval and Military Press, entitled *Soldiers died in the Great War 1914-19* (Version 1.1, 1999), includes details of over 700,000 officers and men.

If you find that you have army ancestors, then the range of available records for you to consult is potentially very great. You are strongly recommended to obtain one of the modestly-priced guides to the subject and to read it carefully before venturing into a record office. Once you visit the Public Record Office you will be able to pick up a number of relevant information sheets.

Militia ancestors

Until the establishment of a standing army in 1660, it was expected that every able-bodied adult male would make himself available for the defence of his country should the need arise. To this end, periodic muster rolls were compiled to record the names of available men and the weapons that each possessed or could use. Militia muster rolls from 1522 to 1640 are at the Public Record Office, and a number of muster rolls and 'military surveys' for various counties have been published.

By the early eighteenth century the importance of the militia force had declined, but with the regular army being away from Britain once the Seven Years' War began in 1756, it was decided that there was a need to resurrect it.

A militia substitute at Kinver, Staffs, 1808. *Edward Meredith, a servant, was chosen by lot to serve in the militia, but provided a substitute. His home parish is ordered to pay him £12 out of the rates, being half the current price for a volunteer.*

By an act of 1757 every county was obliged to provide a certain number of men to join a local regiment of militia, serving within Britain but not abroad. To this end, a ballot was held in every parish and the men drawn were obliged to serve a period of years, the chosen man or his parish being offered the option of finding and paying a substitute to serve in his stead. Some men would even volunteer to serve of their own free will.

Records relating to militia officers and other ranks are mainly held in the Public Record Office and in County Record Offices. With luck you might find an ancestor's name and a full description of his height, the colour of his hair and

DESERTED

From his MAJESTY's Service, and also charged with having committed a Capital Offence,

MICHAEL BYRNE,

BELONGING TO THE

Corps of Ulfter Volunteers,

(Now on March to Chatham)

ABOUT five Feet and five or fix Inches high, fhort black Hair, dark Eyes, dark Complexion, flightly marked with the Small Pox, about 25 or 26 Years of age, ftout and well made.

Whoever will apprehend the faid Michael Byrne and give Notice thereof to the Magiftrates or Town Clerk of the Borough of Marlborough, fhall receive a Reward, over and above the Reward for apprehending Deferters.

Oct. 10, 1799.

Harold, Printer, Marlborough.

A reward is offered for the apprehension of a deserter, 1799. (Wiltshire Record Office)

eyes, details of any distinguishing marks and, occasionally, the name of his next-of-kin. Allowances paid to dependent wives and children can also be discovered in these records.

Air Force ancestors

The Royal Air Force was formed in 1918, an amalgamation of the Royal Flying Corps and the Royal Naval Air Service. The only complete muster list of the Royal Air Force was compiled at the time of this amalgamation. Officers' careers can be traced through the Air Force Lists. The Public Record Office has some RAF personnel records from the 1920s, and will steadily be acquiring more as these are released into the public domain. Enquiries about officers' records should be addressed to Royal Air Force Personnel Management Centre, PM (AR1b), Eastern Avenue, RAF Barnwood, Gloucestershire GL4 7PN and about other ranks to Royal Air Force Personnel Management Centre, P Man 3e(2), RAF Innsworth, Gloucestershire GL3 1EZ. A large quantity of miscellaneous records (photographs, log books, officers' records, etc) relative to the Air Force is held at the Royal Air Force Department of Aviation Records (Archives), Hendon Aerodrome, London NW9 5LL, which has issued a series of information leaflets: 1. *Personnel Records (pre-1918)*; 2. *Personnel Records (RAF: WAAF: WRAF)*; 3. *Royal Air Force Unit Records*; 4. *Royal Air Force Stations: Information Sources*; 5. *Aircraft - Service Histories*.

Police ancestors

The post of parish constable had been established since early days; he was elected annually and had a wide range of duties which varied over the years. By 1842 the vestries were officially responsible for the election of constables, subject to approval by the Justices of the Peace, and lists of those appointed from this time until the post was abolished in 1862 will be discovered in the records of a county Clerk of the Peace.

In 1829 the Metropolitan Police Act established a police force for London (with the exception of the City itself), and from this time the Home Secretary had jurisdiction over the Metropolitan Police. Many of their records are now in the Public Record Office.

During the ten years following the 1829 Act, it was seen by the authorities that there was a need to create local constabularies to serve English and Welsh counties, with the result that the Rural Constabulary Act was passed in 1839. There were problems along the way: many country folk thought there was no need for a costly police force when the parish constable had sufficed for so many years, and around 1841 certain counties presented petitions signed by their parish ratepayers to Parliament, demanding that the Act be abolished. These petitions, where they survive, should be found in a county Clerk of the Peace collection.

In 1856 the County and Borough Police Act required a force to be established for those parts of the country still not covered. The Local Government Act of 1888 abolished borough police forces where the population was less than 10,000. It was not until 1857 that county police forces were established in Scotland under the same guidelines as those for England and Wales.

It is very likely that one or more of your ancestors will have served either as a parish constable or in a police force, thereby playing an essential role in the community.

Some police force histories such as those for Shropshire, Hereford and

Leominster, Caernarvon and Wiltshire have been published. Many police records have now been deposited in County Record Offices, whilst some still remain at County Police Headquarters. Certain police forces have placed a closure rule of up to one hundred years on some of their records.

For those seeking ancestors who served in the Royal Irish Constabulary, which was established as a peace-keeping force in 1836, records of service, allowances and pensions will be found in the Public Record Office. Those of the Irish Revenue Police are with Customs records.

Some records exist in the PRO Colonial Office collection for the South African Constabulary for a very short period from 1902-1908.

The British Library Newspaper Library at Colindale holds relevant periodicals such as *The Police Review [and parade gossip]* (1893 onwards); *The Police Gazette* (1828 to date); *The Police Service Advertiser* (1866-1959) and the *Hue and Cry*, a periodical which gave descriptions of wanted persons, escaped prisoners and deserters.

There is a Police History Society; enquiries should be made to the Secretary, 37 Green Hill Road, Timperley, Altrincham, Cheshire WA15 7BG. One or two county or area police museums have been set up in recent years, such as the Essex Police Museum in Chelmsford, the Thames Valley Police Museum at Sulhamstead near Reading, and the Metropolitan Police Museum in London.

Further reading

(Navy)

Barriskill, D.T. *A guide to the Lloyd's Marine Collection and related marine sources at Guildhall Library.* (2nd.Ed.) 1994.
Bevan A. *Tracing your ancestors in the Public Record Office.* (5th.Ed.) 1999.
Hocking, C. *Dictionary of disasters during the age of steam (including sailing ships and ships of war lost in action) 1824-1962.* 1969.
Hogg, P.L. *Basic facts about using Merchant Navy records.* 1997.
Imperial War Museum: family history notes from the Imperial War Museum: *Tracing Royal Navy Ancestry. Tracing Merchant Marine Ancestry.*
PRO Pocket Guide. *Using Navy records.* 2000.
Rodgers, N.A.M. *Naval records for genealogists.* 1998.
Smith, K. & Watts, C.T. & M.J. *Records of merchant shipping and seamen.* 1998.
Society of Genealogists. *Trinity House Petitions. A Calendar of the records of the Corporation of Trinity House, London, in the Society of Genealogists.* 1987.
Society of Genealogists. *Maritime sources in the library of the Society of Genealogists.* 1997.
Thomas, G. *Records of the Royal Marines.* 1994.
Watts, C.T. and M.J. *My ancestor was a merchant seaman: how can I find out more about him?* (2nd.Ed.) 1991.

(Army)

Cantwell, J.D. *The Second World War: a guide to documents in the Public Record Office.* 1972. Reprint 1993.
Crowder, N.K. *British army pensioners abroad 1772-1899.* 1995.
Fowler, S. *Army records for family historians.* (2nd.Ed.) 1998.
Fowler, S., Spencer, W. and Tamblin, S. *Army service records of the First World War.* PRO Readers' Guide no.19. (2nd.Ed.) 1997.
Gibson, J. and Peskett, P. *Record Offices: How to find them.* (8th.Ed.) 1998.

Hamilton-Edwards. G. *In search of army ancestry.* 1977.
Holding, N. *World War One army ancestry.* (3rd.Ed.) 1997.
Holding, N. *More sources for World War One army ancestry.* (3rd.Ed.) 1998.
Holding, N. and Swinnerton, I. *Location of British Army Records 1914-18.* (4th.Ed.) 1999.
Imperial War Museum: family history notes from the Imperial War Museum: *Tracing Army Ancestry.*
Kitzmiller, J.M. *In search of the 'forlorn hope': a comprehensive guide to locating British regiments and their records, 1640 - World War I.* 1988.
Public Record Office. *Battlefront: 1st July 1916. The first day of the Somme.* (Document Study Pack). 1996.
Public Record Office. *Records of officers and soldiers who have served in the British army.* (2nd.Ed.) 1985.
Swinson, A. *A register of the regiments and corps of the British army.* 1975.
Swinnerton, I. *The British army: its history, tradition and records.* 1996.
Watts, C.T. *My ancestor was in the British army: how can I find out more about him?.* Reprint, with addenda. 1996.

(Militia)
Cole, J.A. *Wiltshire militia orders 1759 to 1770.* 1994.
Cole, J.A. *Wiltshire militia courts martial 1759 to 1770.* 1997.
Gibson, J. and Dell, A. *Tudor and Stuart muster rolls.* 1991.
Gibson, J. and Medlycott, M. *Militia lists and musters 1757-1876.* (4th.Ed.) 2000.
Spencer, W. *Records of the Militia and Volunteer forces from 1758-1945.* PRO Readers' Guide no.3. (2nd.Ed.) 1997.
Thomas, G. *Records of the militia from 1757.* 1993.

(Air Force)
Fowler, S., Elliott, P., Nesbit, R., Goulter, C. *RAF records in the Public Record Office.* 1994.
Imperial War Museum: family history notes from the Imperial War Museum: *Tracing Royal Air Force Ancestry.*
Nesbit, R. *The RAF in camera* series. Volumes for 1903-1939; 1939-1945; 1946-1995. 1995.
Spencer, W. *Air Force records for family historians.* 2000.
Williamson, H.J. *The roll of honour, Royal Flying Corps and Royal Air Force, for the Great War, 1914-1918.* 1992.
Wilson, E. *Records of the Royal Air Force: how to find the few.* 1991.

(Police)
Bridgeman, I. and Emsley, C. *A guide to the archives of the police forces of England and Wales.* 1990.
Critchley, T.A. *A history of police in England and Wales 900-1966.* (2nd.Ed.) 1978.
Emsley, C. *Crime and society in England 1750-1900.* 1989.
Emsley, C. *The English police: a political and social history.* 1991.
Forester, C. 'Metropolitan Police Consolidated Index' in *Family Tree Magazine,* July 1994.
Shearman, A. *My ancestor was a policeman.* 2000.
Waters, L. *Police History Society: notes for family historians.* 1987.
Wilkes, J. *The London police in the nineteenth century.* 1977.

CHAPTER 16

Emigrants and Immigrants

Emigrants

One feature of life in centuries past which might surprise you when you take a close look at your ancestors is that families were very mobile. Despite our view of idyllic country life in times past, it was unusual for a family to stay in one parish for more than three generations - that is, a hundred years or so. You must expect your ancestors to disappear from one place and to reappear somewhere else, near or far.

Some more adventurous spirits made journeys farther afield, and set off across the world's oceans to seek a new life abroad. Others had no choice: condemned as criminals, often for quite minor crimes, they were transported to America and the West Indian plantations. Once the American War of Independence had removed this option in the late eighteenth century, convicts were shipped to Australia and Tasmania.

Entrepreneurs or the younger sons of gentry families were migrating to Virginia from the seventeenth century, often alongside the servants and labourers who made up the great bulk of emigrants to the New World. Those who were escaping religious persecution, meanwhile, headed to the New England states. Great numbers of Presbyterian Irish had emigrated to North America during the eighteenth century, many along with their ministers, but in 1846 and the years following the potato famine, there was massive movement from Ireland across the Atlantic. These 'Famine emigrants' sometimes sailed direct to the United States, while others came to England first; some who had intended to continue on to America ended up by settling in England.

You may well find Cornish tin-miners who had made the Atlantic crossing in search of work, and Welsh emigrants who settled not just in North America, but also in more far-flung locations such as Patagonia in southern Argentina.

Lack of work in the northern and midland industrial districts of England, particularly around the time of the American Civil War, forced many cotton workers to emigrate to a new life overseas. Some emigrants believed they would be able to make a better life for their families in another country, and were able to travel by way of assisted passages. In other cases, parishes would pay any necessary expenses from the rates to allow some of their paupers to leave England for a life elsewhere.

Many voluntary emigrants, of course, did not settle happily abroad and would return home, thus sometimes posing a problem for you as you compile the

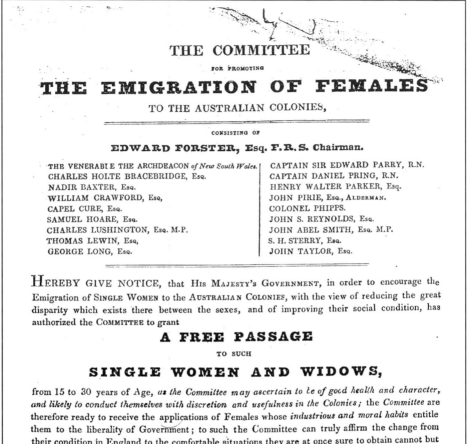

THE COMMITTEE

FOR PROMOTING

THE EMIGRATION OF FEMALES

TO THE AUSTRALIAN COLONIES,

CONSISTING OF

EDWARD FORSTER, Esq. F.R.S. Chairman.

THE VENERABLE THE ARCHDEACON *of New South Wales.*	CAPTAIN SIR EDWARD PARRY, R.N.
CHARLES HOLTE BRACEBRIDGE, Esq.	CAPTAIN DANIEL PRING, R.N.
NADIR BAXTER, Esq.	HENRY WALTER PARKER, Esq.
WILLIAM CRAWFORD, Esq,	JOHN PIRIE, Esq., ALDERMAN.
CAPEL CURE, Esq.	COLONEL PHIPPS.
SAMUEL HOARE, Esq.	JOHN S. REYNOLDS, Esq.
CHARLES LUSHINGTON, Esq. M.P.	JOHN ABEL SMITH, Esq. M.P.
THOMAS LEWIN, Esq,	S. H. STERRY, Esq.
GEORGE LONG, Esq.	JOHN TAYLOR, Esq.

HEREBY GIVE NOTICE, that HIS MAJESTY'S GOVERNMENT, in order to encourage the Emigration of SINGLE WOMEN to the AUSTRALIAN COLONIES, with the view of reducing the great disparity which exists there between the sexes, and of improving their social condition, has authorized the COMMITTEE to grant

A FREE PASSAGE

TO SUCH

SINGLE WOMEN AND WIDOWS,

from 15 to 30 years of Age, *as the Committee may ascertain to be of good health and character, and likely to conduct themselves with discretion and usefulness in the Colonies;* the Committee are therefore ready to receive the applications of Females whose *industrious and moral habits* entitle them to the liberality of Government; to such the Committee can truly affirm the change from their condition in England to the comfortable situations they are at once sure to obtain cannot but prove highly advantageous; and those who persevere in a right course, not only in time obtain liberal wages, but may look forward, in a country where the disparity between the sexes is so great, to marry under circumstances of provision and comfort, far beyond what they can hope for in the crowded population of Great Britain. *The Committee particularly recommend Servants accustomed to the duties of a Farm-house in England to emigrate to these Colonies,* the Colonial Farmers being in great want of young women of steady and industrious habits to fill situations in their families; House-Maids, and Servants of All-work, too, are much in demand; indeed all who proceed with a determination to conduct themselves with industry and propriety, are certain to do well in these prosperous Colonies.

The Ship "CANTON," of 510 tons register, will sail from the Thames for SYDNEY on the 30th of April next (beyond which day she will on no account be detained), fitted up under the direction of the EMIGRATION COMMITTEE. *This fine Ship is quite new, and her superior heights and ventilation render her peculiarly eligible for this Service.*

Notice sent to the overseers of St Peter's, Marlborough in 1835. *The offer of a free passage for women was an attempt to redress the imbalance between the sexes 'down under'.* (Wiltshire Record Office)

family tree. Realising, perhaps, that the grass was greener in the colonies after all, some returning emigrants may have set off from Britain for a second time, in a spirit of hope triumphing over experience. Census returns, of course, can be invaluable in such cases as you wrestle with the to-ings and fro-ings of a family with itchy feet.

Tracing the movements of an emigrant at any period and in any place is never easy. Clerk of the Peace records in County Record Offices such as bonds and contracts for those transported, Quarter Sessions records, vestry minutes in parish chests and letters and diaries may provide essential details. Sometimes records kept at the country of arrival are helpful, as is the case with various censuses and surveys made in Australia in the first few decades of settlement, where the place of origin (or of trial) of the emigrant is mentioned. You would be well advised to consult David Hawkings' book, *Bound for Australia*, if you have an interest in the Antipodes, and many birth, marriage and death indexes for Australian states are now available on CD-ROM.

From the mid nineteenth century many emigrants chose to go to New Zealand, while a number of British soldiers who had fought in the Maori Wars stayed there and never returned home. Movement of individuals and of families between New Zealand and Australia (as between the USA and Canada) should never be ruled out.

The fishing trade with Newfoundland had long taken temporary or permanent emigrants there from the south-western counties of England in particular, the first English settlers having arrived in the sixteenth century. In recent times, many boys and girls from British children's homes were taken to Canada.

South Africa was settled by people of many nationalities including the British, and very useful lists of names of British emigrants to the Cape, Natal and elsewhere have been published, including Esmé Bull's *Aided immigration from Britain to South Africa, 1857-1867* (1991) and the ongoing series, *British Settlers in Natal, 1824-1857, a biographical register* by Shelagh O'Byrne Spencer (from 1981). The Union of South Africa was established in 1910, and a Republic was proclaimed in 1961. For periodic updates of genealogical matters in South Africa, see Mark Tapping's informative articles in *Family Tree Magazine*.

If you have an interest in emigration from the port of Liverpool, the Maritime Record Centre, Merseyside Maritime Museum, Albert Dock, Pierhead, Liverpool L3 1DN has some relevant records and histories.

Meanwhile, printed details of emigrants to North America, Australia, New Zealand, South Africa and the West Indies abound, and a list of some such publications with brief samples from each appears in *Family Tree Magazine* (November 1996 and January and March 1997) under the title *Emigration from Britain: a selected list of printed, microform and CD-ROM sources* by John Titford.

Chartered companies

Your ancestors may have been involved in the activities of one of a number of companies incorporated by Royal or Parlimentary charter, such as the Virginia Company, the Royal African Company, the Russia Company, the Eastland Company, the South Sea Company or the Merchant Adventurers.

The East India Company was incorporated in the year 1600 and was a powerful and independent force until its demise in 1858. If your ancestors served the EIC in some capacity or other, don't be surprised to find more than one generation involved. Much relevant material is in print: annual *India Lists* from 1803 give names of senior Company servants, and amongst other reference works you will find fascinating volumes such as *List of marine records of the late*

A passport issued to Rev Edward Manners Sanderson, *of Huyton, Liverpool, in 1906. An endorsement on the back by the Turkish Consul General grants permission to enter Palestine.*

East India Company, and of subsequent date, preserved in the record department of the India Office, London (1896), with voluminous lists of the Company's ships from 1605 to 1856, naming each captain and listing journals made on voyages.

Printed works such as these and a sizeable archive of related manuscript material may be found at the British Library, Oriental and India Office Collections, 96 Euston Road, London NW1 2DB. The library holds the archives of the East India Company from 1600 to 1858, including records of those who served in India as servants of the Company or in the armed services; over one thousand volumes of ecclesiastical returns of births, marriages and deaths, 1698 to 1947; records of the Board of Control 1784-1858, the India Office 1858-1947 and the Burma Office 1937-1948.

Following the independence of India, Pakistan and Burma in 1947/8, the official India Office Archive was closed, but there are certain series of papers dating for a few years beyond this date. The collection includes photographs, prints, drawings, official publications, maps and microfilm of archives in South Asia. Some records extend beyond India and Burma to countries such as Aden, Afghanistan and China. The office also holds a large newspaper collection including Indian newspapers in English. There are many lists, indexes, finding aids and microfiche catalogues to the various collections. You are recommended to do at least some background reading before consulting original manuscript material in this field.

The records of the Levant Company and microfilmed records of the Hudson Bay Company are in the Public Record Office.

Passports

Although various types of passport were in use from medieval times, they were not made compulsory until 1914. During the sixteenth and seventeenth centuries (to 1677) those who travelled abroad would sometimes make use of a 'Licence to Pass Beyond the Seas'.

The Public Record Office has a Register of Passports from 1795 in class FO16, with indexes of names for part of this period, and Licences to Pass Beyond the Seas are in class E157.

Immigrants

Just as people emigrated to new lives overseas, so many others came into Britain as immigrants - see the sections in this book on Huguenots and Jews. Many French émigrés escaped to England after the French Revolution, and more recent years have seen the arrival of West Indian immigrants and those from the Indian sub-continent. Where immigrants have decided to become naturalised, relevant papers should be found in the Public Record Office. Some chose to anglicize their surnames in order to fit in with the rest of the population - and this can catch the researcher unawares.

Further reading

(Emigration and immigration)

Anglo-German FHS. *Tracing German-speaking ancestors*. Research Guide No.2. 1999.

Baxter, A. *In search of your Canadian roots.* 1989.
Baxter, A. *In search of your European roots.* 1985.
Baxter, A. *In search of your German roots* (3rd.Ed.) 1996.
Bevan, A. *Tracing your ancestors in the Public Record Office.* (5th.Ed.) 1999.
Bromell, A. *Tracing family history in New Zealand.* 1991.
Chorzempa, R.A. *Polish roots.* 1993.
Coldham, P. *The complete book of emigrants, 1607-1776.* 1986-1993.
Coldham, P. *The complete book of emigrants in bondage, 1614-1775.* 1988. With a *supplement*, 1992.
Cole, T.R. *Italian Genealogical Records.* 1995.
Coletta, J.P. *Finding Italian roots.* 1996.
Cunningham, W. *Alien immigrants to England.* 1897, reprinted 1969.
Filby, F.W. [with various co-editors]. *Passenger and immigration lists index.* 1981, with annual supplements thereafter.
Fitzhugh, T.V.H. (Ed. Lumas, S.). *The dictionary of genealogy.* (5th.Ed.) 1998. Includes a comprehensive listing of emigrants' records.
Frykberg, P. 'South African connections'. In *Grinz Yearbook*, Genealogical Research Institute of New Zealand, 1994. pp.7-20.
Glazier, I.A. *The famine emigrants: lists of Irish immigrants arriving at the port of New York 1846-1851.* 1983-86.
Grannum, G. *Tracing your West Indian ancestors: Sources in the Public Record Office.* 1995.
Guildhall Library research guide. *The British Overseas.* (3rd.Ed.) 1994.
Hawkings, D. *Bound for Australia.* 1987.
Kershaw, R. and Pearsall, M. *Immigrants and Aliens: A guide to sources on U.K. immigration and citizenship.* 2000.
Lombard, R.T.J. *Handbook for genealogical research in South Africa.* 1984.
Marshall, L. and Mossong, V. *Genealogical research in New Zealand.* (Society of Genealogists' leaflet no. 11). 1982.
Pontet, P. *Ancestral research in France.* 1998.
Pontet, P. *Ancestral research in France: A-Z of genealogical references and sources.* 1998.
Riemer, S.J. *The German research companion.* 1997.
Ryskamp, G.R. *Finding Hispanic roots.* 1997.
Smelser, R.M. *Finding your German ancestors.* 1991.
Towey, P. *An introduction to tracing your German ancestors.* 1999.
Vine Hall, N. *Tracing your family history in Australia: a guide to sources.* (2nd.Ed.) 1994.
Whyte, D. *A dictionary of Scottish emigrants.* 1973.
Whyte, D. *The Scots overseas: a selected bibliography.* 1995.

(East India Company)

Baxter, I.A. *India Office library & records: a brief guide to biographical sources.* (2nd.Ed.) 1990.
Foster, W. *A guide to the India Office records, 1600-1858.* 1919. Reprinted 1966.
Moir, M.I. *A general guide to the India Office records.* 1988.
Taylor, N.C. *Sources for Anglo-Indian genealogy in the library of the Society of Genealogists.* 1990.

CHAPTER 17

Local Records:
County Record Offices

Many record offices, specialised or general, have significant local or national archival holdings which will be of interest to family historians. We only have space here to treat some of these in rather more detail.

A County Record Office is likely to be one of your first ports of call once you start making headway with your family history research. If you're very lucky this will be one near your home - but it's just as likely that you will have to travel some considerable distance in order to spend a precious few hours or days in a CRO in some far-flung corner of the country. You could always pay a local researcher to do some work for you there, but there's no substitute for making a personal visit; perhaps that's where you will take the family on holiday at the next opportunity? Do be aware that some counties contain more than one County Record Office; check in advance.

When County Record Offices were first established, it was not to make life easier for genealogists, but to house important county records such as those of Quarter Sessions. These record offices have been designated as official archival repositories by the Master of the Rolls, and many of them now incorporate Diocesan Record Offices. Their function is to store and to conserve archives relative to their own county area and beyond, and they will often act as repositories for family or business archives on temporary or permanent loan. Many record offices have published catalogues of all or part of their holdings, and such publications should enable you to familiarise yourself with the range of archives available.

Over the years visits to CROs by family history researchers who are keen to examine parish and county records have increased quite dramatically. You will find knowledgeable staff there to help you, but it really is incumbent upon you to establish your research needs before you pay a visit; 'Can you help me? My grandfather came from Worcestershire...' may not be the appropriate starting-point.

All offices have rules and regulations concerning their archives, and it is wise to enquire about facilities, opening hours and the need for appointments before contemplating a visit. Most record offices operate a readers' ticket system, and this may necessitate your having proof of your identity; it is probably best to use a driving licence for this purpose, since it carries your address. Some offices choose to use the County Archive Research Network (CARN). A CARN ticket may then be used at all offices operating within the scheme.

Here is a representative sample of the kind of archives you would normally expect to find in a County Record Office. Do allow for local variations; for example, in some areas county libraries will have significant holdings:

● Parish registers. These are mostly now available on microform; many have been transcribed and will exist in typescript or print. Also look for banns books.
● Parish chest records.
● Nonconformist records of many denominations.
● Copies of census returns 1841-1891, and unofficial census returns pre-1841.
● Records of the Clerk of the Peace, Petty Sessions, Quarter Sessions, Special and Brewster Sessions.
● Records relating to County Councils and to Urban and Rural District Councils.
● City and borough records, town and Parochial Church Council records.
● Poll books and electoral registers.
● Records of Poor Law Union workhouses, Boards of Guardians' minute books, etc.
● Coroners' records.
● Records of land, window and other taxes.
● Enclosure and tithe maps and awards; other maps and plans.
● School records: charity schools, board schools, church schools, district schools, Sunday schools and Local Education Authority schools.
● Records of hospitals and asylums: admissions, discharges, deaths and (for asylums) details of those who absconded.
● Records of charities.
● Records of barges, canals, roads, bridges and turnpikes.
● Militia records.
● County Police Force records from 1839: admissions, discharges, allowance books; details of ticket-of-leave prisoners, wanted notices, etc.
● Prisons, prisoners and related documents.
● Manorial court records.
● Newspapers.
● Business, factory and industrial archives.
● Solicitors' records. These vary considerably from solicitor to solicitor, and often contain a 'mixed bag' of papers such as deeds, wills, inventories, correspondence and business records.
● Family and estate archives, sometimes on temporary or permanent loan. These may include manorial documents and much else.
● Miscellaneous leases and deeds.
● Diocesan records (where the CRO is also a Diocesan Record Office), including bishops' transcripts, probate records, marriage allegations and bonds, records of church courts, etc.

Much material of family history interest will be held by local studies and reference libraries; in some cases these are sited close to the relevant County Record Office for the convenience of everyone concerned. Many museums, including military museums, have a wealth of archival material, diaries, photographs and artefacts. There is a very fine dividing line between local history and family history. If you make an in-depth study of a family which interests you within the context of a town or village, you will be criss-crossing such a line at regular intervals. Books and collections which are of interest to local historians will often contain material which is of use to family historians, and vice-versa.

Do remember, finally, that many significant collections of great family and local history interest are still in the muniment rooms of present or former landowners. See our reference to the Royal Commission on Historical Manuscripts in Chapter 18.

Further reading

Blatchford, R. *Family and Local History Handbook: The Genealogical Services Directory*. (5th.Ed.) 2001.
Campbell-Kease, J. *A companion to local history research*. 1989.
Cole, J. and Church, R. *In and around record repositories in Great Britain and Ireland*. (4th.Ed.) 1998.
Emmison, F.G. *Introduction to archives*. 1977.
Emmison, F.G. *Archives and local history*. 1988.
Hey, D. *Family history and local history in England*. 1991.
Hoskins, W.G. *Local history in England*. 1973.
Iredale, D. *Enjoying archives*. 1985.
Iredale, D. *Local history research and writing*. 1980.
Lumas, S. *Basic facts about archives*. 1997.
Richardson, J. *The local historians' encyclopedia*. (2nd.Ed.) 1986.
Riden, P. *Record sources for local history*. 1987.
Rogers, C. and Smith, J. *Local family history in England*. 1991.
Stevens, W.B. *Sources for local history*. 1973.
West, J. *Town records*. 1983.
West, J. *Village records*. (3rd.Ed.) 1997.
Wood, T. *Basic facts about using record offices for family historians*. (2nd.Ed.) 1999.

CHAPTER 18

National Records

The Public Record Office

The Public Record Office, first established in 1838 but having recently brought together the great majority of its holdings on one site in Kew (Ruskin Avenue, Kew, Richmond, Surrey TW9 4DU), constitutes a vast and unrivalled storehouse of archive material stretching back to the Domesday Book of 1086. As its title suggests, it is a repository of public records - not a collection of genealogical material as such. Your ancestors will almost certainly feature in PRO records - somewhere - but a lot of careful study and preparation will be necessary if you are to track them down, to find where they are lodged among records which fill many miles of shelving. The PRO could overwhelm you if you're not careful, but will yield up riches beyond measure to the careful and methodical researcher. Let the book *Tracing your ancestors in the Public Record Office* by Amanda Bevan (5th Edition, 1999) be your constant companion until you are familiar with the classes of records held by the PRO - and, indeed, those which are NOT held there! Then, and only then, attempt your first foray into this most remarkable of all research centres.

Much of the material held by the PRO may be very old, but the way in which you order and collect records owes everything to new technology; you place your order by way of a computer, and a bleeper made to fit your pocket or handbag will sound when your documents are ready for collection.

Space will only allow us here to list a few of the more frequently-used records held by the PRO. A significant number of researchers will want to consult military records, some will sneak a look at one or more of the registers of marriages celebrated in the precincts of the Fleet Prison, while others will be interested in records of their ancestors being apprenticed. These areas of research have all been referred to elsewhere in this book, but mention must be made here of the voluminous legal records held by the PRO.

Legal records

Our ancestors must often have felt that the long arm of the law was forever reaching out to touch them. Those who infringed the law risked being punished if caught - by the manorial courts, the church courts, Petty Sessions, Quarter Sessions or the Assizes. You didn't have to be a criminal, however, to be involved in the legal process, and many of the most fascinating records which put flesh on the bones of our ancestors concerned disputes between individuals,

Chancery deposition, 1661, *in the case of Grinsell v. Browne et al. Charles Tittford gives his address, occupation and age, and signs at the bottom. There is also an account of his occupancy of a house near Charing Cross during the Civil War and Interregnum.* (PRO C24/850)

not between the state and an individual.

Various local courts of law have already been covered in this book, but the Public Record Office houses a significant proportion of all other legal records which have survived throughout the centuries. Here you will find a wealth of material which features people in all walks of life settling disputes over land ownership, property rights, contested wills, the payment of tithes, and much else. A huge quantity of sheets or rolls of parchment or paper has been preserved over hundreds of years, forming the records of the courts of common law and of equity, such as the Court of Common Pleas, the Court of Star Chamber, the Court of Chancery, the Court of the Exchequer, the Court of Requests, and so on.

Much of this legal material is unindexed and thus all but impenetrable, but a significant quantity of printed and manuscript indexes does exist, many published as PRO *Lists and Indexes* or by the List and Index Society, which is still very active. Chancery records are particularly well served in this regard, and the Bernau Index, held on microfilm at the Society of Genealogists, may well help you find an ancestor who was a plaintiff (the person instigating the case), a defendant (the person responding to the charge) or a deponent (a person giving evidence on behalf of either the plaintiff or the defendant).

On open shelves at the PRO itself and elsewhere (such as at the British Library) you will find printed calendars, transcripts or summaries, frequently with indexes. *British National Archives: sectional list 24* gives an impressive listing of such publications, and you will see that the medieval period is particularly well covered. The names of many such volumes will mean little to you as a beginner in family history, and can even seem daunting, but as you pull a few volumes off the shelves and consult the indexes, you'll slowly become familiar with them. Here are printed works on charter rolls, patent rolls, close rolls, fine rolls, liberate rolls, treaty rolls, Gascon rolls, memoranda rolls, curia regis rolls, assizes, inquisitions post mortem, state papers, colonial records, treasury books and papers, privy council registers - and the excellent series of *Public Record Office Lists and Indexes*, which cover chancery proceedings and much else. Scotland and Ireland are featured in these printed volumes, alongside England and Wales.

Palatinates
Palatinates or Counties Palatine were areas of England situated near the vulnerable borders with Wales and Scotland, and were originally ruled and administered by an Earl or Bishop, the term deriving from the word 'palace'. Examples are Chester, Durham and Lancaster. If you have ancestors in these counties, do be aware that they had their own significant jurisdiction, including chancery courts. Surviving records are held in the Public Record Office. Palatinates were abolished in 1835.

The private muniments of the Duchy of Lancaster were transferred to the PRO for safe keeping in 1868, and are quite separate from the records of the County Palatine of Lancaster. Nearly every county in England and Wales had at least some territory which came under the jurisdiction of the Duchy, and you will find references to it in some unexpected places, many miles away from the county of Lancashire.

Office-holders in the Duchy and County Palatine of Lancaster from 1603 by R. Somerville (1972) contains a useful list of names with brief career details.

Inquisitions Post Mortem
When a tenant-in-chief of the Crown died, an Inquisition Post Mortem would be held by a regional official known as an 'escheator' to determine details of the land holding of the deceased and the identity and age of an heir, information which was provided on oath by neighbours. If the heir was a minor, the Crown would become his guardian and would take the revenue of his lands until he came of age. IPMs were carried out from 1235 to 1662. The written inquisition would be sent to the Court of Chancery, with a copy to the Exchequer. So in theory, at least, a researcher has two chances of a particular inquisition having survived and being available for consultation at the Public Record Office. Most such inquisitions will establish family relationships and provide at least some detail concerning the sworn informants. Many indexed volumes of IPMs have appeared in print.

Tontines
One particularly fascinating set of records held in the PRO which can be of real value to genealogists is that which features tontines. A tontine was a form of annuity organised by the state in which the interest paid remained constant, but as nominees of the subscribers died, those remaining collected a larger share. Eventually a sole survivor would receive all the available interest. The idea proved most popular with the wealthy - and with those who liked a bit of a gamble.

Certificate of appointment to the Royal Mews, 1700/1. *William Titford is admitted as Page of the Back Stairs to King William III, probably thanks to his wife Ann's connections with Henry de Nassau, Master of the Horse.* (Crown copyright. HMSO)

The first state scheme dates from 1693, and the last from 1789. Surviving registers show the names and parishes of the subscribers and nominees, together with nominees' ages, dates of death and executors. Records of the eighteenth century tontines will be found in PRO classes NDO2 and NDO3, and a printed list of the nominees of the 1693 scheme is in the British Library.

Here is a sample of other holdings of genealogical value in the PRO:

- Births, marriages and deaths of Britons overseas
- Records relative to genealogy in Wales, Scotland, Ireland, the Isle of Man and the Channel Islands
- Records of emigration and immigration
- Oaths of allegiance
- Electoral registration
- Changes of name
- The coastguard service

- The police
- Crown employees and civil servants
- Railway workers
- Apprentices
- Lawyers
- The medical profession
- Teachers and school records
- Prisoners of war
- Coroners' inquests
- Land ownership and occupancy
- Taxation
- Debtors and bankrupts

Many records are subject to a closure rule of thirty years or more, and may not be consulted until the appropriate time has elapsed. There is a closure rule of one hundred years for census returns and seventy-five years for coroners' records.

Public Record Office opening hours are as follows: 9.30 am to 5 pm (Monday, Wednesday, Friday – last order time, 4 pm – and Saturday – last order time, 12 noon), 10 am to 7 pm (Tuesday – last order time, 4.10 pm) and 9.30 am to 7 pm (Thursday – last order time, 4.10 pm). The office is closed on public holidays (including the relevant Saturdays), and also for stock-taking during the first two weeks in December. A reader's ticket is required, and must be applied for in person; you will need some proof of identity such as a driving licence.

The Kew site can accommodate six hundred researchers, who will be consulting indexes and calendars, original documents or microform, or the books in the extensive PRO library.

Facilities include a large car park, a shop with a wide range of products and publications, and a refreshments area.

The same rules apply at the PRO as at any other record office: eating, drinking, smoking and the use of pens are prohibited in the search rooms.

For those unable to visit the Public Record Office in person, the Reader Services Department will carry out paid research in certain classes of records for members of the public. The fee is inclusive of postage and copies of documents.

The British Library
The British Museum was originally founded on the basis of a number of priceless collections of major national importance, and its unrivalled accumulation of books and manuscripts, significantly augmented year by year, now constitutes the British Library.

The Library has now moved its holdings, including the largest collection of printed books in the country, together with manuscript collections, photographs, maps, music and philatelic material, from its original site in Great Russell Street to new purpose-built premises at 96 Euston Road, London NW1 2DB, near St Pancras Station. Many visitors familiar with the world-famous reading room in Great Russell Street may never learn to love its replacement in Euston Road, but here you will find an excellent range of reference books on open shelves, many of them of great genealogical value.

Although the British Library Newspaper Library at Colindale houses the largest collection of newspapers, the British Library has the Thomason and

Burney collections of newspapers and ephemera.

The British Library has published extensive catalogues covering its book and manuscript holdings over the years, and now has available an on-line Public Access Catalogue of Printed Books. You will need a reader's ticket, with photograph provided, in order to visit the book library, and permission to access the manuscript collections can be granted for those whose *bona fides* can be guaranteed.

The National Monuments Record Centre

This centre is the public archive of the Royal Commission on Historic Monuments and is situated at Churchward Village, Kemble Drive, Swindon, Wiltshire SN2 2GZ. No appointment is needed, but you are advised to ring NMR Customer Services in advance of any visit so that library or search room desk space and appropriate archive material can be ready for you on your arrival. Photocopying facilities are available.

You will find much here of social, topographical and family history interest. There are 500,000 oblique aerial photographs of architectural, archaeological and landscape subjects, together with three million vertical air photographs derived from RAF, Ordnance Survey and commercial sources. There is a large reference collection of maps, lists of historic buildings (including those of some Poor Law Union workhouses) and of archaeological sites, historic parks and gardens, and some original drawings and plans of railways. A large reference library covering all English counties may also be used by the public, and MONARCH, the NMR's database of architectural and archaeological information, can be consulted. The London office and search rooms of the NMR are at 55 Blandford Street, London W1H 3AF, and a fax and a free phone line has been installed between the Swindon and London search rooms. The London office records include 75,000 photographs of London buildings ranging from Westminster Abbey to council houses, with specialist accumulations such as the Rokeby Collection of railway stations, the Maltby Collection of Odeon Cinemas and the Survey of London archive.

Similar centres exist for Scotland and Wales:

NMR for Scotland, John Sinclair Terrace, 16 Bernard Terrace, Edinburgh EH8 9NV

NMR for Wales, Crown Building, Plas Crug, Aberystwyth, Dyfed SY23 1NJ

Royal Commission on Historical Manuscripts

The Royal Commission on Historical Manuscripts was established in 1869 with the brief of locating records in private or institutional ownership and making their existence and contents known to a wider public. The Commission has published over 200 detailed reports and appendices which include calendars and summaries of the records it has examined. There are separate index volumes. In 1945 the RCHM was given the task of directing the National Register of Archives, and it maintains the register of manorial documents. The Commission may be found at Quality House, Quality Court, Chancery Lane, London WC2A 1HP.

The National Register of Archives

It is the function of the National Register of Archives to locate and compile a record of historical papers of significance still remaining in private hands, obtaining permission from the owners, where possible, for their records to be accessed by researchers or for information about their collections to be made publicly available.

The NRA's coverage includes papers of people of note and of estates, businesses, local authorities, societies, churches, and so on. Their lists and indexes include holdings of various record offices, universities, national libraries and museums. The NRA records have been computerised with three main indexes (a personal index, a business index and a subject index) together with a file featuring over 1,500 repositories. Most record offices hold copies of NRA material relevant to their own area of interest, and the NRA itself has a set of information sheets available.

The NRA for England, Wales and the Channel Islands is at Quality House, Quality Court, Chancery Lane, London WC2A 1HP. The National Register of Archives for Scotland operates from West Register House, Charlotte Square, Edinburgh, but any postal enquiries for information or advice should be addressed to The Secretary, National Register of Archives (Scotland), HM General Register House, 2 Princes Street, Edinburgh EH1 3YY.

Further reading
(Public Record Office, RCHM)

Atherton, L. *'Never complain, never explain': records of the Foreign Office and State Paper Office 1500-c1960*. 1994.

Atherton, L. *Top secret: an interim guide to recent releases of intelligence records at the PRO*. 1993.

Bevan, A. *Tracing your ancestors in the Public Record Office*. (5th.Ed.) 1999.

Colwell, S. *Dictionary of genealogical sources in the Public Record Office*. 1992.

Cox, J. *New to Kew*. 1997.

Fowler, S. *Sources for labour history*. 1995.

[Giuseppi, M.S.] *Guide to the contents of the Public Record Office*. 3 vols., 1963-1968. The last attempt to produce a printed guide to PRO records, updating earlier works by F.S.Thomas and by S.R.Scargill-Bird. Now out of date but still enormously useful. The PRO *Current Guide* on microfiche is now the most comprehensive guide to holdings.

Grannum, G. *Tracing your West Indian ancestors (PRO)*. 1995.

HMSO: *Publications of the Royal Commission on Historical Manuscripts*. Government publications: sectional list no.17. 1985.

Prochaska, A. *Irish history from 1700: guide to sources at the PRO*. 1986.

RCHM: *Guide to the location of collections described in the reports and calendars series, 1870-1980*. 1982.

Reports and appendices of the RCHM. 1870 onwards. Separate index volumes of names and places.

Wood, T. *Basic facts about using record offices for family historians*. 1996.

Public Record Office Information Leaflets can be of enormous help to researchers, and are classified as: Records Information Series, Family Fact Sheets, General Information Series, Census Information, Domestic Records, Legal Records, Military Records, Overseas Records, etc. These are brief but full of detail, and may be obtained free of charge during a personal visit or accessed on the PRO web site on the Internet at: www.pro-gov.uk. Useful addresses and ideas for further reading are often included.

(Legal records and tontines)

Cale, M. *Law and society: an introduction to sources for criminal and legal history from 1800.* 1996.

Carter, A.T. *A history of the English courts.* 1927.

Garrett, R.E.F. *Chancery and other legal proceedings.* 1968.

Gerhold, D. *Courts of Equity: a guide to Chancery and other legal records.* 1994.

Guy, J.A. *The Court of Star Chamber and its records to the reign of Elizabeth I.* 1985.

Leeson, F. *A guide to the records of the British State Tontines and Life Annuities of the 17th and 18th centuries.* 1968.

Potter, H. *A short outline of English legal history.* (4th.Ed.) 1945.

Radcliffe, G.R.Y. and Cross, G. *The English legal system.* 1937.

CHAPTER 19

Publications to Aid Research

Published works

It is a golden rule of family history research that you should always make yourself aware of the existence of relevant printed books before launching into a time-consuming search in original records (parish registers, wills, marriage licences and the like) which might duplicate work which has already been done.

There are one or two bibliographies for family historians with nationwide coverage, but in recent years the county-by-county genealogical bibliographies compiled by Stuart Raymond and published on a continuing basis by the Federation of Family History Societies have made life much easier for researchers.

In any case, you should always look carefully at the publication lists issued by Family History Societies or local record societies, and determine whether there are any volumes of the Victoria County History for your area of interest, many of which abound in details of manorial ownership and much else. Local *Notes and Queries* or similar publications may produce useful information, as may the once-popular national publication with the same title. Various publications under the name of 'Burke's' constitute a vast storehouse of information on families of wealth or prestige. The various editions of *Burke's Peerage, Baronetage and Knightage* are complemented by *Burke's Landed Gentry* (which began life in the 1830s as *Burke's History of the Commoners*) and by *Burke's Family Records* of 1897. Editions of the *Landed Gentry* which appeared during the 1850s have an exceptionally useful index of over 100,000 names of individuals. Other editions of the *Landed Gentry* have no such index, alas, and the *Peerage* has never carried a full name index. An easy way to determine whether any family is featured in a Burke's publication (including the volumes of extinct and dormant peerages and baronetcies) is to refer to *Burke's Family Index*, published in 1976 with an introduction by the *doyenne* of genealogical booksellers, Rosemary Pinches. Various other publishers have produced peerages and the like over the years, principally Debrett's, who concentrate more on collateral branches of each family than on a detailed genealogy of earlier generations.

The Dictionary of National Biography and *Who Was Who* have recently appeared on CD-ROM, and contain a great wealth of biographical information.

If you can, visit a good local reference library or spend time simply scanning the shelves of the British Library or the library of the Society of Genealogists;

give yourself time, and become acquainted with the range of printed works which exists.

You might be surprised to discover just how many books of genealogical value are offered for sale on the second-hand book market. Visit good local bookshops, or get on the mailing list of one or more of the bookdealers specialising in this field.

Printed books may contain the names of your ancestors, or they may not; in any event, they are essential if you want to broaden your understanding of the lives led by those ancestors within the contexts of place and time. If you hope one day to write an account of your own family - and we hope you will - then wide reading in printed books will help you turn a family tree into a family history.

Further reading

Filby, P.W. *American and British genealogy and heraldry: a selected list of books.* (3rd.Ed.) 1983. Also later supplements.
Fitzhugh, T.V.H. (Revised Lumas, S.). *Dictionary of genealogy.* (5th.Ed.) 1998.
Humphery-Smith, C.R. *A genealogist's bibliography.* 1977.
Kaminkow, M.J. *A new bibliography of British genealogy with notes.* 1965.
Mullins, E.L.C. *Texts and calendars: an analytical guide.* 1978.
Raymond, S. County and other bibliographies for the family historian, most published by the FFHS. Ongoing.
Richardson, J. *The local historian's encyclopedia.* (2nd.Ed.) 1986.
Saul, P. *The family historian's enquire within.* (5th.Ed.) 1995.
Titford, J. *Writing and publishing your family history.* 1996.

Journals and magazines

Family historians are well served by periodicals designed to suit their needs and interests - and have been for many years.

Some excellent and scholarly genealogical journals began to appear in the 1830s, offered in parts over a period of time to loyal bands of subscribers. Many concentrate on families of note and distinction, but none should be ignored, especially since the genealogical guides by Marshall and Whitmore will refer you to material contained in them. The principal journals of early date, most containing substantial indexes, are as follows:

- *Collectanea Topographica et Genealogica.* 8 volumes. 1834-43.
- *The Topographer and Genealogist.* 3 volumes. 1846-58.
- *The Herald and Genealogist.* 8 volumes. 1863-74.
- *Miscellanea Genealogica et Heraldica.* 31 volumes. 1868-1938.
- *The Genealogist.* 44 volumes, 1877-1921.
- *The Genealogical Magazine.* 7 volumes. 1897-1904.
- *The Ancestor.* 12 volumes. 1902-5.

In more recent times, various family history and other societies have published regular journals and/or newsletters, most of which go from strength to strength. The Society of Genealogists' *Genealogists' Magazine* and the Institute of Heraldic and Genealogical Studies' *Family History* are proven and long-standing favourites (as is the American publication, *Everton's Genealogical*

Helper), while 1995 saw the arrival of two new illustrated magazines, *Family History Monthly* and *Family Researcher Magazine*.

In November 1984 *Family Tree Magazine* made its first appearance and immediately filled a need in the market for an informative and well-illustrated magazine suitable for family historians whatever their previous knowledge and experience. Originally a bi-monthly publication, popular demand was such that it now appears monthly, being sold in thirty-eight countries world-wide. Each issue carries informative articles and other helpful features, a computer section, a beginners' series, questions and answers, readers' letters, book reviews, a 'readers' interests' section with long lists of surnames being researched, and a postal book service. *Practical family history*, a monthly product from the same stable, aimed at beginners, arrived in 1997. For details of both publications write to: *Family Tree Magazine*, 61 Great Whyte, Ramsey, Huntingdon, Cambs PE17 1HL.

Members' interests and genealogical directories

Most Family History Societies publish or include in their quarterly journals lists of members' interests. Members supply the surnames which they are researching, together with areas and approximate dates, hoping that others may contact them for an exchange of information. Long-lost relationships may even be established in this way. *Family Tree Magazine* publishes a similar list each month, and several journals have a *Connections sought* feature in which researchers pay to have a more detailed appeal for help published.

Genealogical directories are altogether more substantial, and are published on a subscription basis. *The Genealogical Research Directory* (GRD), also now available on CD-ROM, is a key reference work for world-wide family history research. Edited by Keith Johnson and Malcolm Sainty, it has been published annually since 1982. Everyone who contributes details of surnames being researched, together with the appropriate fee, receives a copy of the directory which contains his or her entries. The aim is to put family historians in touch with one another, not only so that information can be confirmed or expanded, but also to avoid unnecessary duplication of research.

Using the GRD is simple. Once you have found a surname in the list which interests you, use the number alongside it to establish the name and address of the relevant subscriber from a separate list arranged in numerical order.

In the event it is worth purchasing a recent copy of the GRD simply in order to determine the localities in which certain surnames are being researched. You may not know that anyone with your family name of 'Hawley', for example, ever lived in Shropshire - but looking at the GRD you could find that someone has found Hawleys, or hopes to find them, in that county.

If you write to a GRD subscriber, mention the edition in which you found your reference, and give the subscriber's number. Do include a stamped addressed envelope or the appropriate number of International Reply Coupons. You are advised to limit your first letter to specific and concise details; don't send off copies of everything you have unearthed, and never send original research which might get lost. The subscriber may know a lot already - or may be ignorant and be hoping for help. Do give freely of your knowledge, but don't be exploited by someone who wants to benefit from the fruits of your labour and will give little or nothing in return.

In 1994 the Federation of Family History Societies published the results of a major project which registered surnames being researched in the British Isles by over 17,000 family historians worldwide. It is called the British Isles Genealogical Register (*BIG R* for short), and is available on microfiche. The Register for England is published in county sections, each listing surnames being researched in that county only, plus names and addresses of researchers. There are separate sections for the Isle of Man, the Isle of Wight and the Channel Islands. The rest of the British Isles is published in national sections for Ireland, Scotland and Wales. The microfiche is available for consultation in various record offices and libraries, and may be purchased from the FFHS by individual researchers. The *BIG R* is an ongoing project, and is now in its second edition.

CHAPTER 20

Societies, Associations and Institutions

You are not alone. Even if you enjoy working on your family history in the privacy of your own home, you are bound to benefit from at least occasional contact with fellow-researchers. Family historians tend to be gregarious, keen to share their discoveries with others. Why not join a group of people who share your interests and enthusiasms?

Family History Societies and the Federation of Family History Societies

If you enjoy the pursuit of your ancestors, it may not be long before you decide to join at least one Family History Society. You may wish to belong to a society which covers the county or area from which your ancestors originate, but do also consider joining a society near you. Here you may choose to contribute to the work being done, and you should enjoy the sharing of ideas and experiences with others in a congenial atmosphere. Many FHSs are run and organised by people who live in a locality, whether or not that is where their own ancestral roots lie. Society membership usually costs only a few pounds annually, and for this sum you can expect to be offered a series of interesting lectures on a variety of subjects, a quarterly journal and, perhaps, outings to places of interest including main London repositories. Out-of-county members can be helped with their research problems by members living in the locality, either free of charge or for a small payment to cover expenses. Reciprocal research arrangements are often possible. Most societies have projects in hand, such as indexing census returns and recording monumental inscriptions or transcribing and publishing parish registers and other records - work which can prove to be of great value to fellow genealogists far and wide. Many Family History Societies all over the world are now members of the Federation of Family History Societies (FFHS), which was formed in 1974 to join together the various Family History Societies throughout the country. Twice each year it falls to one of the member societies to host a week-end conference for the Federation on its own territory, to include a council meeting and/or the Annual General Meeting and a festival of lectures, static displays and outings. These conferences are usually attended by two to three hundred people, of whom seventy or so are official representatives of individual societies, charged with attending the council meetings.

The Federation publishes a large number of reasonably-priced specialist books and a twice-yearly journal, *Family History News and Digest*, which carries an account of recent activities of member societies and offers a listing of key articles which have appeared in FHS journals, together with book reviews, details of new publications and a list of member societies.

Details of your local Family History Society may be obtained by writing to the Administrator of the FFHS, PO Box 8654, Shirley, Solihull B90 4JU. Please enclose a stamped addressed envelope or three International Reply Coupons.

The Association of Family History Societies for Wales is also a member of the FFHS, and can be contacted at the Birmingham and Midland Institute address, above.

The Scottish Association of Family History Societies has similar aims to those of the FFHS. For information about member societies, publications and holdings write to: 51/3 Mortonhall Road, Edinburgh EH9 2HN, enclosing a stamped addressed envelope or three International Reply Coupons.

The Society of Genealogists

This Society was founded in London in 1911, and its first meetings were held in a room in Fleet Street. This eventually became too small to hold its fast-growing collection of genealogical books and materials, and after various moves to larger premises throughout the years, the Society is now based in Goswell Road, London, not far from Barbican underground station.

The Society owns the largest collection of genealogical material and books in Britain, and only a personal visit can give you a true impression of the wealth of resources it contains, including the 'Great Card Index' containing over three million names and Boyd's Marriage Index with its six million entries. Every county has its own section in the library, with innumerable books of genealogical and topographical interest, copies of parish registers and other records, original manuscripts and a wide range of material on microform and CD-ROM. A complete inventory would be impossible, but thanks to a grant from the Lottery Fund, the Society is currently computerising its catalogue.

The reading rooms are open from Tuesday to Saturday, and many happy hours can be spent browsing and researching; to do so you need either to be a member or to pay an hourly or daily fee. A comfortable lounge is provided for use by members and visitors, where refreshments may be obtained. Membership of the Society could be of great benefit to you, whether you live near London or not. Members receive the quarterly *Genealogists' Magazine*, and the Society has produced a large number of publications and information leaflets of its own, offered for sale in its well-stocked bookshop alongside books from other publishers. For details of the Society, please send a stamped addressed envelope to the Director, Society of Genealogists, 14 Charterhouse Buildings, Goswell Road, London EC1M 7BA, or visit the Society's web-site at www.sog.org.uk which includes useful information, a membership application form and an on-line bookshop ordering facility.

The Institute of Heraldic and Genealogical Studies

The Institute of Heraldic and Genealogical Studies is dedicated to a study of the family in all its aspects; genealogy and heraldry alike are grist to its mill. The origins of the Institute lie in the pioneering work of Cecil Humphery-Smith, who in turn was inspired by his godfather, Canon Julian Bickersteth. Determined in its efforts to ensure quality and probity in matters of genealogical research, the Institute organises a number of day and residential courses, and its comprehensive correspondence course, supported by well-qualified tutors, is a time-honoured route for those who wish to make an in-depth study of genealogy and heraldry at home. A structured system of examinations, from the basic level to the award of the Licentiateship of the Institute, can be taken by candidates who feel they have reached the required level of competence. The Institute also conducts genealogical research to help geneticists who are involved with families whose members suffer from a number of inherited medical disorders.

The Institute has a very large collection of genealogical and heraldic books and manuscripts, and its publications include the series of county maps for genealogists and its own journal, *Family History*.

The well-known Pallot Index is housed at the Institute, and searches from it may be made on payment of a fee. The index was begun in 1818 by a firm of London record agents, and consists chiefly of references to marriages. In all, 101 of the 103 ancient parishes of the City of London are included, as well as many Middlesex parishes and a certain number from other counties. It is particularly useful in tracking down marriages which took place in the years immediately before the beginning of General Registration in 1837.

The Institute has recently acquired the long run of Lang family marriage registers from Gretna Green (see 'Clandestine and irregular marriages', above).

For details of membership of the Institute and of the services it offers, including a current examination syllabus, send a stamped, addressed envelope to The Institute of Heraldic and Genealogical Studies, Northgate, Canterbury, Kent CT1 1BA.

The Association of Genealogists and Record Agents

The Association of Genealogists and Record Agents (AGRA) was founded in 1968 in order to promote and maintain high standards of professional conduct and expertise amongst genealogists (those who direct overall programmes of research) and record agents (those who carry out specific research commissions). Only well-qualified persons with several years' experience are eligible for membership, and they subscribe to the Association's Code of Practice.

Members of AGRA have a variety of specialisms, a fact which is reflected in the list of members, a copy of which may be obtained for a small charge from the secretaries of the Association at 29 Badgers Close, Horsham, West Sussex RH12 5RU. Details of AGRA membership and affiliate membership may be obtained from the same address.

The Association of Scottish Genealogists and Record Agents (ASGRA) can be contacted by writing to 51/3 Mortonhall Road, Edinburgh EH9 2HN, Scotland. For the Association of Ulster Genealogists and Record Agents write to Glen Cottage, Glenmachan Road, Belfast BT4 2NP, Northern Ireland, and for the Australian Association of Genealogists and Record Agents write to PO Box 268, Oakleigh, Victoria 3166, Australia.

The Guild of One-Name Studies

The Guild of One-Name Studies (GOONS) is an organisation of one-name family history researchers or groups who collect all references to a particular surname but who are prepared to help fellow members of the Guild when they come across references to surnames being sought by others.

One person working alone on such a project may soon find others with a similar interest, and a group is formed; such a group may be the first to specialise in their particular surname of interest, and membership of the GOONS may be the next natural step to take.

To date, there are well over a thousand members of this 'one-name' guild. Perhaps your own surname is already registered? A GOONS prospectus may be obtained by sending a stamped, addressed envelope to The Guild of One-Name Studies, Box G, 14 Charterhouse Buildings, Goswell Road, London EC1M 7BA.

Projects and indexes

Many organisations, societies and individuals have compiled and maintain family history indexes of all kinds. Some people prefer to work completely on their own, transcribing and indexing a variety of records and archives, whilst others work in groups on larger projects. Many Family History Societies transcribe and index monumental inscriptions, census returns and non-conformist and parish registers. So it is that dedicated people endeavour to put something back into their hobby for the advantage of other researchers. Using indexes or transcripts can save you a great deal of time and effort, but these must be treated as 'finding aids' only, and you are strongly recommended to refer to the original source material wherever possible; even conscientious transcribers and indexers make the occasional mistake. Many individuals who have compiled an index will expect enquirers to pay a small fee to cover their running costs, but will offer excellent value in return.

Two particularly important indexes are currently in progress. The Strays' Index organised by the Federation of Family History Societies features births, baptisms, marriages, deaths, burials and census entries which occur in a county or country outside that of an individual's normal place of abode. All members of Family History Societies are encouraged to gather up any such 'strays' found during the course of their own research, and to submit details to the appropriate Strays' Co-ordinator for eventual publication on fiche by the FFHS. It is surprising just how many 'lost' ancestors may be tracked down in this way.

The National Burials Index Project (NBI) is being co-ordinated by the FFHS for England, Wales and Ireland, and by the Scottish Association of Family History Societies for Scotland. The NBI database will include the name of the deceased, age, date of burial, parish, county and a source code which will allow the reader to trace the particular entry to the originator of the material. A DOS-based computer program has been created which will allow the information to be accessed by county, region or country.

Further reading

(One-name studies)

Christmas, B.W. *Sources for one-name studies and for other family historians.* 1991.
GOONS: *Register of one-name studies.* (12th. Ed.) 1996.
Marker, I.J. and Warth, K.E. *Surname periodicals, a world-wide listing of one-name genealogical publications.* 1987.

Palgrave, D. *Forming a one-name group.* (4th. Ed.) 1992.
Ulph, C. *Organising a one-name gathering.* 1988.

(Projects and indexes)

FFHS. *Current publications by member societies* and *Current publications by member societies on microfiche.* New editions published regularly.

FFHS. *The strays clearing house and the national strays index.* Leaflet available from: FFHS Administrator, PO Box 8654, Shirley, Solihull B90 4JU on receipt of a stamped, addressed envelope or three international reply coupons.

Gibson, J. and Hampson, E. *Marriage, census and other indexes for family historians.* (7th.Ed.) 1998.

Jones, B. *Index of indexers: a directory showing the location of indexes for the family historian.* Published in various editions from 1994. Write to: 32 Myers Avenue, Bradford, West Yorks BD2 4ET.

For the names and addresses of other societies, organisations, federations, institutes, associations, councils, commissions, archives, record offices, libraries and museums, see Appendix One.

CHAPTER 21

Computers in Genealogy

Family historians collect a considerable amount of data as their researches progress; such data needs to be stored, retrieved, classified, analysed and organised. Little wonder, then, that the computer has been a boon to the world of genealogy, both to those who wish to operate at the simplest level and to those who hunger after ever more complex and sophisticated programs, from those who enjoy a bit of computing with their genealogy to those who like a bit of genealogy with their computing. Computers can be a great asset to your work, providing that you remain in control - and that you remember that you are recording information about human beings, not collecting telephone numbers!

As to hardware, most computer users opt for an IBM-compatible PC, an Apple Macintosh or the rather more modest Amstrad PCW, together with whatever printer seems the best for the job, given restraints of cost.

Genealogy programs may be purchased outright or obtained on a shareware basis. Here you can record information concerning the lives of your ancestors, and then arrange and present your findings by way of a printed report such as a drop-line pedigree. If you wish your data to be transferable, you would be well advised to produce it in the standard GEDCOM format. Look at the December and March issues each year of the Society of Genealogists' quarterly publication, *Computers in genealogy*, for a listing of available programs together with prices.

Genealogical databases will enable you to store family history information and to extract it with great speed and in ways which suit your needs. Indexing by field, for example, should be an easy enough matter. Several Family History Societies are now publishing indexes and other material on disk, and developments in CD-ROM technology mean that the International Genealogical Index (IGI) may be obtained in this form by institutions as part of the *FamilySearch* package. Other readily-available CD-ROMs include the LDS *Source Guide*, the LDS *Vital Records Index: British Isles* (containing over 5 million births, christenings and marriages, 1538-1888), Ancestry.com's *Periodical Source Index* (PERSI), the *Dictionary of National Biography, Who Was Who, Palmer's Index to The Times* newspaper, *Biography Database 1680-1830, The Genealogical Research Directory*, P.W. Coldham's *Book of Emigrants*, Australian state birth, marriage and death records, and various national telephone directories.

If you have a modem and the appropriate software, you can use an access provider to connect into the burgeoning world of the Internet. You will find

Email a fast, simple and cheap way of corresponding with family historians world-wide, you can join a genealogy forum or visit genealogical sites on the World Wide Web, such as GENUKI. Computer interest groups are organised by various Family History Societies and by the Society of Genealogists in London, and you can always advance your skills by attending a computer course at a local college.

There are many exciting family history databases and indexes available on-line. The LDS Church web site at http://www.familysearch.org allows you to access 'FamilySearch', which includes the IGI, Ancestral File, the US Social Security Death Index and the US Military Index. Also available on-line is the LDS Family History Library Catalog, and a modest but growing 'Free Births Marriages and Deaths' database taken from the original indexes to English and Welsh civil registration records, 1837-1897 (http://FreeBMD.RootsWeb.com/).

In any event, you might content yourself with using a word processing program to record family history information and to conduct your correspondence. The choice is a wide one, and you will delve into computers as deeply as you feel able.

The Society of Genealogists publishes *Computers in genealogy* every quarter, *Computer news* is produced by the Birmingham and Midland Society for Genealogy and Heraldry, and *Family Tree Magazine* has a computer section each month.

Further reading

Bloore, J. *Computer programs for the family historian.* Ten volumes to 1994.
Christian, P. *Finding Genealogy on the Internet.* 1999.
Clifford, K. *Complete Beginner's Guide to Genealogy, the Internet and Your Genealogy Computer Program.* 2001.
Hawgood, D. *An introduction to using computers for genealogy.* 1994.
Hawgood, D. *Computers for family history.* (5th.Ed.) 1994.
Hawgood, D. *Family Search on the Internet.* 1999.
Hawgood, D. *Genuki: UK & Ireland on the Internet.* 2000.
Hawgood, D. *Internet for genealogy.* (2nd.Ed.) 1999.
Lawton, G. *Spreadsheet family trees.* 1994.
Taylor, N.C. *Computers in genealogy: beginners' handbook.* 1994.

CHAPTER 22

Heraldry

Heraldry delights the mind and delights the eye, rekindles the atmosphere of jousting knights in days of yore, yet can be seen around us every day in prosaic as well as grand settings. If you refuse to be intimidated by its more obscure aspects, a mastery of the basics of heraldry will guarantee you a lifetime's fun and fascination.

What does heraldry have to do with family history? It has everything to do with family history, given the fact that personal armorial bearings make a statement about an individual and about his or her family alliances (his wife, her husband, his or her ancestors). Corporations, councils, companies, colleges, dioceses - all may have armorial bearings, but what will interest the family historian most of all is arms borne by an individual. You may well see advertisements in which what were once known as 'bucket shops' offer to sell you a computer-generated armorial display of your family coat of arms. There is a fundamental dishonesty at work here: throughout the centuries, arms have been officially granted by the College of Arms in London - and that grant is made not to a family, but to an individual and thereafter usually to his male offspring.

From the earliest years of heraldry 'canting' or punning arms have been favoured - so a Mr Hancock may choose cockerels for his arms, and Mr Lucy may choose 'lucies' (an earlier term for the fish we now know as a pike). An individual's greatest lifetime achievements may be featured on his arms - as in the case of the cluttered and even clumsy arms of Lord Nelson, which carry an 'augmentation' (a special grants of arms) showing a disabled ship and a 'ruinous battery' in celebration of the great man's victory at the Battle of the Nile. In more recent times, arms are quite likely to represent the bearer's interests or profession (the professional astronomer's arms may feature a telescope, the amateur musician's arms may include an oboe...).

Of more direct genealogical interest are those arms which indicate a marriage union between two people. Suppose that a man has the right to bear arms, and that he marries a woman who is the daughter of an 'armiger' with arms of his own. The married man's arms during his wife's lifetime will now consist of a shield divided in half vertically. The man's arms will appear in the 'dominant' position on the heraldic shield, which is the left-hand side - known as the 'dexter' (Latin for 'right') because arms are described from the point of view of the person carrying a shield, not from the perspective of a person looking at that shield from the front. The wife's arms, or rather those of her father, will appear

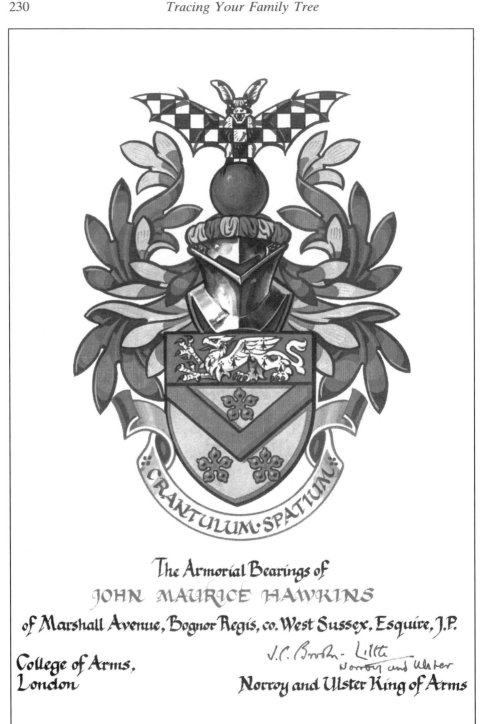

The Armorial Bearings of
JOHN MAURICE HAWKINS
of Marshall Avenue, Bognor Regis, co. West Sussex, Esquire, J.P.

College of Arms,
London

Norroy and Ulster King of Arms

A modern example of armorial bearings. (John Hawkins Esq, JP)

on the right of the shield as you look at it, the 'sinister' side. To divide a shield vertically in this way is to 'impale', in the language of heraldry. If a wife is an 'heraldic heiress' - that is, her father had no sons to carry his armorial bearings on to the next generation - then her arms will appear on a small shield in the centre of her husband's arms on what is known as an 'escutcheon of pretence'. In this situation, the children of such a couple will be entitled to display the arms of both their father and their mother, 'quartered' on a shield with father's arms shown top right and bottom left, and mother's shown at top left and bottom right. By this means, the arms of the mother's side are perpetuated in succeeding generations, and do not die out with the death of her father. 'Quartering' has nothing to do with a 'quarter' meaning a fourth part - rather, it is similar to the expression 'living quarters', that is, a place in which a home for something may be found. Several ancient families have numerous quarterings on their armorial bearings; try and look at the illustration on the back of the dust jacket of *Debrett's family historian* by Noel Currer-Briggs and Royston Gambier, which shows in full colour a shield containing no fewer than 323 quarterings!

So heraldry has everything to do with genealogy - with husbands and wives, fathers and mothers, children and grandchildren. If you want to know whether arms have been used by individuals of a particular surname, look at Burke's *General Armory* (available in several editions, the best dating from 1884, frequently reprinted), which is arranged alphabetically and includes both official and unofficial arms. You may well wish to work in reverse - that is, you may have seen arms on a silver spoon, a signet ring, a bookplate or a stone monument in a church, and want to know whose arms they may have been. Here you need *Papworth's Ordinary of British Armorials* (published in 1874 and several times reprinted), which is in effect Burke's *General Armory* in reverse.

One of the glories of heraldry is that any armorial achievement can be 'blazoned' - that is, expressed in words. So a green St Andrew's cross on a silver background would be blazoned like this: 'Argent, a saltire vert'. Using the written blazon, a heraldic artist can draw the relevant arms; providing he or she keeps to the spirit of the written description, a good deal of artistic licence is permitted, and the artist can allow his or her own creativity and sense of style to shine through. Once you have learned to blazon, you should be able to use Papworth's *Ordinary*. You would locate the section dealing with 'saltires', find 'argent' followed by 'a saltire vert' - and discover that such arms have been borne by individuals with the following surnames: BLOXAM, Chester Square, Pimlico; BLOXAM or BLOXHAM; KIRKBRIDGE, Northumberland; KIRKEBY; Sir Richard KIRKEBY; KIRKBY; NOONE, Norfolk. Your search is narrowing. If the arms which interest you are impaled and include those of the bearer's wife, use Papworth again. Let us suppose you come up with the surname YATES this time. Now you know that you are looking for a man surnamed Blox(h)am, Kirkbridge, Kirk(e)by or Noone who married a woman surnamed Yates. Let's say that the arms which interest you are dated 1682, or at least have a late seventeenth-century feel about them. After a bit of searching through printed books in a well-stocked library, you'll eventually stumble across a Bloxham-Yates liaison: Richard Bloxham of Offenham, lieutenant under Sir William Keyt, Bart., a lieutenant-colonel of foot in the Worcestershire militia, aged 55 in 1682, married Hannah, daughter of Robert Yates of Yardley, Worcestershire, a sister of Captain Robert Yates of Yardley. This appears in *The Visitation of Worcestershire 1682-2*, edited by W.C. Metcalfe, 1883.

What could be more fun than being a heraldic and genealogical detective and solving a riddle in this way? This is the glory of heraldry - that it pleases our intellect as well as our eye, carries genealogical clues within the aesthetic of its pleasing form and its glorious profusion of colour.

The other parts of a heraldic achievement of arms will become familiar to you as you progress: the helm placed above the shield will give you a clue as to the status of the bearer, as will the coronet which surrounds it in the case of peers of the realm; you'll learn that the mantling, the cape lapping around the shield, reflects the principal colour and metal or fur used on the shield itself; you'll pay attention to the 'supporters' who may appear at right and left of the shield, and you may use any motto as a short-cut to identifying the name of the bearer. You'll learn that a woman's shield is displayed on a lozenge and that those glorious heraldic boards sometimes displayed in churches are called 'hatchments' and reveal a great deal about those whom they commemorate.

No matter if your own family were not armigerous; as you trace your family tree you'll find that it's important to know something about the nobility and landed gentry who lived cheek-by-jowl with your more humble forebears, and who acted as their employers or owned the land or the property they occupied. Society, after all, has always been interdependent - and in any case, the English class system has been very fluid throughout the centuries, with individuals rising and falling in successive generations. Your humble village wheelwright grandfather may have gentry or noble ancestry after all!

Heralds' Visitations

Heraldry and genealogy come together in a most dynamic and useful way in what are known as the Heralds' Visitations. In 1530 a warrant issued by Henry VIII granted permission for Thomas Benolt, Clarenceux King of Arms, to travel throughout his province in the south of England and to seek out those who were using arms and to establish their right to do so - given the fact that abuse of arms by then had become widespread. Benolt's 'Visitation' established a practice which continued until the late seventeenth century, as each county was visited periodically by the heralds, with arms and pedigrees being recorded.

Most original visitation records are at the College of Arms; many have been published with name indexes, some based upon original records, others taken from copies and pseudo-visitation collections of varying provenance and authenticity held in the British Library and elsewhere. To gain some clear understanding of the worth of any particular printed visitation, you should refer to *Visitation pedigrees & the genealogist* by G.D. Squibb (2nd.Ed. 1978). The Harleian Society has been publishing visitation volumes since 1869, and continues to do so to this day.

Thanks to the work of the heralds, then, we have an unrivalled collection of pedigrees made during a period of just less than two hundred years. Not all of them are strictly accurate, of course, and some may be based upon hearsay or even deliberately fabricated, but they are still a wonderful resource.

If you come across a reference in an early parish register, a will or some other document to an ancestor who is termed 'Gent.', 'Esquire' (or even 'Mr' or 'Mrs') then you should consult the relevant printed visitation for the period in question. Be aware that errors and discrepancies may still be found even in such august tomes as these, and try to refer back to original records wherever possible.

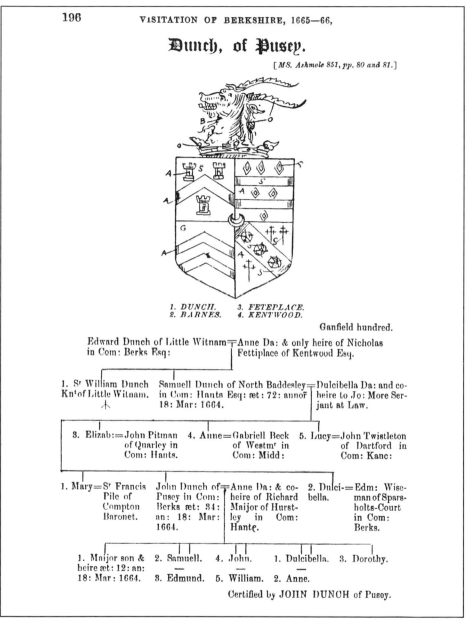

196   VISITATION OF BERKSHIRE, 1665—66,

𝔇𝔲𝔫𝔠𝔥, 𝔬𝔣 𝔓𝔲𝔰𝔢𝔶.

[*MS. Ashmole 851, pp. 80 and 81.*]

1. *DUNCH.*   3. *FETEPLACE.*
2. *BARNES.*   4. *KENTWOOD.*

Ganfield hundred.

Edward Dunch of Little Witnam ⊤ Anne Da: & only heire of Nicholas
in Com: Berks Esq: Fettiplace of Kentwood Esq.

1. Sᵣ William Dunch   Samuell Dunch of North Baddesley ⊤ Dulcibella Da: and co-
Knᵗ of Little Witnam.   in Com: Hants Esq: æt: 72: annoᵣ   heire to Jo: More Ser-
     18: Mar: 1664.   jant at Law.

3. Elizab:=John Pitman   4. Anne=Gabriell Beck   5. Lucy=John Twistleton
of Quarley in   of Westmᵣ in   of Dartford in
Com: Hants.   Com: Midd: Com: Kane:

1. Mary=Sᵣ Francis   John Dunch of=Anne Da: & co-   2. Dulci-=Edm: Wise-
Pile of   Pusey in Com: heire of Richard   bella.   man of Spars-
Compton   Berks æt: 34:   Maijor of Hurst-   holts-Court
Baronet.   an: 18: Mar: ley in Com: in Com:
     1664.   Hante.   Berks.

1. Maijor son &   2. Samuell.   4. John.   1. Dulcibella.   3. Dorothy.
heire æt: 12: an: —   —   —
18: Mar: 1664.   3. Edmund.   5. William.   2. Anne.

Certified by JOHN DUNCH of Pusey.

A Dunch family pedigree from the Visitation of Berkshire 1665–6; *from vol 56 of the
publications of the Harleian Society 1907. The visitation was made by Elias Ashmole,
Windsor Herald, for Sir Edward Bysshe, Clarenceux, and the details are from Ashmole
Manuscript 851 in the British Museum. Note that the arms are 'tricked', the colours being
indicated by letters: O is 'or' (gold), A is 'argent' (silver), S is 'sable' (black), G is 'gules'
(red), and B is 'blue' (the normal heraldic name for which is 'azure'). The arms show four
quarterings for the families of Dunch, Barnes, Feteplace and Kentwood. The crescent at the
centre indicates that the bearings are those of a second son.*

Several catalogues and indexes relating to Heralds' Visitations have appeared in print over the years, but with the publication of C.R. Humphery-Smith's *Armigerous ancestors: a catalogue of visitation records together with an index of pedigrees, arms and disclaimers* in 1997, the researcher is now able to access the results of forty years' research into existing manuscript and printed visitation sources, augmented by editorial commentary and indexes.

If you are attracted by the idea of combining old and new technologies, you could always experiment with a computer program such as 'BLAZONS!' or 'Blazon' (see 'Digital coats of arms' in *Family Tree Magazine,* Computer Section, December 1996), and if you have a general interest in heraldry, contact the Institute of Heraldic and Genealogical Studies, Northgate, Canterbury, Kent CT1 1BA or the Heraldry Society, PO Box 32, Maidenhead, Berkshire SL6 3FT.

The College of Arms, Queen Victoria Street, London EC4 4BT, has a vast and unrivalled collection of heraldic and genealogical manuscripts and printed works. If you seek specific information from these records you will need to contact an officer of the College, who will undertake work for you for a fee.

Further reading

A large number of books have been published on heraldry in many different languages from the sixteenth century onwards. Amongst the most useful more recent publications are the following:

Bedingfeld, H. and Gwynn-Jones, P. *Heraldry.* 1993. Includes a large number of facsimiles from documents in the College of Arms in full colour.

Chesshyre, D.H.B., Woodcock, T. and others. *Dictionary of British arms: medieval ordinary.* The first two volumes of this long-planned work were published in 1992 and 1996.

Fairbairn's Book of crests of the families of Great Britain and Ireland. The fourth and best edition of 1905 has been reprinted several times.

Fox-Davies, A.C. *Armorial families.* The seventh and best editon was published in two volumes, 1929.

Fox-Davies, A.C. *The art of heraldry.* 1904, reprinted 1986. (This is the most gloriously-illustrated book on heraldry of recent times).

Friar, S. *A new dictionary of heraldry.* 1987.

Friar, S. *Heraldry for the local historian and genealogist.* 1992.

Gough, H. and Parker, J., *A glossary of terms used in heraldry.* 1894 (several times reprinted).

Humphery-Smith, C.R. *Anglo-Norman armory.* 1978. *Anglo-Norman armory two.* 1984. The second volume consists of a substantial illustrated and indexed ordinary of thirteenth-century armorials.

Humphery-Smith, C.R. *General Armory Two.* 1973.

Moncreiffe, Sir Iain and Pottinger, D. *Simple heraldry.* 1953.

Rylands, J.P. *Disclaimers at the Herald's Visitations.* 1888.

Summers, P. (later volumes with Titterton, J.E.). *Hatchments in Britain.* A ten-volume series, 1974-1994.

Swinnerton, I. *Basic facts about heraldry for family historians.* 1996.

Wagner, A.R. *The records and collections of the College of Arms.* 1952.

Appendix One

Useful addresses
[For a full list of Family History and other societies which belong to the Federation of Family History Societies, see the latest issue of *Family History News and Digest*.]

Great Britain
Anglo-French FHS, Patrick Pontet, 31 Collingwood Walk, Andover, Hants SP10 1PU

Anglo-German FHS, Mrs J.Towey, 20 Skylark Rise, Plymouth, Devon PL6 7SN

Anglo-Jewish Association, Woburn House, Upper Woburn Place, London WC1H OEZ

Association of Genealogists and Record Agents, 29 Badgers Close, Horsham, West Sussex RH12 5RU

Bank of England Archive, Archive Section HO-M, The Bank of England, Threadneedle Street, London EC2R 8AH

Belfast Library and Society for Promoting Knowledge, Linen Hall Library, 17 Donegal Square North, Belfast BT1 5GD

Borthwick Institute of Historical Research (University of York), St Anthony's Hall, Peasholme Green, York YO1 2PW

British Association of Local History, PO Box 1476, Salisbury, Wiltshire SP2 8SY

British Library, 96 Euston Road, London NW1 2DB

British Library Newspaper Library, Colindale Avenue, London NW9 5HE

British Library, Oriental and India Office Collections, British Library, 96 Euston Road, London NW1 2DB

British Records Association, 18 Padbury Court, London, E2 7EH

British Record Society, Stone Barn Farm, Sutherland Road, Longsdon, Stoke-on-Trent, Staffs ST9 9QD

British Telecommunications (BT) Archives, 3rd Floor, Holborn Telephone Exchange, 268–270 High Holborn, London WC1V 7EE

British Waterways Archive, Llanthony House, Gloucester Docks, Glos GL1 2EJ

Business Archives Council, 101 Whitechapel High St., London E1 7RE

Catholic FHS, Mr and Mrs T. Goggin, 45 Gates Green Road, West Wickham, Kent BR4 9DE

Charity Commission for England and Wales, St Alban's House, 57/60 Haymarket, London SW1Y 4QX

Church of Jesus Christ of Latter-day Saints, Family History Centre, 64/68 Exhibition Road, South Kensington, London SW7 2PA [For a list of LDS Family History Centres in the British Isles, see Appendix II to Tom Wood's

An introduction to British Civil Registration (2nd.Ed.) 2000 or *The Family Historian's Enquire Within* by Pauline Saul (5th.Ed. 1995) pp.51-53]

College of Arms, Queen Victoria Street, London EC4 4BT

Corporation of London Records Office, PO Box 270, Guildhall, London EC2P 2EJ

Court of the Lord Lyon, New Register House, Edinburgh EH1 3YT

Dr. Williams's Library, 14 Gordon Square, London WC1H OAG

Family Records Centre, 1 Myddelton Street, Islington, London EC1R 1UW

Federation of Family History Societies, Administrator, PO Box 8654, Shirley, Solihull B90 4JU

Genealogical Society of Utah (UK), 185 Penns Lane, Sutton Coldfield, West Midlands B76 1JU

General Register Office, 1 Myddelton Street, Islington, London EC1R 1UW

General Register Office (Northern Ireland), 49-55 Chichester Street, Belfast BT1 4HL

General Register Office (Scotland), New Register House, Edinburgh EH1 3YT

Grand Lodge Library and Museum, Freemasons' Hall, Great Queen Street, London WC2B 5AZ

Guildhall Library, Aldermanbury, London EC2P 2EJ

Guild of One-Name Studies, Box G, 14 Charterhouse Buildings, Goswell Road, London EC1M 7BA

Heraldry Society, PO Box 32, Maidenhead, Berks SL6 3FT

Historical Association, 59a Kennington Park Road, London SE11 4JH

House of Lords Record Office, House of Lords, London SW1A OPW

Huguenot and Walloon Research Association, Mrs J. Tsushima, 'Malmaison', Great Bedwyn, Wilts SN8 3PE

Huguenot Society, Huguenot Library, University College, Gower Street, London WC1E 6BT

Imperial War Museum, Department of Documents, Lambeth Road, London SE1 6HZ, (records from the First World War onwards only).

Institute of Heraldic and Genealogical Studies, Northgate, Canterbury, Kent CT1 1BA

Irish Genealogical Research Society, 82 Eaton Square, London SW1W 9AJ

Jewish Genealogical Society of Great Britain, PO Box 13288, London N3 3WD

Jewish Historical Society, 33 Seymour Place, London W1H 5AP

London Metropolitan Archives, 40 Northampton Road, London EC1R OHB

London Museum of Jewish Life, The Sternberg Centre, 80 East End Road, London N3 2SY

Methodist Archives and Research Centre, John Rylands University Library, Deansgate, Manchester M3 3EH

National Archives of Scotland. HM General Register House, Princes Street, Edinburgh EH1 3YY

National Army Museum, Royal Hospital Road, London SW3 4HT

National Library of Ireland, Kildare Street, Dublin 2

National Library of Scotland, Department of Manuscripts, George IV Bridge, Edinburgh EH1 1EW

National Library of Wales, Aberystwyth, Ceredigion SY23 3BU

National Maritime Museum, Romney Road, Greenwich, London SE10 9NF

National Museums and Galleries on Merseyside, Merseyside Maritime Museum (Archives and Library), Albert Dock, Liverpool L3 4AQ

Post Office Archives and Records Services, Freeling House, Mount Pleasant Complex, Phoenix Place entrance, London EC1A 1BB

Presbyterian Historical Society of Ireland, Room 220, Church House, Fisherwick Place, Belfast BT1 6DW

Principal Probate Registry of the Family Division, 1st Avenue House, 42–49 High Holborn, London WC1V 6NP

Public Record Office, Ruskin Avenue, Kew, Richmond, Surrey TW9 4DU

Public Record Office, Census Reading Rooms, 1 Myddelton Street, Islington, London EC1R 1UW

Public Record Office of Northern Ireland, 66 Balmoral Avenue, Belfast BT9 6NY

Quaker FHS, 32 Ashburnham Road, Ampthill, Beds MK45 2RH

Romany and Traveller FHS, Mrs. Janet Keet-Black, 6 St James Walk, South Chailey, East Sussex BN8 4BU

Royal Air Force Museum, Dept. of Research and Information Services, Grahame Park Way, Hendon, London NW9 5LL

Royal Marines Museum, Eastney, Southsea, Hants PO4 9PX

Scots Ancestry Research Society, 8 York Road, Edinburgh EH5 3FH

Scottish Association of Genealogists and Record Agents, 51/3 Mortonhall Road, Edinburgh EH9 2HN

Scottish Genealogy Society, Library and Family History Centre, 15 Victoria Terrace, Edinburgh EH1 2JL

Scottish Maritime Museum, Laird Forge, Gottries Road, Irvine, Strathclyde KA12 8QE

Société Jersiaise, 7 Pier Road, Saint Helier, Jersey, Channel Islands

Society of Friends, Library of the Religious Society of Friends, Friends House, Euston Road, London NW1 2BJ

Society of Genealogists, 14 Charterhouse Buildings, Goswell Road, London EC1M 7BA

United Reformed Church History Society, 86 Tavistock Place, London WC1H 9RT [see page 91].

Australia

Australian Association of Genealogists and Record Agents, PO Box 268, Oakleigh, Victoria 3166

Australian Federation of Family History Organisations, c/o 6/48 May Street, Bayswater, WA 6053, Australia

Australian Institute of Genealogical Studies, PO Box 339, Blackburn, Victoria 3130

National Library of Australia, Parkes Place, Canberra, ACT 2600

Society of Australian Genealogists, Richmond Villa, 120 Kent Street, Observatory Hill, Sydney 2000, New South Wales

Canada

Canadian Federation of Genealogical and Family History Societies, 227 Parkville Bay, Winnipeg, MB, R2M 2J6

Family History Assoc. of Canada, PO Box 398, West Vancouver, BC, V7V 3P1

National Archives of Canada, 395 Wellington Street, Ottawa, ONT, K1A ON3

Ireland

Association of Ulster Genealogists and Record Agents, Glen Cottage, Glenmachan Road, Belfast BT4 2NP, Northern Ireland

General Register Office, 8-11 Lombard Street East, Dublin 2
Irish FHS, The Secretary, PO Box 36, Naas, Co. Kildare, Eire
National Archives of Ireland, Bishop Street, Dublin 8
National Library of Ireland, Kildare Street, Dublin 8

Netherlands
Centraal Bureau Voor Genealogie, PO Box 11755, NL2502 AT'S-Gravenhage

New Zealand
Genealogical Research Institute of New Zealand, PO Box 12-531, Thorndon,
   Wellington 6038
New Zealand FHS Inc., Mrs J. Lord, PO Box 13301, Armagh, Christchurch
New Zealand Society of Genealogists, PO Box 8795, Symonds St., Auckland 1035

South Africa
Genealogical Society of South Africa, Suite 143, Postnet X2600, Houghton 2041
West Rand FHS, Mr Mark Tapping, PO Box 760, Florida 1710

United States of America
British Isles FHS of Los Angeles, 2531 Sawtelle Boulevard, #134 Los Angeles,
   CA 90064-3163
Family History Department (LDS), Family History Library, 35 North West
   Temple, Salt Lake City, Utah 84150
International Society for British Genealogy and Family History, PO Box 3115,
   Salt Lake City, Utah 84110-3115
Irish Genealogical Society Int'l, PO Box 16585, St Paul, Minnesota 55116-0585
National Genealogical Society, 4527 17th St. North, Arlington, Virginia 22207-
   2363
New England Historic Genealogical Society, 101 Newbury Street, Boston MA
   02116-3087

For further relevant addresses and other details you should refer to:
ASLIB. A guide to sources of information in Great Britain and Ireland.
Bentley, E.P. *The genealogist's address book.* (1995-6 Ed.) [Covers USA only.]
Cole, J. and Church, R. *In and around record repositories in Great Britain and
   Ireland.* (4th.Ed.) 1998.
Foster, J. and Sheppard, J. *British Archives.* (4th.Ed.) 2001.
Harrold, A. *Libraries in the United Kingdom and the Republic of Ireland.* 1997.
O'Neill, R.K. *Guide to libraries and archives of Ulster.* N.d.
Pinhorn, M. *Historical, archaeological and kindred societies in the United
   Kingdom.* 1986.
Royal Commission on Historical Manuscripts. *Record repositories in Great
   Britain.* (11th.Ed.) 1999.
Saul, P. *The Family Historian's Enquire Within.* (5th.Ed.) 1995.
The Libraries, Museums and Art Galleries Year Book
The World of Learning. Annually (51st.Ed.) 2001.

Appendix Two

Glossary of terms, abbreviations and colloquialisms used in Family History

General glossary

Abstract Summary of the essential details from a document

Affidavit Written declaration on oath

Allegation Statement made on oath

Anabaptist A derogatory term; when found in a parish register usually refers to a Baptist or a Quaker

Badgeman A person responsible for ensuring that all paupers receiving parish relief wore badges

Badger Pauper, from the badge a pauper was obliged to wear; also licensed pedlar, hawker or chapman

Bargain & Sale A procedure whereby property was conveyed secretly

Blanket search A search through a set of records looking for specific references - e.g. to a particular surname

Boyd's Marriage Index Compiled by Percival Boyd. Available for consultation at the Society of Genealogists, with a few copies elsewhere. Individual county sections are often held by county libraries

Brewster Sessions Annual sessions held to license victuallers from 1729

Bridewell A gaol or house of correction

Brief Letter commending a charitable appeal, or written summary of facts in a law case

Calendar A précis full enough to replace an original document for most purposes. Also commonly used for a list of names which is only alphabetical by the first letter of each surname

Canon Law Church law

Catalogue Calendar or descriptive list

Chattels Personal goods

Churching Ceremony of purification of a woman after the birth of a child

Codicil An addition to a will; has to be signed and witnessed

Consanguinity Of the same blood, related by birth

Cordwainer Shoemaker; originally one who used leather from Cordova

Cousin A general term for a relative

Cousin German A first cousin

Curtilage Small courtyard or piece of ground attached to a dwelling place

Dame School A small private school usually run by an elderly woman for a small fee.

Deed poll Deed made by one party, needing no duplicate (and therefore different from an indenture)

Deposition Testimony given under oath in a court case

Descriptive list List with brief abstract of documents

Diocese Area of a bishop's jurisdiction

Dissenter A person who did not conform to the beliefs and practices of the established Church of England

Emigrant Person leaving one place to live elsewhere

Executor/Executrix Person appointed by a testator to ensure that the provisions of a will were carried out

Extract Selected details taken from any document or class of records

Facsimile An exact copy

Farlieu Money payment

Father-in-law/Mother-in-law Sometimes used to mean stepfather/stepmother

Foundling Abandoned infant, often left in a public place

Genealogy The study of descent from ancestors

Glebe terrier Survey of church lands and benefices

Gossip A god-parent

Half-baptised Baptised privately, very soon after birth

Hundred Administrative division of a county. Alternative terms include 'Lathe' in Kent, 'Leet' in East Anglia, 'Liberty' in the Isle of Wight, 'Rape' in Sussex, 'Ward' in Cumberland, Durham and Northumberland and 'Wapentake' in Derbyshire, Leicestershire, Lincolnshire, Nottinghamshire and Yorkshire. In Wales the word 'Cantrev' is used

Husbandman Small farmer, usually a tenant farmer

Immigrant A person arriving in a place to settle

Incumbent A parson, vicar, rector or perpetual curate

Indenture Deed entered into between two or more parties, each party having a copy (so unlike a deed poll)

Index Alphabetically-arranged references to people, places or subjects (index nominum, index locorum, index rerum)

Interregnum The time between two reigns (such as that between the reigns of Charles I and Charles II)

Intestate (Both adjective and noun) used when a person died not having left a will

Journeyman One whose apprenticeship was complete and who hired his labour out by the day (from French, *journée*) or the week

Lady Day 25 March, a Quarter Day; until 1752, the first day of the new year

Michaelmas 29 September, a Quarter Day

Nephew Until the end of the seventeenth century, could mean a grandson or kinsman

Niece Until the end of the seventeenth century, very often used to denote any younger female relative

Palaeography Study of old handwriting

Pallot Pallot's Index of Marriages (and some baptisms) held by the Institute of Heraldic and Genealogical Studies

Parish chest The chest used for storing church records and communion silver; used as a term for parish records in general

Petty Sessions Meeting of two or three local magistrates for local business

Phillimore Long-established publishers of genealogical books; often used to refer to the series of printed marriage registers edited by W.P.W. Phillimore and others

Poll tax Tax levied on a person, rather than on his lands or goods

Presentment Statement of fact made on oath (for example, churchwardens' presentments made to an ecclesiastical official at the time of a visitation)

Ragged School School for poor children, provided free in cases of real poverty

Recognizance Legal document with certain stated conditions and a financial penalty for non-compliance

Recusants Nonconformists, especially Roman Catholics

Relict Widow

Rose's Rose's Act of 1812, instituting printed baptism, marriage and burial registers for use in parishes

Sojourner Temporary resident in a parish

Somerset House Term often used to refer to the Principal Probate and Divorce Registries which are housed there

Special Sessions Sessions held monthly in each division of a county, informal meetings of magistrates

Spurious Illegitimate

Stray Person found referred to in a place other than his or her place of birth or settlement

Substitute Person provided by another person or parish to replace a parishioner chosen by ballot to serve in the militia

Surrogate Clergyman or other person appointed to deputise for a Bishop

Terrier Record giving details of land holding

Testamentary Pertaining to a testament or will

Testator One who makes a will

Three Denominations The three nonconformist denominations, Presbyterian, Baptist and Congregational, sometimes known as the 'Old Dissent'

Transcript Exact copy of the text of an original manuscript or document

Tyburn Ticket Certificate granting exemption from the need to serve a parish office, the bearer having helped in the capture and successful prosecution and conviction of a felon

Vagrant Person of no fixed abode

Yeoman A more substantial farmer than a husbandman; the two terms were often interchangeable

Some abbreviations used in Family History, including census returns

Admon	Letters of Administration
Ag lab	Agricultural labourer
AGRA	Association of Genealogists and Record Agents
Ann	Annuitant
App	Apprentice
B	Born
Bach	Bachelor

Ban	(Marriage by) Banns
Bap	Baptised
Bd	Bond OR buried
BMD	Births, Marriages and Deaths
Bro	Brother
BTs	Bishops' transcripts
Bur	Buried, burial
C	Circa [about]: e.g. c.1645 - or Christened
Chr	Christened
CMB	Christenings, Marriages and Burials
Cod	Codicil - an addition to a will
C of E	Church of England
Cog	Consent of Guardians
Co-h	Co-heir/co-heiress
Cop	Consent of Parents
CRO	County Record Office
Ct	Court
D	Died OR daughter (sometimes 'dr')
Dat	Dated
Dau	Daughter
Div	Divorce(d)
DNB	Dictionary of National Biography
Dom	Domestic servant
DRO	Diocesan Record Office
Dsp	Decessit sine prole (died without issue)
D.unm	Died unmarried
Emp	Employed
Exec	Executor/executrix
FFHS	Federation of Family History Societies
FHS	Family History Society
FRC	Family Records Centre
FS	Female servant
FTM	Family Tree Magazine
FWK	Frame work knitter
GRD	Genealogical Research Directory
GRO	General Register Office
H	Heir/heiress or head of the household (census)
HMSO	Her Majesty's Stationery Office
Husb	Husband OR husbandman (small farmer)
IGI	International Genealogical Index (LDS church)
IHGS	Institute of Heraldic and Genealogical Studies
Illeg	Illegitimate
Ind	Of independent means
Inf	Infant
Inv	Inventory
Lab	Labourer
LDS	Church of Jesus Christ of Latter-day Saints
Lic	(Marriage) licence
M (or '=')	Married
MI	Monumental Inscription OR Marriage Index

MS	Male servant
N	Natal or birth date
NK	Not known
NLW	National Library of Wales
NPRs	Non-Parochial Registers (at the Public Record Office)
NS	New Style (Gregorian calendar, 1752 onwards)
ONS	Office for National Statistics OR One-Name Study
OPCS	Office of Population Censuses and Surveys (now ONS)
OS	Old Style (Julian calendar, up to 1751)
Otp	Of this parish
PCC	Prerogative Court of Canterbury
PCY	Prerogative Court of York
PLU	Poor Law Union
PPR	Principal Probate Registry
PRO	Public Record Office
Prob	Probate
QS	Quarter Sessions
RDC	Rural District Council
S	Son
S & H	Son and Heir
Sis	Sister
SoG	Society of Genealogists
Soj	Sojourner
Sp	Sine prole (without issue) - or Spinster
Temp	Time of (eg, 'Temp. Henry VIII')
U/Unm	Unmarried
UDC	Urban District Council
USD	Urban Sanitary District
Ux	Uxor (i.e. wife)
VCH	Victoria County History
Vid	Vidua (i.e. widow)
Vis	Visitor
W	Wife OR will
Wid	Widow or widower
Wit	Witness
Wp/Wpr	Will proved
Z	Sometimes used for 'births' (eg, 'ZMD' for 'births, marriages and deaths')

Appendix Three

Useful dates

1534:	Act of Supremacy. Henry VIII became head of the Church of England
1536:	Union of Wales with England
1538:	Earliest parish registers begin; in principle, all christenings, marriages and burials to be recorded in a book to be kept in a 'sure coffer'
1597/8:	Parish registers to be entered on parchment; previous paper registers to be copied onto parchment. Copies of each year's entries (bishops' transcripts) to be sent to the Diocesan Registry within a month after Easter
1601,1640:	Poor Law Acts
1653:	Clerks ('parish registers') to make entries in parish registers. All wills to be proved in the Court of Civil Commission
1660:	Restoration of King Charles II
1662-1689:	Hearth Taxes
1662,1671,1697:	Settlement Acts
1667,1678:	Burials in Woollen Acts
1692:	Land Tax
1694:	Tax on births, marriages and burials, bachelors and widowers without children
1696:	Window Tax
1707:	Union of England and Scotland
1710:	Stamp duty on apprentice indentures
1722/3:	Parishes encouraged to build workhouses
1751/2:	Lord Chesterfield's Act; change from the Julian to the Gregorian calendar. Year to commence on 1 January, not 25 March
1753:	Hardwicke's Marriage Act, largely intended to end clandestine marriages. Effective from 1754
1760-1797:	Enclosure Acts. 1,500 private enclosure acts passed
1777-1852:	Male Servants' Tax (employers only named)
1778:	Catholic Relief Act; Roman Catholics allowed to own land after taking oath of allegiance
1783:	Tax on all baptisms, marriages and burials. Paupers exempt. Repealed 1794
1785-1792:	Female Servants' Tax (employers only named)

1795:	Speenhamland system of outdoor relief adopted; wages made up to subsistence level
1801:	Union with Ireland. First British census (statistics only)
1801:	General Enclosure Act
1812:	Parochial Registers' Act (Rose's Act). Enforced 1813. Separate printed registers for baptisms, marriages and burials
1829:	Metropolitan Police Force Act
1832:	Parliamentary Reform Act
1834:	Poor Law Amendment Act - parishes to combine into unions to provide workhouses for the destitute
1836:	Enclosure by consent without private legislation if two-thirds of the interested parties agreed
1836:	Tithe Commutation Act
1837:	Civil Registration, 1 July 1837. Returns of births, marriages and deaths to be sent to the Registrar General
1837:	Commission appointed to call in all existing non-parochial registers to be authenticated
1839:	County Constabulary Act
1840:	Non-parochial Register Act; surrendered registers of nonconformists deposited with the Registrar General's Office
1841:	First national census return with names. Decennial censuses made available for public consultation after one hundred years.
1845:	Enclosure Acts. Commissioners to consider applications for enclosure and given powers to allocate land for 'exercise and recreation'
1851:	Ecclesiastical census, listing every place of worship in England and Wales
1852/3:	Burial Acts. Local authorities to open cemeteries, various churchyards being overcrowded and to be closed to future burials
1855:	General Registration of births, marriages and deaths in Scotland
1857:	Matrimonial Causes Act, which allowed for divorce on the grounds of adultery by the wife and various 'offences' by the husband
1857:	Probate Act. All wills and administrations for England and Wales to be proved at the Principal Probate Registry from January, 1858
1864:	General Registration of births, marriages and deaths in Ireland
1876:	Curtailment of enclosures
1882/3:	Married Women's Property Act; married women to have control over their own property and goods and allowed to make wills in their own right
1926:	Adoption of children legalised in England. Permission for illegitimate children to be re-registered after the marriage of their parents
1929:	Marriage Act. Marriage age with consent of parents or guardians raised to sixteen for boys and girls (previously boys were able to marry at fourteen and girls at twelve with consent of parents or guardians)

Appendix Four

Registration District reference numbers at the General Register Office (Family Records Centre)

1837 to 1851		1852 to 1946	
Anglesey	XXVII	Anglesey	11b
Bedfordshire	VI	Bedfordshire	3b
Berkshire	VI	Berkshire	2c
Brecknockshire	XXVI	Brecknockshire	11b
Buckinghamshire	VI	Buckinghamshire	3a
Caernarvonshire	XXVII	Caernarvonshire	11b
Cambridgeshire	XIV	Cambridgeshire	3b
Cardiganshire	XXVII	Cardiganshire	11b
Carmarthenshire	XXVI	Carmarthenshire	11a
Cheshire	XIX	Cheshire	8a
Cornwall	IX	Cornwall	5c
Cumberland	XXV	Cumberland	10b
Denbighshire	XXVII	Denbighshire	11b
Derbyshire	XIX	Derbyshire	7b
Devonshire	IX,X	Devonshire	5b
Dorsetshire	VIII	Dorsetshire	5a
Durham	XXIV	Durham	10a
Essex	XII	Essex	4a
Flintshire	XIX,XXVII	Flintshire	11b
Glamorgan	XXVI	Glamorgan	11a
Gloucestershire	XI,XVIII	Gloucestershire	6a
Hampshire	VII,VIII	Hampshire	2b,2c
Herefordshire	XXVI	Herefordshire	6a
Hertfordshire	VI	Hertfordshire	3a
Huntingdonshire	XIV	Huntingdonshire	3b
Kent	V	Kent	1d,2a
Lancashire	XX,XXI,XXV	Lancashire	8b-8e
Leicestershire	XV	Leicestershire	7a
Lincolnshire	XIV	Lincolnshire	7a
London	I,II,III,IV	London	1a-1d

Merionethshire	XXVII	Merionethshire	11b
Middlesex	I,II,III	Middlesex	1a-1d,3a
Monmouthshire	XXVI	Monmouthshire	11a
Montgomeryshire	XXVII	Montgomeryshire	11b
Norfolk	XIII	Norfolk	4b
Northamptonshire	XV	Northamptonshire	3b
Northumberland	XXV	Northumberland	10b
Nottinghamshire	XV	Nottinghamshire	7b
Oxfordshire	XVI	Oxfordshire	3a
Pembrokeshire	XXVI	Pembrokeshire	11a
Radnorshire	XXVI	Radnorshire	11b
Rutland	XV	Rutland	7a
Shropshire	XXVI,XVIII	Shropshire	6a
Somersetshire	X,XI	Somersetshire	5c
Staffordshire	XVI-XVIII	Staffordshire	6b
Suffolk	XIV-XIII	Suffolk	4a,3b
Surrey	IV	Surrey	2a,1d
Sussex	VII	Sussex	2b
Warwickshire	XXV	Warwickshire	6b-6d
Westmorland	XXV	Westmorland	10b
Wiltshire	VIII	Wiltshire	5a
Worcestershire	XVIII	Worcestershire	6b,6c
Yorkshire	XXI-XXIV	Yorkshire	9a-9d

Appendix Five

Public Record Office: Group letters

Records in the Public Record Office are classified under Group letters; a list of the principal groups is as follows:

A	Alienation Office
AB	United Kingdom Atomic Energy Authority
ACT	Government Actuary's Department
ADM	Admiralty
AE	Royal Commission on Historic Monuments, England
AF	Parliamentary Boundary Commission
AH	Location of Offices Bureau
AIR	Air Ministry
AJ	Consumer Council
AK	County Courts
AN	British Railways Board
AO	Exchequer and Audit Department
AP	Irish Sailors' and Soldiers' Land Trust
AR	Wallace Collection
ASSI	Clerks of Assize
AST	National Assistance Board
AT	Department of the Environment
AVIA	Ministry of Aviation
AX	Local Government Boundary Commission for England
AY	Research Institutes
B	Court of Bankruptcy
BA	Civil Service Department
BC	Law Commission
BD	Welsh Office
BE	Iron and Steel Board
BF	Pensions Appeal Tribunal
BH	Hudson's Bay Company
BJ	Meteorological Office
BK	National Dock Labour Board
BL	Council on Tribunals

BM	Remploy Ltd
BN	Department of Health and Social Security
BP	Royal Fine Art Commission
BR	British Transport Docks Board
BS	Defunct Temporary Bodies
BT	Board of Trade
BV	Parole Board
BW	British Council
BX	Coal Industry Social Welfare Organisation
C	Chancery
CAB	Cabinet Office
CAOG	Crown Agents for Overseas Governments and Administrations
CB	National Playing Fields Association
CHES	Palatinate of Chester
CJ	Northern Ireland Office
CK	Commission for Racial Equality
CL	Certification Office for Trade Unions and Employers' Associations
CO	Colonial Office
COAL	National Coal Board
COPY	Copyright Office
CORB	Children's Overseas Reception Board
COU	Countryside Commission
CP	Court of Common Pleas
CRES	Crown Estate Commissioners
CRIM	Central Criminal Court
CSC	Civil Service Commission
CSPR	Civil Service Pay Research Unit
CT	Social Security Commissioner
CUST	Board of Customs and Excise
CV	Value Added Tax Tribunals
CW	Advisory, Conciliation and Arbitration Service
CX	Prime Minister's Office
CY	Royal Commission on Environmental Pollution
D	Development Commission
DB	Council for National Academic Awards
DD	Local Government Boundary Commission for Wales
DEFE	Ministry of Defence
DEL	High Court of Delegates
DG	International Organisations; records of International Whaling Commission and Western European Union
DJ	Post Office Users National Council
DK	National Ports Council
DL	Duchy of Lancaster
DM	Occupational Pensions Board
DN	Public Health Laboratory Services Board
DO	Dominion Office and Commonwealth Relations Office
DPP	Director of Public Prosecutions
DR	Civil Aviation Authority
DSIR	Department of Scientific and Industrial Research

DT	General Nursing Council
DURH	Palatinate of Durham
DV	Central Midwives Board
DW	Council for Education and Training of Health Visitors
DY	Joint Board of Clinical Nursing Studies
E	Exchequer
EA	Department of Education and Science
ECG	Exports Credits Guarantee Department
ED	Department of Education and Science
EF	Health and Safety Commission and Executive
EG	Department of Energy
ET	Manpower Services Commission
F	Forestry Commission
FCO	Foreign and Commonwealth Office
FEC	Commissioners of Forfeited Estates
FO	Foreign Office
FS	Registry of Friendly Societies
GFM	Captured Enemy Documents
HCA	High Court of Admiralty
HLG	Ministry of Housing and Local Government
HMC	Historical Manuscripts Commission
HO	Home Office
IND	INDEX Volumes
INF	Central Office of Information
IR	Inland Revenue
J	Supreme Court of Judicature
JUST	Justices Itinerant
KB	Court of King's Bench
LAB	Ministry of Labour
LAR	Land Registry
LC	Lord Chamberlain's Department
LCO	Lord Chancellor's Office
LO	Law Officers' Department
LR	Auditors of Land Revenue
LRRO	Land Revenue Record Office
LS	Lord Steward's Department
LT	Lands Tribunal
MAF	Ministry of Agriculture, Fisheries and Food
MEPO	Metropolitan Police Office
MH	Ministry of Health
MINT	Royal Mint
MONW	Royal Commission on Ancient and Historic Monuments in Wales and Monmouthshire
MT	Ministry of Transport
MUN	Ministry of Munitions
NATS	Ministry of National Service
NDO	National Debt Office
NIA	National Insurance Audit Department
NICO	National Incomes Commission
NSC	Department for National Savings

OD	Ministry of Overseas Development and Overseas Development Administration
OS	Ordnance Survey Department
PALA	Palace Court
PC	Privy Council Office
PCAP	Judicial Committee of the Privy Council
PCOM	Prison Commission
PEV	Court of the Honour of Peveril
PIN	Ministry of Pensions and National Insurance
PL	Palatinate of Lancaster
PMG	Paymaster General's Office
POWE	Ministry of Power
PP	Privy Purse Office
PREM	Prime Minister's Office
PRIS	King's Bench Prison
PRO	Transcripts, Gifts and Deposits
PROB	Prerogative Court of Canterbury
PSO	Privy Seal Office
PT	Public Trustee Office
PWLB	Public Works Loan Board
QAB	Queen Anne's Bounty
RAIL	British Transport Historical Records
RECO	Ministry of Reconstruction
REQ	Court of Requests
RG	Registrar General
SC	Special Collections
SO	Signet Office
SP	State Paper Office
STAC	Court of Star Chamber
STAT	Stationery Office
SUPP	Ministry of Supply
T	Treasury
TITH	Tithe Redemption Office
TS	Treasury Solicitor
UGC	University Grants Committee
WALE	Principality of Wales
WARD	Court of Wards and Liveries
WO	War Office
WORK	Ministry of Public Buildings and Works
ZHC	House of Commons Sessional Papers
ZHL	House of Lords Sessional Papers
ZJ	The London Gazette
ZLIB/ZPER	British Transport Historical Records Office Library
ZSPC	British Transport Historical Records

Acknowledgements

Co-operation and mutual help being hallmarks of any family history enterprise, we are pleased to acknowledge in all gratitude and humility the sterling assistance offered to us in the writing of this book by a number of friends and colleagues. Michael Armstrong, the original co-author, had a major part to play in the book's initial publication, and his wife Mary has done us the great service of proof-reading the text of the present edition. Jeremy Gibson offered helpful suggestions following the publication of the original edition, and Mark Herber, Cecil Humphery-Smith and Pauline Litton have each contributed above the call of duty in checking the text for inaccuracies and omissions. Their accumulated knowledge and careful attention to detail have stood us in good stead. Our thanks also extend to all those people who have offered us moral and professional support and advice, including John Draisey of the Devon Record Office, Steve Hobbs of the Wiltshire Record Office and Neil Staples of the Registrar General's Office of Shipping and Seamen in Cardiff.

In particular our heartfelt thanks go to our partners, Reg and Heather, who have been so patiently supportive of us in our endeavours.

Illustrations:

We acknowledge the fact that copyright in various illustrations we have used is vested in the record offices holding the original material in question.

Crown copyright material is reproduced by permission of the Controller of Her Majesty's Stationery Office; IHGS maps and the illustration from the Gretna Green marriage register are reproduced by permission of the trustees of the Institute of Heraldic and Genealogical Studies, Northgate, Canterbury, Kent. Our further gratitude for permission to reproduce material by way of illustration is extended to the following: Centre for Kentish Studies; The Church of Jesus Christ of Latter-day Saints; Devon Record Office; *Family Tree Magazine*; Heather Flockton; Captain J.W.H. Goddard of Rendcomb, Glos.; Terry Green; Hertfordshire Record Office; John Hawkins, Esq, JP; Huntingdonshire Record Office and the Vicar of Yaxley and Yaxley Church Council; Lambeth Palace Library; Office for National Statistics; Registrar General for Scotland; Representative Body of the Church in Wales and the National Library of Wales; Somerset Record Office and Wiltshire Record Office.

Our thanks must also go to various correspondents who have written to *Family Tree Magazine* over the years and have drawn our attention to a number of fascinating documents which we have been able to reproduce here: Mr G. Anthony Foster of Bury, Lancashire (birth certificate of Arthur Pepper, 1883; Norman Holding of Caddington, Bedfordshire (1881 census return featuring Master Lovelock); Mrs G. Lawes of Leighton Buzzard (1881 census return featuring Nell Gwynne); Joan Lehman of West Vancouver, Canada (baptism entry for Christopher Leach, 1818); Winifred Waterall of Loscoe, Derbyshire (death certificate of John Massey, 1910). Duncan Harrington, who is currently preparing an edition of the Hearth Tax returns for Kent, very kindly arranged for us to obtain a copy of part of the returns for Faversham.

All other illustrations are taken from originals held by the authors.

Index